RAVEN CHRONICLES

JOURNAL, VOL. 26

# LAST CALL

# Raven Chronicles

## Journal, Vol. 26

# Last Call

*Editors*

Kathleen Alcalá

Anna Bálint

Phoebe Bosché

Gary Copeland Lilley

Priscilla Long

Raven Chronicles Press
Seattle, Washington

FIRST EDITION

ISBN 978-0-9979468-4-0
Library of Congress Control Number: 2018950109

*Cover:* "Last Call," photograph, 2017, Magnuson Park, Seattle, by Alfredo Arreguín

*Book Design*: Phoebe Bosché, using 12/14 Adobe Jenson Pro typeface
*Cover Design*: Tonya Namura
*Raven Press Logo*: Scott Martin

Established in 1991, *The Raven Chronicles* is a Seattle-based literary organization that publishes and promotes artistic work that embodies the cultural diversity and multitude of imaginations of writers and artists living in the Pacific Northwest, other regions of the United States, and abroad.

Raven Chronicles Press
15528 12th Avenue NE
Shoreline, Washington 98155

editors@ravenchronicles.org
http://ravenchronicles.org

Somewhere the sky touches
the earth and the name of that place
is the end—in between
is the journey.

—African Saying

# Closing Time

## Kevin Miller

*—for PB & Co.*

Same again, make it doubles,
the black feathered songs,
the raven's wood block tok
is rolling thunder, the deepest
dark marks the gray. Cedar
and fir leave sliver shafts
for sky light, arbutus offers
its red hue to evergreen,
hardwood arches overhead.
Salal, huckleberry, sword fern
underscore, the south wind
is rain, north brings cold.
Sly dogs live in the time
between bar time and real,
old dogs find the hearth.

# TABLE OF CONTENTS

VIII   Rants, Raves, and Reviews

IX   Raven Notes

# LIST OF ARTISTS AND ILLUSTRATORS
Pages art/illustrations appear on:

Alfredo Arreguín, Washington: Cover, 125
Kree Arvanitas, Washington: 19
Anna Bálint, Washington: 91, 155
Toni La Ree Bennett, Washington: 27, 195
Angela Boyle, Washington: 46-47
Anita Boyle, Washington: 41
Gregg Chadwick, California: 86, 170
Manit Chaotragoongit, Thailand: 58, 200, 285, 323
E. Grace Dager, Washington: 48, 78
Patrick Dixon, Washington: 37
Kathleen Gunton, California: 293
Katsushika Hokusai, Japan: 156
Jury S. Judge, Arizona: 208, 302, 388
Julia Justo, New York: 139, 354
J.I. Kleinberg, Washington: 227
vivian linder levi, Washington: 51
Kevin J. O'Conner, Washington: 384
Organization for Prostitution Survivors: 85
Willie Pugh, Washington: 66 (photo of Donald W. Butler)
Red Sky Poetry Theatre flyers, Seattle: 366-368
Rayn Roberts, Washington: 307, 349
Sabrina Roberts, Washington: 63, 64, 65
John Timothy Robinson, West Virginia: 247, 359
Joel Sackett, Washington: 75, 76, 77
Judith Skillman, Washington: 221, 263
Marilyn Stablein, Oregon: 69
George L. Stein, Indiana: 217
Don Swartzentruber, Indiana: 242-243
Drake Truber, Indiana: 233, 341
Theodore C. Van Alst, Jr., Montana: 101, 112, 131, 181, 253, 275
Daniel Staub Weinberg, Illinois: 317
Jack Williams, England, UK: 325
Saint James Harris Wood, California: 369
Judy Xie, New Jersey: 287
Mary Zore, New Hampshire: 269

# Preface

For Raven's Vol. 26 issue, we chose the theme "Last Call." In the United States, in a bar, "last call" by the bartender means your last chance to order a drink. This is important, because the next public announcement will be the bar closing and you and your friends will be heading for the door. Well, this is our last call. *The Raven Chronicles*, after chronicling the literary antics of tricksters and dreamers, the underheard, the underserved (and probably underage), since 1991, will no longer publish a regularly-scheduled, subscription-based magazine. Yes, you read that right: the chronicles part of *The Raven Chronicles* is subsiding back into the Northwest tree pulp from whence it came. Starting with the 2016 publication of *Words From the Café, An Anthology*, edited by Anna Bálint, *Raven Chronicles* will live on as a book publisher: Raven Chronicles Press. Our first anthology, *Stealing Light: A Raven Chronicles Anthology, Selected work from 1991-1996*, is due out October, 21, 2018.

Here is what our editors have to say about editing this particular theme:

**Kathleen Alcalá** (Fiction Editor): After all these years of reading your stories late into the night, I am going to miss it. Yes, we grumble, but there is nothing quite like that jolt that says, this is familiar, but entirely new. This is exceptional. Now *this*, this is real writing.

The happiness of being able to accept and publish your work is, in my opinion, as good as getting my own work published. We've had contributors refuse to cash their checks, flaunt them in the faces of their families, change their majors to Creative Writing.

In the case of "Last Call," I feel the theme for the fiction I ended up selecting is about being the lonely child, the one who reinvents themself, or is destined to be reinvented. Maybe it took the last call to motivate you, because we had an unusually high number of good manuscripts, more than we could publish. I hope you enjoy this sampling.

Now our managing editor wants Raven to fly to another corner of the forest and try some new stuff. Publishing books, maybe publishing prisoners (more prisoners), branching out to see where this rapidly evolving world of publishing will take her. And Raven.

**Anna Bálint** (Safe Place Writing Circle): In SPWC I presented the theme of "Last Call" like a town crier, as in "Hear ye, Hear ye! *Caw caw caw!* The Raven is calling! Submit your work for the last ever issue of *Raven Chronicles Journal!*" The immediate response was "Oh no!" at the news that the journal will soon be no more. After all, Safe Place Writing Circle has had a special relationship with *Raven Chronicles* for the past four-plus years. During this time Raven's ongoing commitment to publishing emerging writers has translated into both the "Words From the Café" section of the journal, as well as the 2016 publication of *Words From the Café*—the book. So for Safe Place writers, Raven has provided a vital opening, a bridge linking what happens in a Recovery Café classroom each week with the larger literary world.

In the spirit of Raven's call for "daring, unpredictable work ... that takes risks ... and stretches to startle the reader" I encouraged students to look back over their past as well as recent writing, and send me pieces that reflected experimentation of one sort or another, and different ways of engaging with language and story. I ended up with a lot of work to choose from, and a final selection that includes:

In "Tongoy," vivian linder levi makes use of lyrical language to recreate the magical beauty of a childhood haunt in Chile. Megan McInnis turns her hand to fiction writing with her story, "Waiting," in which a young boy sits and waits for his drug-addicted mother to wake up. Suicide is a potent subject in Safe Place, but Hamlet's famous to-be-or-not-to be soliloquy brought it sweeping into the room, along with much discussion of the Bard's use of language and rhythm. Cathy Scott responded by trying her hand at parody to write her own "suicidal soliloquy."

In "Please Officer"—written in response to the 2017 police murder of Charleena Lyles in Seattle—Elliott Villarreal expresses the vulnerability of mentally ill people in relation to the police, and the fear that his own mental illness might make him a target.

Finally, Taumstar's two poems reflect very different sides of her. Where "Awake Alive Aware" uses a simplicity of language to express a down-to-earth sense of accomplishment and well-being, "Anything But" is a playful rebellion against the writing of poetry and that afternoon's writing prompt.

**Phoebe Bosché** (Managing Editor): *The Raven Chronicles* began in 1991, when Kathleen Alcalá and Philip Red Eagle guest-edited several King County Arts Commission Newsletters. They realized that there was a lack of diverse, multicultural writing being published in Seattle and the Northwest region in general. They thought: let's start our own magazine! Phil knew me through my work with Red Sky Poetry Theatre, editing *SkyViews* and other Red Sky Press Publications, so he asked me to join them. The result of this initial collaboration has been a magazine that "is not so much a collective as a dialectic magazine—we hope to reflect several sides of each topic," according to Kathleen.

We chose the name *Raven* because—as we learned from Upper Skagit storyteller Vi Hilbert (now deceased)—in northern Northwest Coast mythology Raven is a powerful figure who transforms the world, by accident or on purpose, yet he is also a trickster, a shape-shifter who is mischievous, often selfish, but brings light to the world. We added *Chronicles* because we intended the magazine to be a chronicle of how time passes, *chronos*, and us with it.

Since 1991, we have had numerous (too numerous to name here) editors, interns, and volunteer staff. While I have been the Raven Factotum-In-Chief (editing, proofing, magazine design, grant writing, event organizing, etc.), there are several folks to thank who have worked tirelessly over the years: Paul Hunter, proof reader and poetry editor extraordinaire; Jody Aliesan and Elizabeth "Beth" Myhr, who were poetry editors for so many years; Matt Briggs, who brought our website into the modern era; Kathleen Alcalá, for her incredible cheerfulness and longstanding dedication to publishing multicultural literature;

Thomas Prince, for patiently videotaping all Raven readings over the past few years; Thomas Hubbard, for his ongoing support of Raven activities; Anna Bálint, for her dedication to help dispell stereotypes of folks "struggling with addiction or mental illness or homelessness;" Larry Laurence, for ongoing emotional and financial support; Irene H. Kuniyuki, who was our staff photographer for many years, for her visonary photos; Alfredo Arreguín, for sharing with us photos of his beloved crows; and Scott "Scotty" Martin, for his humor and perseverance. Check our website for names of other editors of past issues: *http://www. ravenchronicles.org/staff/*.

Like many small press publications, we published *Raven* from our office jobs, homes, or Xerox offices for the first few years. Then, in 1997, we moved into the Richard Hugo House, and spent ten wonderful years, until 2007, working in a vibrant literary community. Those first couple of years RHH co-founder Frances McCue, her husband Gary Greaves, and their daughter Madeline (Maddy) lived in the building—a former mortuary, complete with a child's coffin in the basement. Raven became a vibrant, community-based magazine in those ten years, and we hosted a long-running reading series there, "City Chronicles, Raven Chronicles Live!" In 2007 we had the good fortune to find a new home when RHH made interior changes: at the Jack Straw Productions' building in the University District. We shared an open office space with Floating Bridge Press for ten years, 2007-2017. The hard-working and tireless folks at Jack Straw, Joan Rabinowitz, Levi Fuller, et al, were incredibly supportive. We miss them. Raven Chronicles Press is now, for the time being, located in Shoreline and in Georgetown, Seattle.

We published forty-eight issues of *Raven*, from *Vol. 1, No. 1, Summer/Fall 1991* to *Vol. 26, Last Call, Summer 2018*. Up to and including *Vol. 22, Celebration, Summer 2016*, we published in regular magazine format, 8-1/2 x 11 inches. Starting with *Vol. 23, Jack Straw Writers Program, 1997-2016*, we switched to book format, 6 x 9. As Raven Chronicles Press, we will continue to publish work which embodies the cultural diversity of writers and artists living in the Pacific Northwest, and elsewhere.

**Gary Copeland Lilley** (Poetry Editor): The Last Call—a celebration to the rest of the night, after the music, the flirtations, the fails and the successes, the noise of a bar reeking with the stains of everything that declares we are alive. So appropriate a theme for *The Raven Chronicles* as it transitions from lit and art journal to a book publishing press.

I am honored to be the poetry editor for Volume 26. I wanted to curate an issue of poetry that had a keen edge, the grit of a dive, because who isn't intrigued by a dive filled with the people that most of our mamas warned us about. I envisioned poems that spoke to this particular critical time with an urgency that good writing always has. I wanted people that weren't afraid to talk on the possible situations that would inhabit such a place. But man, was the task tough. Thank you to y'all who submitted your wonderful works. I'm never careful of what I wish for. I am truly grateful to you poets. There was an outpouring of nearly 900 poems, which put me through a beautiful ordeal of making these selections. Thank you *Raven Chronicles* for this opportunity. Alright you fellow denizens, drink up.

**Priscilla Long** (Nonfiction Editor): I am proud of this group of essays. "Last Call," the issue's theme, means things are over, finished, done, about to close down, but not forgotten, maybe never forgotten. So we have Stephen Grigg's incisive reconstruction of the Seattle Police shooting of Native woodcarver John T. Williams, and we have Anne Frantilla's moving elegy for her father. Memoir cannot be subtracted from history, and two essays—by Kaye Linden and Sharon Goldberg—evoke the traumatic legacy of the Holocaust as it continues to unfold in two families—never to be forgotten.

Last Call also means we are done with sexual harassment or, if not, its perpetrators will be called out, revealed, excoriated. Consider "We Too" by Loreen Lilyn Lee, "Just a Kiss" by Janet Yoder, and "Battle Cry of the Survivor" by Rebeka Fergusson-Lutz. There are other imbrications here (meaning overlapping of edges, as in the shingles of a house). "Rakija" by Ana Vidosavljevic (who lives in Indonesia) recalls childhood in Serbia, and "Zabavnik" by

Vladimir Vulović recalls childhood in Socialist Yugoslavia (also Serbia). Both pieces are funny and at moments hilarious.

In "Daddy Volcano" Loreen Lilyn Lee makes vivid her Chinese-American childhood in Honolulu. After childhood comes old age, during which it is never too late to run a marathon, as related in Alice Lowe's "Running While Old." Her abecedarian mixes the internal—feelings and perceptions—with science, and this internal/external dichotomy is also the concern of "The External Me," Sue Gale Pace's poignant memoir of living with temporal lobe epilepsy.

This is the "Last Call" for *Raven Chronicles* in journal form (I salute the vibrant role it has played in the culture of our region). But let us hope and—more than hope—struggle, rage, and work steadily against the grim possibility that we are undergoing the last call for democracy, justice, and human rights in our country. In his astonishing memoir, "The Realm Between," writing about Club 870 in Detroit, 1973, John Mifsud reminds us that in the struggle there can be sweetness—even delirious joy. As to the civic derangements we are dealing with, I invite you to read Jack Remick's "The Arrogance of the Princely Mind" and Chris Espenshade's cry of outrage in "The Blood on Your Fingers." Both reach the level of poetry. Finally, returning to art, we finish with Jack Remick's "The Wisdom of Finishing." May you savor, in this last issue, a rich and rewarding read. 📖

# I

# FROM THE
# RAVEN'S ROOST

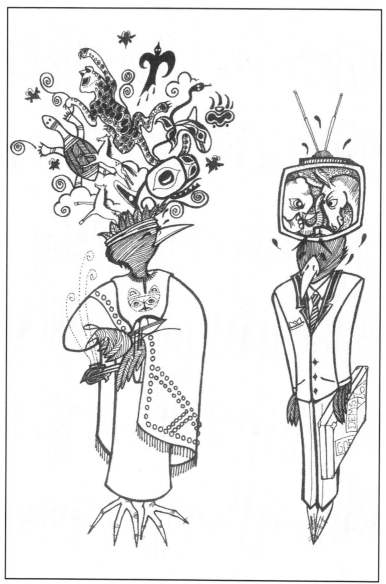

*Two Ravens,* Pen and Ink Drawing, by Kree Arvanitas

# Jury Duty

## Thomas Hubbard

He parks in the public lot and begins the two block walk past the town's movie house and past a department store where naked window mannequins await the day's clothing with mysterious half smiles, a few the color of milk chocolate and all the rest pinkish. Most show a few chipped places where the plastic peeps through.

He stops momentarily at the corner, then crosses the street and steps inside the town's favorite restaurant and sits at the counter.

"Yessir, what'll ya have this morning?"

"Just coffee. Black."

The waitress turns to pick up a glass coffee pot, then faces him to fill the cup in front of him with steaming coffee. Shifting her weight to one foot, still holding the glass pot, she raises her other hand and brushes bleach-blond hair back from her eyes. "Haven't seen you before. New in town?"

"Nah. Moved here about a year ago for the new factory. I stay a few miles out toward the Interstate. Jury duty this morning."

"You're early. Courthouse doesn't open til nine."

"That's what I figured, but wasn't sure. And I don't wanna be late. This is my first time."

"You have time for breakfast. . . ."

"Maybe lunch. Ate before leaving the apartment. You got a good lunch here?"

"Best in Town." She writes his bill, tears it off her pad and lays it on the counter. "May I ask . . . are you Native American?"

He chuckles, "Are you white?"

"Too-shay!" She turns to greet another customer, a tall grandmotherly woman whose reddish blond hair makes a halo of tight curls around her head. "G'mornin' Lashana. Sit anywhere."

The woman sits in a booth by the window, setting her purse on the table in front of her. She orders coffee and whole wheat toast, and the waitress heads for the kitchen.

The man finishes his coffee, lays money on the counter, steps outside the door and heads for the courthouse, where he sits on a bench in the yard until a janitor unlocks the doors. After waiting a few minutes more he goes inside, follows the taped-up paper signs into a room with a few rows of folding chairs. He sits in the back row, alone in the room.

People begin filing in and sitting. Before long the woman from the restaurant steps through the door, scans the crowd, and stops near him by the back row. "Aren't you the man I saw in the restaurant?"

"I am." Meeting her hazel eyes as they peer from a face the color of the café au lait he used to sip in N'Orleans cafes, he motions to the chair beside him. "Have a seat, cousin. I'm Joe. Heard the waitress call you Lashana."

She remains standing. "Cousin. . . ?"

"Distant, but cousins nevertheless."

"What makes you think so?"

"That reddish 'fro and hazel eyes. And you're tall, kind of stately. My ancestors probably sheltered some of yours after their escape."

"Oh. . . ?" She sits, leaving one empty chair between them. "So . . . which are you, a fortune teller or a voyeur? Or just a wiseguy?"

"Neither. I'm a mixed-blood like you, except I didn't inherit as much from my black ancestors, if I had any. You and I both have some Cherokee blood."

"Well I don't really know and I care less, but you're right about one thing. My name's Lashana. And I've been called for jury duty, just like you." She moves her purse from her lap, placing it under her folding chair.

By this time most of the chairs are occupied by prospective jurors. A middle-aged woman dressed in a skirt and blouse with a jacket and high heel shoes steps to the front, a sheaf of papers in her hand. "Good morning everyone. If you haven't signed in already, please sign your name on the attendance list as it comes around." She hands a clip board to one of the people in the first row.

Joe and Lashana both sign when the clipboard finally comes to them. He frowns at Lashana, "I'm missing a day's work for this. I hope I don't get chosen, 'cause I can't afford to miss any more."

The woman at the front of the room clears her throat loudly and announces, "We had three jury trials on the docket, however two have been settled by plea changes. For the one jury we have to fill, I'll call twelve names." She picks up the clipboard and calls out the names, including both Joe and Lashana. "If I called your name, please step through the door behind me and have a seat."

Joe and Lashana stand and begin moving toward the door with the ten other prospects, all white. The woman continues, "Everyone else please remain seated while the prosecution and defense asks a few questions of the prospective jurors."

Lashana turns toward Joe. "This trial must be for the cop who shot a young man in my neighborhood last year. A traffic stop. The kid died for a broken tail light. His case has finally come up."

Joe grimaces and nods, "Happens way too much, and they always get off. Maybe not this time. Guess I want to be chosen after all."

When the twelve prospects are all seated, the prosecutor stands, looking over the prospects. "Please raise your hand if a police officer is among your family members. One woman raises her hand. "Your name?" The prosecutor asks.

"Laura Davis, sir."

"No more questions." The prosecutor sits back down, and the defense attorney stands.

Circling the seated prospects, he stops at the end of each row to look over the prospects. He stops by Joe. "Your name please."

"Randall Joseph Redhorse. Folks call me Joe."

"Thank you." He addresses Lashana, "Your name?"

"Lashana Lee Jones."

Your address?

"Nine-oh-two Jackson Street."

"That's over on the east side, isn't it?"

"Yes sir."

"Thank you. No more questions."

The prosecutor and defense both hand papers to the woman in the skirt and jacket.

She steps into the other room and calls out three more names, then returns. "Laura Davis, Lashana Lee Jones, and Randall Joseph Redhorse are excused. You may leave the courthouse, and we thank you for your time. Everyone else please remain in your seats.

Outside the courthouse, Joe and Lashana pause.

Joe glances up from staring at the ground. "How about that?"

Lashana shrugs. "The cop will get off."

Joe starts away, then turns. "Lunch?"

"No. I'm good. Maybe some other time. . . ."

"Yeah, I guess I'm not hungry now, either. See ya around." 📖

# Thirsty

## Paul Hunter

Their first real fight caught Charlie
at a low spot tractor broken down
just with the wheat coming on
golden heads nodding in the sun
no room time money for anything
but this toothless gear to mend

when Evaleen had most need of him
with her firstborn just starting to show
he loaded up sold half the pigs
they were fattening for the fall
counting on said not one word
until there was the check in his hand

to squander on tractor parts
the deed done an announcement
she met with absolute silence
which meant he slept in the hayloft
took a couple days' quiet thought how
to lift the whole thing on his shoulders

carry on like he knew best
somehow with or without her
ignore her while she calmed down
forgetting how good she was figuring
things close which only meant
his first mistake he compounded

so there they were both broken down
stuck in the road where life went
on around them silent in slow motion
untouched untasted all but meaningless
each put-upon staggered like a young
mule overburdened scared to take a step

then he recalled how folks used to say
looks like you threw both your
bucket and rope down the well
better hope you don't never get thirsty
which to look at her he surely was
so got out his heart's longest ladder

in the cobwebby dark after supper
got set to climb down that hole
sundown on the porch apologize
down on his knees like he meant it
purely ask her forgiveness and vow
from now on to forever ask her first

# Inhabited

## John Olson

A m I my habits? Are my habits my habitation? Is the habit of living a syllabus of silly routines? The answer, of course, is yes. Sort of. And no. Habits regulate our behavior, but they don't define us. We're the art, habits the frame.

The world of the habitual is generally divided into two categories: bad habits and good habits.

Bad habits are burdens. The logical thing is to get rid of them. But it's not that simple. Far from it. Bad habits are the burdens that make us feel lighter, assuaged and blithe. For a minute or two. Be it booze, drugs, or compulsively tweeting, the feeling is counterfeit. It dissipates fast. And then we feel hoodwinked until the next craving comes along and the eternal debate called temptation fires up again.

Bad habits cheat us every time. As soon as we satisfy their cravings, we get dumped. That gurgle we hear is our self-esteem going down the drain.

But they're sexy, so enticing, so nasty. As in, say, porn. Or popcorn. Or chocolate chip cookie dough ice cream.

Bad habits are always exciting: cheap thrills. We know we get cheated, but that's part of the fun. Good habits are well-groomed and squeaky clean; they promote our well-being, but there's little excitement in a yoga mat or a mug of herbal tea.

Not all habits are bad, not all habits are good, but all habits are deeply rooted. Habits are punctuation, semicolons joining moment to moment like cigarette breaks or pen clicking. They structure our day. They envelop us in form. They give a shape and a shell to that inner convolution we call ourselves.

Good habits are hard to get going, but once going, they burrow into our lives like instincts. They must be performed. They become engines fueled by consummation. They demand, but they

*Bus Tunnel*, Seattle, Washington, 2013, Photograph, by Toni La Ree Bennett

reward. They renew, but they badger. They can be a drag. And they can redeem.

Good habits can be cumbersome in their own way. They have the potential for becoming a little maniacal. A habit, when all is said and done, is still a habit. It's a behavior that has to be performed in order to feel OK. It can be a little OCD or it can be a lot OCD. It can be a routine of checking the stove once before one leaves one's abode. Or it can be a routine of checking the stove twelve consecutive times with a ritual or two thrown in for good measure.

Ritual and habit have a lot in common. Both are repetitive, both have a pattern. Rituals are performed solemnly and ceremoniously. Habits are performed routinely, almost unconsciously. But not always. There are habits that border on ritual, rituals that border on habit. Some habits are performed with purposeful rigor, some with gleeful regularity. Habits can restrain us. They can also individualize and differentiate us.

What makes habits good? Good habits rejuvenate. Good habits expand our living. Appeasing the dictates of a good habit can sustain and empower us. Good habits feed on solar energy like leaves photosynthesizing light. They savor the sun and put gold in the blood.

Good habits sanction the kind of decisions that promote health and well-being. Some people go a little crazy with their habits and perform them with the devotion of a zealot, in which case a good habit can acquire the sheen of lunacy and cease to be, strictly speaking, a good habit. You can get carried away with a good habit to the point of obnoxiousness but a good habit turned weird habit is more likely to keep you afloat than a bad habit, which will definitely torpedo you.

Changing habits is a tough but regenerative restructuring of your life. I will attest to that.

I've quit drinking and smoking. I miss drinking, I don't miss smoking. Drinking is a wonderful luxury until it isn't. Until it becomes a howling need and enslaves and degrades you. I remember enjoying smoking quite a bit; a shot of whiskey would have been unthinkable without a wraith of smoke flowing in, flowing out, flavoring everything with the mellowing dawdle of smoke. Cigarettes were like having a buddy in my breast pocket. If I was new to a job or feeling lonely while out on the road I could pull out a cigarette and feel like someone was there musing and ruminating right along with me. We shared a rhythm. We shared a mutual pause of truancy.

Cigarettes were a subtle pleasure, but booze, booze was electrifying.

There are few things in life as pleasurable and gratifying as pouring a glass of wine after a hard day at work and feeling all those little injuries and disappointments and frustrations dissipate like methane—leaving the climate of your brain free of swampy miasma for a while.

Few things in life as exciting as tequila, as congenial as bourbon, as sexy as a martini in a Nevada saloon.

Few things in life are as jubilant as beer, as exhilarating as whiskey, as delectable as brandy. The ensuing euphoria grows, cheerfully endorsing another drink. And another and another and another. And the next morning you awaken to that godawful bone-aching malaise that is the hangover. It's called a hangover because you find yourself hanging over a dark abyss, moaning with headache and nausea.

Drinking is great until you lose control and it controls you.

And so I stopped those things and it was hard but liberating and I've been able to do a lot of things without their slyly undermining cajolery.

Then there's coffee: unthinkable to begin a day without coffee. Two full mugs, at least. My favorite mug is a frosted glass affair with red polka dots. I got it at the Seattle Art Museum. It was linked with a show by Yayoi Kusama called *Infinity Mirrors: Doors of Perception*. One would enter a room full of mirrors that would extend surreal, sculpted objects into infinity, polka-dotted pumpkins or polka-dotted phalluses. Kusama is obsessed with polka dots. She relates of once staring at a red, patterned tablecloth and then looking up to find the entire room—floor, walls, and ceiling—dappled with the same pattern. She discovered her own body besprinkled with polka dots. It made her feel obliterated.

And so she created an obliteration room: a stark white interior in which people are invited to stick a colored dot anywhere they want: a table, a bowl, a couch, a bookcase. Kids love it.

I'm polka-dotted with habits. I have habits piled on habits, like books. Good habits, mostly, but some bad. Some neutral. Some balsamic, some cumbersome, some nonsensical. Good habits include running a minimum of three miles every day, doing one hundred push-ups, forty sit-ups, and rinsing my mouth with mouthwash before going to bed.

Bad habits include sleeping far more than I need, eating meat (I've tried embracing a vegetarian regime a number of times), and overreacting to minor annoyances.

Most of my habits are in the realm of the methodical. They help structure my day, but are essentially neutral, neither good nor bad. They're just habits. Things I like to do whose consequences are fairly innocuous.

I'm in the habit, for example, of listening to podcasts when we go to bed at night. This is a recent habit. More accurately, it is the elaboration of a habit: I used to listen to talk shows. My favorite was AM 1090 KPTK, particularly Mike Malloy, who came on about 10:00 p.m. and helped me get through the Bush years. He softened on Obama, who not only continued Bush's militaristic policies but expanded them, quite dramatically. Few so-called progressives seemed to mind, because Obama was smart, affable, refreshingly eloquent, and (like his wife Michelle) intensely charismatic. He was also our first black president. A lot of progressives went silent about the accelerated erosion of civil rights, escalated drone strikes, militarization of U.S. police, unprecedented federal crackdown on whistleblowers, and the spectacular criminality and fraud of Wall Street in 2008, which went unpunished. Rather than send anyone to prison, Obama packed his economic team with Wall Street insiders. I stopped listening to KPTK some few years before they went off the air and became a sports format.

In 2013 I bought a tablet with Bluetooth which, paired with a Sangean Bluetooth radio, provided me access to a gazillion podcasts. Favorites now include *Stuff To Blow Your Mind*, hosted by

Robert Lamb and Joe McCormick, which covers a broad, eclectic range of topics from "The Nature of Heroism" to "The Evolution of the Anus," and *The Partially Examined Mind*, a discussion of philosophy.

Bluetooth also provides access to a French radio station, France Culture Radio, which also offers a broad array of subject matter, everything from politics to philosophy. I enjoy listening to these podcasts and pretending I can understand French.

We've also long been in the habit of watching the French news on our French cable TV station, TV5 Monde. French journalism has been pretty much as corporatized as mainstream American news, but to a much lesser extent. If there is a strike or protest, however marginalized or disproportionately small the group may be, they receive generous coverage. Today, for example, TV5 Monde reported on a letter to an oak tree written by Cécile Duflot, a former member of the National Assembly of Paris and leader of the Green political party in France, in support of the recent triumph of ZAD (Zone à Defendre), a group of activists who formed a commune in a rural region a few miles northwest of Nantes to block the development of an airport in Notre-Dame-des-Landes.

I'm in the habit of running every day. Runners will tell you it's an addiction. They're right. I've gotten to know a lot of people via my running. I've been running in this neighborhood for over twenty years. People often tell me how enthused and impressed they are to see me out there every day, rain or shine, even in the bitter cold and snow. I appreciate hearing that, of course, but I can't really go into specifics about why I run. It's personal. It's not that I shy away from expressing personal issues, I'm mostly unembarrassed about expressing interior experience, it's one of the reasons I enjoy writing, but the truth of my answer can be disconcerting. I run because I suffer from depression and anxiety. If I don't run, I feel crappy. I just don't feel right. Running is the best antidote I have found for coping with anxiety and depression. Running lifts my mood. It's invigorating. And it *is* addictive.

People tend to squirm and look away at the mention of depression. We live in a culture obsessed with the positive. I had to laugh when I saw Michael Shannon, playing the villainous Colonel Strickland in *The Shape of Water*, reading *The Power of Positive Thinking* by Norman Vincent Peale. I've long thought that there was something fundamentally deleterious about that book, a form of magical thinking that is childish and woefully simplistic.

I like my habits. Most of them. Some aren't so great. I've gotten into the habit of eating candy lately. That one I could do without.

But here's the deal: habits can get in the way of being in the world. I mean, really being in the world. Not just living robustly and intensely, but creatively. That's the hard part. Habit and creativity don't really go together. Creativity is more about destruction: destroying habits. Undermining cognitive bias. Subverting prejudice, one's proclivity to judge. It's hard. This is difficult because it's so deeply rooted. These are invisible habits. These are habits that are so integrated into the fabric of our being that we don't even know they're there.

Living, for example. I'm in the habit of living. Big time. I'm not aware of it being a habit because it's not something I'm tempted to do and either avoid it or break down and say, what the hell, and do some living. That's not how I live. It's not how anybody lives. Nobody thinks about living they just do it.

Breathe, pump blood, blink our eyes. That's how it's done. There's just one thing: we're not the ones doing that. Our bodies do it for us.

Unless we're on life support. Then it's the quiet hush of an iron lung or ventilator keeping us going, and a staff of people coming and going as they check on vital signs and intravenous drips and daydream about Paris or last night's date while they're checking the pulse of this strange legume laid out before them on a bed. But who or what are we in relation to the world at that point? Are we the inhabitants of the body even when the body is virtually a vegetable, our eyes shut, our mouths mute, our very being and personality utterly absent? Are we somewhere else, or do we—the inner essence of our bodies—continue to have an existence? If we put together an oxygen atom with two hydrogen atoms we have water; but where does wetness come from? Are we wetness? Are we a witness to the wetness that is consciousness?

Or suppose, rather, that we aren't an essence, a nucleus of being, but a conglomerate of forces, an amalgam of protein and carbohydrate, all of which require a network of nerves and neurons. That is to suppose ourselves as a form of being that finds its life and meaning in interrelation, a wave among other waves, a leaf among leaves.

Am I my body? My body thinks so. I don't know what to think. But I do know this: I don't want to die.

"Let us say aloud to each other here that being alive is habit-forming," writes palliative care author Stephen Jenkinson in Die Wise. "Even when it doesn't go particularly well, still most of us feel the draw of living, and we usually look toward the next new day. It isn't an easy thing to feel otherwise. It is hard as hell, it is counterintuitive, and it is mandatory that *when the time of dying is upon us we have to find a way to stop trying not to die.*"

Have you ever met someone who didn't appear to be alive? Someone with a fully functioning body and a reasonable amount of intelligence, but no one appeared to be home? I've been seeing a lot of that lately. These people are called zombies, and are generally found gazing at a device called a smartphone.

This is another habit: making judgments. The above paragraph is a judgment. It's a judgment I'm choosing to make about people I see walking down the street paying no mind to anything except their smartphone. I make it every day. I know it's a judgment, it's my judgment, and I know I could be way wrong, unfairly wrong, but I don't feel that it's wrong. Still. It's something I have to consider: that judgments like this are preventing a fuller existence, an openness to life that would help me find a deeper humanity and a connection with the rest of my human companions on this sad, polluted planet.

But it's a habit. It's a habit I inhabit. I'm working on it. Trying to do better. Be better. Less habitual. More hospitable. Less inhibited by habit. 📖

# Snapshots of Home

## JT Stewart

*—for Bruce*

I could tell you that home is never
where the heart was / that things are
bad all over / and you would say a little
information never stopped a kettle on
the stove / never shut the petals of a
rose / its blossoms unfolding through
silent urban summer afternoons / rooms
and rooms away

I could take some snapshots of home / for-
ward them to Chelan / but would they help
advance your dialogs with God / Pops as
you call him / or help you combat sun-
stroke / mildew / and love headed for the
skids one more time

Consider the familiars of one's child-
hood / anyone's hometown / some port city
on or off some sound or bay named after
an explorer / Puget Sound / Hudson's Bay /
for instance / and these old men lazing
in arched doorways / spittle dribbling
down their yellow beards / their spongy
minds conjuring up nickle & dime places
of country fried chicken / mountains of
pan gravy / toast – pale / yes paler than Pioneer
Square / paler than local color

Peruse Third & Union/ a spawning ground
for Metro buses/ gen-uine teenagers with
their hair fried / teased / plastered /
purpled / see them do the Diddly Bob
their ghetto speakers ba-booming &
watch them out-wait buses / never lose a
down-beat / never miss a half – step / munch
on tight and tired enchiladas from Taco
Time or Colonel Sander's bleached out
funny bones.

Witness the Courthouse / the old jail's
still upstairs and here's this lady / this
marvelous / elderly lady who sweeps side-
walks & the street across from here / the
Hotel Morrison's still still around the block /
sweeping is what she does best / her avocation /
yes

I could tell you that home was never
where the heart is / that things are bad
all over / with these people sleeping on the
streets / those other people sweeping up
the streets / these crowds of wasted dreams /
these fumes of rotted breath / and those
folks who pay to keep our city clean /
yes

What more is there to understand / except
it's always them & us / these & those /
yours & mine / somebody's / ours/ every-
body's split-leveled nightmares in search
of enough voices / enough postage for the next
Trailways or Amtrack back to the self's lonely
depot / or solitary flagstop / the heart

# a madder red

## Carletta Carrington Wilson

in comes an in-voice
there under phylum, phylum, phylum
the mad roots of madder plantings
stretch across distant trails gnarled/knotting/frayed
the way the business of a day  un/whorls the world

you will never see a fleur-di-lis  study paisley
watch calico grow across yards
wonder how brocade is made or touch velvet's plush
never be tasked to finger damask
the rage of this age is Tinctoria of Diasporia
mollusk-purple cochineal-red
as long as the dye bath lasts it will stink to high heaven
of piss, shit, the dead the dying
infusions of confusion soaking woof-and-weft of your breath

two-head woman don't look back  grab/snatch
pull/drag  weigh this life against the other weight
the one you carried until heaviness slowed the coffle  down

madder red fill'a head come undone
where the threadbare bear patterns of repeating figures
stitched across scrotums embroidered upon wombs
every body pieced out of an incomprehensible cloth whose bolts
unravel become remnant swatch must/be/watched/for/they/run

# II

# The Family Corvidae

*Raven in Snow,* Kodiak, Alaska, 2008, Photograph, by Patrick Dixon

# Beliefs About Ravens

## Yvonne Higgins Leach

Who conjures up such comparisons?
The souls of evil priests trapped
in their black, oily plumage.
Exorcised spirits croaking
in the deep *crruck-crruck-crruck*
of their call. For the flock
to be called an "unkindness."
Seen as only
antics on a telephone wire,
scrabbling on the sidewalk,
or every task composed of selfishness.

When again this day is rollicking fun
with sticks in their heavy-duty beaks,
beaks that just moments ago
preened one another into a tidy bond.
I hear a chorus and not clatter.
I see cool practice at capturing
every potential kernel.
I encounter play in their
cocking glances.
Nothing but pure-magnified existence.
I go outside to replant the empty pots.
The ravens remember my face
and trust I mean no harm.

# Crows

### Bruce Louis Dodson

They go unnoticed overhead
above the supermarket malls and cities
countryside
suburban fields and meadows
watching.
Airborne gangs dressed in black feather jackets
fearless wise guys with a raucous comment
for the goings on below.

# crow poem

## Frank Rossini

five crows unfold & float
from dripping cottonwoods along the roiling
creek to a yard across the street to share
scattered stale crusts cut
from a week's loaves of daily bread
a common meal between good neighbors

a week before  I stopped the car
for a fledgling crow in the middle
of a downtown street
five or six adults urgently cawing
from some overhanging branches

I couldn't move  the crow in front
a line of traffic behind
I opened the door  slowly
approached it  whispering
it's OK  I won't hurt you
a sharp cry exploded by my ear
a sudden sting to the back of my skull
bent my head toward the pavement
hands up I hurried back to the car
the young crow still in the street

a man leaving a nearby shop  suddenly
was in the road bending down
& quicker than my warning his face turned
from solace to pain his hands pressed
against his head he ran
back inside  two adults landed
to guide the young crow
to safety

I started the car  one hand
on the wheel  the other gingerly
touching the back of my head
blood & crowspit on my fingertip
I licked it off   a good mix
for a wild communion   between crow
& human

*Wah!*, 2015, Graphite Sketch, by Anita K. Boyle

# My Morning Crow

## Catherine Sutthoff Slaton

Nearly eight o'clock, the crows have not come
my coffee is cold in its cup.

I ease a weed from between the stepping stones,
pluck a slug, fling it to four frantic hens.

On the fence's top rail I leave
toast corners, an ellipsis of nuts, any affront

to my neighbor who sends my black birds scattering
with her great gonging wind chimes rattling

the flesh of her upper arms flapping
like a pelican's wattle of flopping fish.

I count her among the songbirds' Cerberus
coddling rust-breast birds who plead

for their stolen brood, snug in a crow's black beak—
the meal soft as a stewed plum.

I give one last whistle, long as a train's call.
One crow comes in a stroke of calligrapher's trail—

jet claws upon the board. For my one almond she relinquishes
a twisting stickleback, plucked from our pond, pale as a peeled tree,

two long spines prehistoric in configuration—its ironic armor—
and one wet eye staring skyward.

# Eating Crow, Lessons Learned From the Corvid Community

### Marianne Weltmann

I

Three days the bird has been lying
flattened in the street just off the corner
of the arterial
a geodesic dome of dots that
glisters the concrete and
quickens my breath
I share the shame of the peerless planner
robbed of power
no agile self-respecting North American Crow
would foray for or sequester treasure
in the asphalted cement of my gentrified block

it reminds me of the hopeless hoarse
caw of a mother whose baby fell to its death
from a nest high in the dogwood on my strip
the congregation of corvids that marched
in silent single-file formation
around my house to nominate
a leader who lifted the corpse
then spread its fanned tail in flight

Last night I sat cooling on my stoop
after the movie where the woman's lover
asked, "What's the worst thing you ever did?"
I missed a few frames and came up with a whitewash
descending darkness rolled back the years
on the promise of a breeze

## II

I remember the last suitcase my mother packed for me
between her first and final heart-attacks
her artistic acumen in the arrangement
of socks married in pairs stuffed into
toe-boxes of shoes that rounded out corners
and me neglecting to thank or embrace her
at the airport gate

The time I chose to fly back to my son in Seattle
leaving my father in a hospital room in Cincinnati
not there to hold his hand when he mumbled
final words through oxygen

How I sent others to visit
my little daughter at the cancer ward
of the hospital in Munich
before the terminal call
*Es ist vollbracht*

Sunlight through the window graced
a sheet stopped short at booties
the nuns crocheted to warm her feet
still warm

I read no more
bedtime stories to my son
he taught himself to read
at three
at the moment he hanged himself
I was fast asleep

# III

Thinking of the bird before dawn this morning
I run down the middle of the street
white nightgown and black slides
*New York Times* in hand
a spectre contradicting daylight

After three days and a night
the mound has vanished.
At the curb I feel for oil-scum
under chassis of parked cars
to spot engraved on the rim of a tire
the bas-relief of a beak
a skeleton in two dimensions

One double-take and a tug dislodge
the trophy and newspaper scoops into its blue bag
the infrastructure of a city-state
of maggots feasting on carrion
a sense of finality

I ferry the body-bag to its dumpster descent
a cortege of crows surrounds me
swooping from telephone wires
beaks peck as a team
to free the departed corvid spirit
their chorus keening at the wake
of a kindred who abandoned grass
for concrete and failed to notice
the car speeding down a side street

*Oooh! Shiny,* 2011, Panel Excerpts, pages 8-11, by Angela Boyle

# III

# WORDS FROM THE CAFÉ

*Swallow it Whole*, 2017, Digital Photograph, by E. Grace Dager

# The Recovery Café

## An Introduction

The Recovery Café sits on the corner of Boren and Denny, in downtown Seattle. It is a unique and remarkable place. "Recovery Café and its School for Recovery serve men and women who have suffered trauma, homelessness, addiction and/or other mental health challenges. In this loving community, men and women experience belonging, healing and the joy of contributing. The Café and School for Recovery help participants develop tools for maintaining recovery and stabilizing in mental/physical health, housing, relationships and employment/volunteer service." —*Excerpt from mission statement, Recovery Café website.*

Writer/teacher, Anna Bálint, joined the Café community as a volunteer, teaching writing classes with the School of Recovery. Over time, her classes evolved into "Safe Place Writing Circle," an ongoing and fluid group that has met weekly since fall 2012. Its purpose is to provide a "safe place" for Café members to creatively explore many different aspects of their lives through writing, give voice to their beliefs, hopes and fears, and discover the power of their own voices. Some amazing stories and poems emerge, on a regular basis, from everyone involved in this writing circle. Here are a few of those voices.

*Note*: Raven Chronicles Press published *Words From the Café, An Anthology*, edited by Anna Bálint, in 2016. It includes ten featured writers, a selection of Other Voices, and a CD of the featured writers reading a selection of their work. Check our website *http://www.ravenchronicles.org/shop/* or *Amazon.com* to buy a copy.

# Tongoy

## vivian linder levi

In Chile, there is a place called Tongoy. Shaped like a tongue, it reaches into the warm sea and is surrounded by soft undulating dunes. From there you can walk undisturbed to another beach, lonely and quiet, with just the water, the sand and the luminous sun; the water so translucent, so diaphanous, you see all kinds of creatures. But on the other side of the tongue the waves are huge, with stingrays often stranded on the beach, desperately flapping their fins and emitting dreadful sounds due to asphyxiation.

Tongoy is a place my grandmother took me to as a child. Somewhere I could run to from her small house, which was situated in the outermost part of this odd-shaped quasi-island. There is also a forest close by, with branches so wide you can sleep on them; a mattress of lichen, with soft nuanced colors and big clouds above. It is said, if you get lost in that forest you'd never get out. Forests like that once abounded in Chile, before the Spanish arrived, conquering with the sword and the cross. Now there is just that one. I still miss the light there. And I still miss my grandmother who introduced me to a world full of beauty and enchantment, who cooked me delicious Jewish Greek food, and taught me French with a Greek accent.

In those days, further north, a person could swim for hours and rent a humble room for almost nothing. But all that disappeared with what is called progress, but to me it is really the invasion of the barbarians. My grandmother was the one who explained the origins of the word barbarian. How it is rooted in the Greek word *barbaros*, meaning "that which is not understandable." Now I refer to this "progress" as the war of the north against the south, with the south and its luscious fruits lost to agribusiness and the mighty dollar.

I often think of Tongoy and the mountains behind it, where some of the most isolated and impoverished communities once lived—with just cacti, goats, and nothingness. I should have stayed there, and looked for the remnants of an ancient culture called Diaguita that left behind beautiful pottery, the sweetest apricots, and the delicate smell of jasmine. 📖

*Medicine Woman 1*, Acrylic on Wood, by vivian linder levi

# Waiting

## Megan McInnes

Christopher waited for his mom to wake up. They were in a McDonald's in Frankfurt, a two-hour drive from where they lived with Chris's grandparents on Ramstein Air Force Base. Christopher was ten. He didn't want to leave his mom long enough to look for a pay phone, or know what he would have said when Grandma answered. My mom's asleep with her head on the table and she won't wake up? My mom is passed out? Dead?

The Germans at the tables around him stared. Only an American child would be so irresponsible as to let his mother pass out with her hair in the French fries. Didn't he know this wasn't a place for sleeping? He kept expecting a guard or the manager to come and make them leave. Would they be able to wake up his mom?

Earlier that day, Christopher had waited in the car in an alley while his mother stood behind the car with a bearded, greasy-haired German. The trunk was raised, and he had a partial view through the slit between the lid of the trunk and the car. He saw his mom pull out a gun—most likely her boyfriend Werner's .45—and hand it to the German, who handed her a plastic bag full of powder. Chris had felt a prickling at the back of his neck, and was sick to his stomach.

When his mom got back in the car she was in an excellent mood and drove them straight to McDonald's. She gave Chris some money and said he could order whatever he wanted while she went into the bathroom—but that she didn't want anything herself. It made Chris nervous when his mom wasn't hungry, and made going to McDonald's less of a celebration when she didn't eat. But he ordered a cheeseburger, French fries, Coke, and an apple pie.

While he waited, he watched the door to the restrooms for his skinny mom in her bright-red raincoat and waist-length black hair. She was beautiful from faraway, but up close her face was pock-marked and her eyes were weary and lined.

Only when Chris was seated and had eaten half his meal did his mom come out of the restroom, walking like she was made of liquid. With heavy lids she scanned the restaurant, smiling big when she found him and making her way to his table. It was the smile Christopher hated: the smile she only wore after she'd disappeared for a long time.

She oozed into a chair, put a French fry in her mouth, then closed her eyes and started sort of melting, her shoulders sagging and her head drooping, until her forehead hit the table. She remained there for . . . how long had it been? He guessed about an hour. And everyone stared—the clerks, the customers (parents and children), the guy who was sweeping the floor. He felt disapproval from all of them, for failing to have a normal mom.

What scared him the most was that he didn't know how to drive, or how he would have gotten his mom in the car if he could drive. And he definitely didn't know how to get back to Ramstein Air Force Base. So he waited.

He waited so long that, forty years later, he has no memory of her waking up. And even now that his mom is dead—she died three years ago—it's as if he's still waiting. 📖

# To Be Or Not To Be?
# aka Early Morning Angst

## Cathy Scott

To live the length of one's years
or end it with a stroke of a sharp knife?
Sharp knife? I don't have a sharp knife!
Besides, so much blood is too much mess . . .
Yet, how I suffer the aches and pains of age.
Arthritis tugs at my back. Age weakens
my legs and spreads fat upon my thighs.
Perhaps it is better to cease the suffering,
better to hang myself from a sturdy rope.
Hang myself? Me? I, who can scarcely tie
my shoes, let alone make a knot strong
enough to hold this old body's heft.
And stand on a chair? Not happening, baby!
Ah, but this early morning angst
reminds me of a foul mattress that delays sleep,
offering endless nights of pain and sorrow.
Surely 'tis better to find a high place
and jump to my end? Jump? Me?
High place? How high is Aurora Bridge?
And does the bus even go that way? I think not.
Forget it. High places scare me.
Alas, too tired to live, too scared to die,
I guess I'll see if I have any chocolate around.

# Anything But

## Taumstar

I would rather pound nails,
attempt to saw a board square,
shovel sand and gravel,
dig a good ditch,
clean out the barn,
milk Charlie the cow

I would rather stack lumber,
lay a row of brick,
burn wood on an open fire,
cut grass with a push mower,
prune bushes and make them round,
pick dandelions by the dozen

I would rather wash dishes in hot soapy water,
listen to classics at breakfast,
eat eggs with potatoes and sour cream,
vacuum the floors, dust every surface,
open the doors, throw back the shutters,
drink coffee and eat cake

I would rather drown worms,
catch rats in a trap,
feed crumbs to the pigeons,
chase the cow from the garden,
pet the cat and feed the dog,
play my flute or blow bubbles

So many things I'd rather do
than sit quietly to write poetry.

# Please Officer . . .

## Elliott Villarreal

I am a human being.
A human being with bi-polar disorder.
I am not crazy.
I am not a danger
to myself or others.
I have a disease,
a disease of the brain.
I do not have a disorder.
I am not disorderly.
I take care of myself.
I take my medications.
I see my psychiatrist once a month.
I see my therapist once a week.
I am a spiritual person.
I study both eastern and western
philosophies of religion.
I use my free time to do this.
I am not lazy
I do not just live off the system.
I do not just eat, sleep, shit, and watch TV.
I am productive.
I am part of a community
called the Recovery Café.
We help each other overcome
our mental illness and addictions.
I travel six hours a day
by public transportation to do this.
I have dignity! I should be shown respect!
I am not a criminal! I do not steal!
I do not kill!
I do my best to do no harm!

Please officer, let me give you my ID.
It is in my wallet.
My wallet is in my pocket.
I am not reaching for a gun . . .
I am not reaching for a gun . . .
I am not reaching for a gun . . .


# Awake Aware Alive

## Taumstar

The eclipse is my timeline
for going through the birth canal
eyes wide open,
awake, aware, alive.

I deserve to be tired.
I wrote six pages,
a report taking five hours.
I cleared the movement
out of my mind and put it on paper,
covered all the points of interest,
and turned my paper over
to a friend to proofread.
I'm glad it's Friday.
All my deadlines I have met on time.
The weekend is clear.
The weather is looking good.
The yard is calling for attention.
I deserve to be tired,
awake, aware, alive.

# IV

## FOOD AND CULTURE

*Kitchen*, Photograph, by Manit Chaotragoongit

# Food Dilemmas

## Megan McInnes

One sign of alcoholism is getting back on the wagon; non-alcoholics don't have a wagon. But I've had a sugar-sobriety wagon for thirty-five-plus years. Every morning I climb back on and, by evening, I've fallen off—or, more often, enthusiastically jumped. If you hear an addict say, "I've been good all day long," go ahead and laugh. All day long is the easiest part; once night falls, you're invisible, and if it can't be seen it doesn't go on your record.

But at my worst I've eaten sugar for breakfast, when the birds are singing and the sun is staring right in. I don't mean pancakes with syrup, or the boxed cereals that finance cartoons; I mean cookies with frosting half as thick as the cookie itself. Whole cartons of them. That is, if any are left from the ones I fell asleep chewing.

I never keep sweets in my house—nor soup, bread, salad dressing, or yogurt containing even a gram of added sugar; that would be *looking* for failure. What I do is wait for the craving to start and then go out to buy something sweet. It only stays in my house for as long as it takes me to eat it—even if it's a whole pie. And I'll eat until it's gone; why keep any around to tempt me later? For God's sake, I'm giving *up* sugar!

This disease runs in my family—both sides. I once found a list that my aunt had written as a teenager, long before I was born: "Twenty-seven Reasons Not to Eat Sugar." When I found it, I had already made several dozen such lists myself—always while high on sugar. (There's nothing like that kind of rush to inspire such brave resolve.) Even now, when I see a new article about glycosylation, glycemic index, insulin resistance, or the way sugar forms glass-like shards that lodge in your joints, I read it as if I'd never read anything else on the subject. I'm fascinated, and motivated to change my life. I'm as addicted to giving up sugar as I am to sugar.

When I was eleven my mom said it was time for me to get clean—not because of ADHD or obesity but because I was normal instead of underweight, like her. (She probably said it while taking a guilty bite from an ice cream bar and giving the rest to me, to keep herself from finishing it.) So she put me on a no-sugar diet, but instead of just cutting out desserts she brought me home "dietetic" candies—that's what they called them in 1978—and ice cream sweetened with saccharin. (When you look at Wikipedia's photograph of the active ingredient—the rocky, powdery "sodium salt of saccharin"—your eye automatically fills in a razor blade next to it.)

Every time a new sugar substitute came on the market, she was all over it: aspartame, neotame, sucralose—anything with a long chemical chain and zero calories. (This is the woman who would later get me addicted to prescription drugs: Methadone. Klonapin. Xanax. Oxycontin.) If anything could be substituted with a low-calorie version, my mom stocked up on it. Melba Toast. Figurines. Tab soda. I Can't Believe You Can't Believe It's Not Butter. Sometimes it wasn't even low-calorie; the important thing was that it was fake.

No wonder the first man I married was someone who'd given up sugar and centered his life around not eating sugar. He also inspired me to vegetarianism—a practice I've continued these last thirty years—but at the time it was less about ethics or even nutrition than self-denial. Together we lived a whole life of self-denial, substituting sugar with healthy carbohydrates, and meat with nothing at all—no protein except that found accidentally in the vegetables we ate (sparingly) and the grains (enough to feed a large farm animal). We didn't think about whether two plates each of whole-wheat spaghetti and a shared loaf of whole-wheat bread was much healthier than a smaller meal with dessert.

But that was our dinner each night. And it followed my daily lunch at Nature's Pantry: a quart of vegetarian pea soup—that's four bowls—and up to seven whole-wheat croissants—as many as were on sale, day-old. (The important thing was that the croissants contained absolutely no sucrose.) When day-old croissants weren't available, I bought a bag of whole-wheat rolls and dipped all eight of them into my soup.

But, even though my body turned all this starch into sugar soon enough, it wasn't soon enough to give me the high I was used to. For that, I resorted to dried pineapple sweetened with harmless fruit-juice concentrate. When I could get it (not every store carried it), I went through the sixteen ounce bag in the car on the way home. I wasn't *really* kidding myself—I knew there was something unwholesome about a sweetness that hurt my teeth. I just didn't dwell on that.

With my second husband I gave up the charade: whole boxes of Fun-Size Baby Ruths were my staple. With my third husband (yes, I was also addicted to marriage), I temporarily lost all interest in sugar—or food of any kind—with my cocaine addiction. I seem to have an attraction to white crystals and powders. Crushed Oxycontin is another example. (Later I learned to love powders in other colors: crushed Adderall can be orange or blue. It's just harder to make excuses for why your nose is dripping blue dye.)

These turned out to be unsustainable solutions to my sugar addiction. And I certainly can't say I've mastered it yet. But I spend a lot more time on the wagon now. I think I'll eventually have a good grip on the reins. 📖

# V

## Odes to Persons, Places, and Things

# Remnant

## Joan Fiset

sift through dust
the crumpled fire exaggerates.

*Remnant*, Photograph, by Sabrina Roberts

# Winnowing

## Joan Fiset

fog too thick to see the curb
alive in this

reminiscent of the house
never discerned

all remembered trees
fade when she glanced away

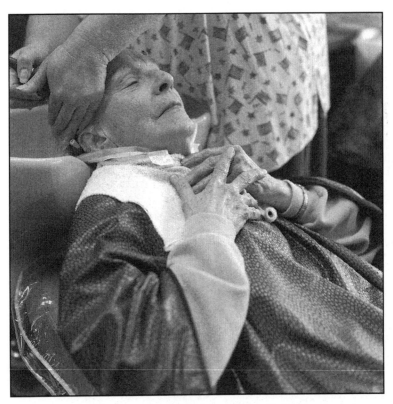

*Winnowing,* Photograph, by Sabrina Roberts

# Posture

## Joan Fiset

late October
plates they shake
nestle in the spine
bend vertebrae
to longitude
homecoming's remind

*Posture,* Photograph, by Sabrina Roberts

# Donald W. Butler
## (December 1964-April 2018)
### Anna Bálint

His slow steady walk, tall, stooped, head low. Slow shy smile. Slow steady movement of hand across paper, pressing the pencil—the words—onto the page; pressing past the pain of gripping the pencil. His words. Their deliberate placement, building blocks to stories. Back into childhood. The one precious day he spent with his father. The death of little brother Merle. Riding with big brother Joe in a beat up Toyota, listening to music. His mother's fried chicken. Her rages, her drinking, the beatings. Home. Holly Park Projects. Bullies, more beatings, a dead body half hidden in grass, broken glass. School. Little boy lost wondering "why am I here?" Drinking behind the gym. Drinking. Drunk.

Discovering dance. The freedom of movement, of moves, of moonwalking. His words now dancing onto the page. Pop-locking contests and dancing at Tacoma Dome. Stories and more stories. Nothing held back. Psychosis, paranoia, the psych ward, prison. The terror of the courtroom. The walls of Walla Walla. Twelve lost years. Release. The joy of walking free. Of seeing children and old people, cats and dogs; of going to the library. Donald the sage. Reading reading reading writing. Self taught.

Writing inspired by Shakespeare. Writing about thermo-dynamics, impulse control, compassion and Buddhism; prison diet and diabetes; about the "sound scape of the sky." His love of music erupting onto the page in bursts of rhythm and rhyme. Donald the gentle, man of endless questions, magic man; death has disappeared you but can never vanquish you. 📖

## Disappearing Act

I am just a fiction
and I am not a fact,
See, I'm going away now
in a disappearing act.
But when you minus zero
from zero minus one
no one is going to tell you
just how the trick is done.

I can pull a rabbit
from out an empty can,
with mind over magic
I am a magic man.
See, from minus to a minus
and now you're having fun,
but it's no longer magic
once you know how it's done.

I am just a fiction
and I am not a fact,
so I have to go away now
in my last disappearing act.
But someone please tell me—
a magic actor ham—
how do you get a big fat rabbit
into an empty can?

—Donald W. Butler

# My Best Friend, Charlie Burks

## (February 6, 1946-January 29, 2018)

### Jeff LaBrache

Who tells their seventh grade friend . . . "This is God's plan for Me . . ." Before I tell you what Charlie said, let me start by saying Charlie had invited me over to his house on Queen Anne Hill to listen to records. I don't mean early rock n roll . . . Yes it was 1956-57 and I was in a band called the Imperials, but Charlie had decided it was time for me to hear some jazz. I had grown up on Big Band music, early rock 'n' rhythm n blues, but NO jazz. Here I was in Charlie's house looking at boxes and boxes of Jazz records. As we listened and drank some hot chocolate, Charlie said, "I know what God's plan for me is." I don't remember exactly what I said but it was probably huh? or oh. . . .

Charlie went on. His father had told him (remember this was the 50s and we all still listened to our parents), "you will live a simple life, never be famous, and never be rich. This is your and my lot in life. You need to accept it and be peaceful with it."

*The early years*: I met Charlie in the seventh grade. I was just drawn to him; he was different than my other classmates. The start was a music connection. I had a rock band; it was 1958. The house where Charlie grew up was old but as warm and comforting as any child's blanket that made them safe in the night. In the front room was a huge, black grand piano, a cheap tiny record player, and boxes full of jazz records. Being with Charlie was like being born again. Not a religious "born again," but born into the amazing world of jazz. Charlie knew more about every jazz and blues musician than anyone I have ever met or seen on PBS. His memory was amazing. Even at the end of his life, he could tell you anything about these historical giants—even the obscure ones.

*Ninth Grade*: Every year in our school there was a talent show. Charlie had written a ten minute production for piano, voice, and drums. It was full of strange chords, lines of poetry about things no other ninth grader (or most high school students) had ever

*Charlie Burks aka Julu El Condor,* 1980s, Seattle,
Bumbershoot Festival, Photograph, by Marilyn Stablein

thought about; then there was me—sitting behind my trap set playing crazy like Keith Moon to accompany Charlie's piano and vocal masterpiece. I remember the teacher, who had organized the event, said "you can't do this!" But we did it anyway. The students sat wide-eyed with their mouths opened in dead silence. It was great. After our act a girl came out and played a piece on the violin. "Ahhh." The crowd went back to normal.

Charlie began writing poetry in elementary school. His hunger for music was never satisfied.

*From Queen Anne High School to the world:* In 1966, we filled a UHaul with band stuff and headed for San Francisco. Charlie, of course, was with us as a friend and musical visionary. We would sit in our apartment in Haight-Ashbury, smoke dope, and talk about what Charlie was sure was coming to the music scene next. He was never wrong. One day I was on the street and found an envelope in a phone booth with $200 in it. I ran back to the apartment to grab Charlie. He put his coat on and we headed for the record store. We bought six albums and spent the rest of the money on "medicine". We spent the next two days locked in our apartment with pinned eyes and records.

*The 1980's*: The next years were hard. Charlie had almost been killed in a car accident at the foot of Queen Anne Hill. He was broke and so became a ward of the state. I was in Texas at the time. In the past month I have read and re-read all the amazing letters Charlie wrote to me at that time. As we wrote back and forth and talked on the phone, Charlie never talked about his troubles. He lived with migraine headaches, stomach problems, and the jail-like conditions he had to live in for the rest of his life. When I would ask about his condition, he would always say, "let's talk about you. How is your wife and tell me what your kids are doing." Although severely disabled, Charlie continued to write. He sent me hundreds of things; second draft of one:

The Program
You used to pretend you didn't like lies
You had the two kinds, pretty lies and ugly lies
Pretty lies were called the Truth and you told them to each other
Now you find you don't have all that time to waste
Lies have to run faster than whoever pays them to run
Ugly lies are like wind sprints, You've got to stay in shape

Charlie, I miss you so much. 📖

# Old Joke

## Stephen Thomas

—*In memoriam Charlie Burks, Stand-up Aphorist,*
*Scholar, and Raconteur*

#1
Skeleton walks into a bar.
Bartender sez, *The usual?*
Skeleton nods.
Bartender pours him a beer,
hands him a mop.

#2
Skeleton sees a woman at the end of the bar.
pretty woman. It's dark.
Sez, *Buy you a drink?*

Husky-voiced woman,
Mae West sort of voice.
*No thanks*
*I drink with men who can hold their liquor.*

#3
Skeleton sez, *Bartender,*
*you heard this one?*
*There were these two guys. See . . .*

A couple of cripples in the corner
pick up their crutches and saunter out.

#4
Skeleton takes his stool at the bar,
sez, *Bartender, what's in the jar?*

Bartender shoots him a look.
*Fingertips, you knucklehead.*

Skeleton drums the bar with his fingers.
Syncopated.

#5
Skeleton's feeling a little eroded.
Wakes up with his jaw on the doorknob.
One of his arms hangs from the door of the fridge.
Can't find most of his ribs.
He puts himself together best he can.

*Whatsamatter!*, he shouts on the street to the starers,
*You never seen a chandelier?*

#6
Skeleton stumbles into a church basement.
There's one of the cripples from Joke #3.
*Where's your buddy?* he asks.

*Died laughing.*

#7
Skeleton looks down the bar.
There's the famous termite.
There's the horse with the long face.
There's the one they call Douche Bag,
sipping her vinegar neat.
The guy who's been called a taxi so many times
he's had a meter installed on his stool.

*I got to start drinking alone.*

#8
Skeleton runs into the bartender at the laundramat.

*Ain't seen you lately.*

*Quit drinkin'.*

You ribbin' me?

#9
Skeleton's scared.
Went to the sink as ever
to scrape the chalk off his chin,
sees skin, lips, a pair of green eyes.

*Shit!* he yelps.
*I'm disappearin'.*

#10
Skeleton walks in the bar.
What'll you have?
Bartender's clueless.
*Soda* he sez
*with a Squeeze.*

Both of them happen to eye Mae West.

*Sorry, stranger.*
Bartender's suspicious.
*This isn't that kinda place.*

# End of An Era:
# Eagle Harbor Liveaboards

## Joel Sackett

E agle Harbor on Bainbridge Island, with its sheltered cove and shallow depth, was known as a friendly port for live-aboards for a century.

They'd often go by nicknames, a liveaboard tradition. Ladder Mike, formerly a skilled house painter, Big Ray, a bosun in the Merchant Marine whose job was "running crews of not so gentle men," Blue-Haired Ryan (not to be confused with Blowhard Ryan), Toothless Jeff, Weird Al, Handkerchief Bill, and Richie Rich because his boat was luxurious compared to the others. And sometimes they weren't around long enough to say their names or reveal a trait that led to a nickname. Others were loners looking down or outlaws looking over their shoulders. Over the decades, many defied homelessness with an old boat in a free harbor.

But this independent living community had struggles with their well-to-do neighbors on the hill overlooking the harbor, many of whom regarded them as freeloaders and an eyesore. It's true that not all of the liveaboards were good environmental stewards. There were derelict vessels, lots of blue tarps, and no adequate waste disposal—all problems that contributed to the demise of the liveaboard community as we knew it before 2011.

That was the year they were finally evicted, about seventeen in all. The newly-devised plan wouldn't work for most of them. They would now be required to meet USCG (U.S. Coast Guard) requirements, pay rent to the city, and be tethered to either lineage moorage or buoy moorage. Gentrification, for all intents and purposes, destroyed this Northwest tradition, now deemed inappropriate for this place.

Most of them scattered to the harbors of more tolerant communities, the woods, Alaska, and who knows where else? I'm glad to see Ladder Mike is still around, even though his dog, Scout, a celebrity in his own right, died. Mike now lives in a wooden container he built in the woods near the Bainbridge Island ferry terminal. I hope the others have found safe havens. 📖

*Dave Ullin on his tugboat and home, named The Spruce.*
Photograph by Joel Sackett

*Gale Williams, retired logger, with his best friend.*
Photograph by Joel Sackett

*A young writer, Big Ray's nephew Jake, is spending a
month on the Wicca to develop his craft.*
Photograph by Joel Sackett

*Big Ray looks out onto Eagle Harbor from inside the Wicca.*
Photograph by Joel Sackett

*Ladder Mike and Scout on their way to town.*
Photograph by Joel Sackett

# VI

## Poetics and Community

*King for a Day*, 2017, Digital Photograph, by E. Grace Dager

# African-American Writers'
# Alliance of Seattle

In January 1991, Californian Randee Eddins called to order the first meeting of the African-American Writers' Alliance (AAWA). Her idea for an informal gathering of Northwest black writers meeting for mutual support and encouragement through the exchange of ideas and concepts became a reality. The warmth and informality of the gatherings provide a forum for both new and published writers, a setting where they can explore both finished works and works in progress among their peers—minus censure. The ready-made audience supports writers by listening and sharing. Attending and presenting workshops also help writers polish their skills.

Writers share their works in a variety of venues in the Puget Sound region: bookstores, libraries, prisons, churches, taverns, festivals, fairs, schools, museums, colleges, and universities. AAWA members are often on television and radio. As AAWA celebrates its twenty-seventh year, more than two hundred writers have participated on a variety of levels. Among venues AAWA has regularly read at are Gallery 110 and Festival Sundiata. AAWA contributors have written poems for Onyx Fine Collective exhibits since 2009, and read at Elliott Bay Book Company since 1992. The group has published five anthologies: *Sometimes I Wander* (1998), *Gifted Voices* (2000), *Words? Words! Words* (2004), *Threads* (2009), and *Voices That Matter* (2018).

The second Sunday of each month AAWA members read at Columbia City Library at 2:00 p. m.; the second Monday at the Seward Park Third Place Books at 7:00 p. m.; Humble Vine Wine Gifts the third Friday at 7:00 p. m.; and at Open Books quarterly. Open mikes are part of all readings. Readings are posted on our website *aawa-seattle.com*.

—Georgia S. McDade

**Margaret Barrie:** "In 2012, I attended a reading at the Elliott Bay Book Company, my first time hearing the AAWA. I was fascinated by the quality of the diverse voices sharing their stories, prose, and poems; some were singing along with their words and others danced; I knew I wanted join. I attended the first Saturday morning meetings, met other writers, who looked like me but didn't write like me. I felt safe to share my short stories and poems. I write to stay healthy, and AAWA have given me many opportunities to grow and develop my skills reading in the larger literary community."

**Minnie Collins:** "AAWA is a concentric of intergenerational writers, published and unpublished. Group members create a positive space for monthly writing, reading, and responding. Desiring their responses raised my writing self-expectations. Being in this writers' circle has transitioned me from personal journal entries to public venues: museums, galleries, libraries, community celebrations, bookstores, and Seattle Reads programs. Encouraged and guided by members, I am the author of two solo poetry collections, and included in several anthologies. More social media visibility is a prerequisite to growth: a city-wide site of all writer's groups, knowledge of and participation with other writers; marketing us to read at city programs, conventions/conferences; network coverage, grant writing workshops, as well as strategies for publishing, marketing, and selling books."

"My name is **Gail Haynes,** a member of AAWA since 2015. The experience has been enlightening, fun, and educational. My association with this group has allowed me to give voice to my silent emotions and feelings. Prior to joining, my writings lived a sedentary life in a binder on a bookshelf. I read them occasionally to family and friends. Since I've joined the Alliance my poems have inspired and empowered audiences throughout Seattle/King County. I've seen people burst out with laughter. I've seen people who appeared to be collecting their thoughts or reflecting on something I said. My poems have taken on a new life and I've joined them for the adventure."

**Georgia S. McDade:** "Without a doubt one of the best moves I ever made was joining the AAWA. Although I kept journals for years and had written stories, poems, and plays for decades before the 1991 inception of AAWA, I had never written regularly, never thought of publishing. An early agreement was that each of us bring a piece of writing to share at each meeting. I had a story for every meeting, some old, some new! One day we decided each of us would read five minutes at an upcoming venue. The story I had written required twenty-one minutes; the group voted to allow me twenty-one minutes. I soon decided I had to make my points in fewer words; that was the beginning of regularly writing poems, to date almost 1,000. I have published four books of poetry and a collection of stories. I'm working on a pamphlet, two biographies, three books of poetry, and the publication of my doctoral dissertation. Being in the company of persons who understand and appreciate what I write has emboldened me. AAWA encourages me to express myself. Because of AAWA, writing has become and most likely will remain an integral part of my life."

**Merri Ann Osborne:** "As a new member of AAWA, I'm inspired and encouraged from the support I have received from other members. The organization has allowed me to develop as a writer through their feedback sessions, book reading opportunities, and professional development. It's also a great place for writers of the African diaspora to get together, hone their craft, and share their personal and universal stories with the global community."

**Lola E. Peters:** "After moving back to the Seattle area in 1998, I test-drove many writing groups: dropping in for a few sessions, listening to their critiques of one another's writing, and finally bringing my work to share. Their critique processes always felt competitive and tinged with humiliation, rather than supportive and nurturing. I was always the only person of color in the group and received much more criticism on my subjects than on my actual writing. A group in Tacoma, run by the extraordinary writer/editor/teacher Val Dumond, was wonderful, but driving between Seattle and Tacoma in rush hour traffic was exhausting, therefore unsustainable. In 2003, I heard about a reading by local African American writers at Elliott Bay Book Company in Seattle. During the reading, their fearless leader and indomitable spirit, Georgia McDade, explained the origins of the African American Writers' Alliance, and invited other writers of African descent to attend their monthly meetings. I did. Home at last. The environment was friendly, welcoming of both subject and style, with supportive and thoughtful critique aimed at improving my writing. With AAWA's encouragement I have published two books of poetry, and one of essays. As an incubator for new talent, and an infrastructure for those who want to branch out and challenge the boundaries of their own potential, the group continues to grow and evolve. The readings at Elliott Bay continue as testament to its success."

**Jacqueline Ware:** "AAWA entered my life at a critical time. My dearest friend and fellow poet passed away on the Sunday the Seahawks won the Super Bowl. Linda arranged all of our events and appearances. I felt alone without her kind and positive encouragement and support, but then I found the Alliance. The environment was different, forcing me to step out of my comfort zone. Dr. McDade was passionate about the group and constantly arranged appearances, performances, and open mike opportunities. Her pushing pushed and motivated me. My writing and confidence steadily improved and I received my first grant because of her example. The role the Alliance played in my development as a writer was a necessary boost." 📖

# The OPS Art Workshop,
# An Agent of Change

## Martha McAvoy Linehan

The Organization for Prostitution Survivors (OPS) is a social service agency and an agent of change. We offer holistic accompaniment to female-identifying people who have been victims of commercial sexual exploitation (CSE), co-creating and sustaining efforts to heal from and end this practice of gender-based violence.

The first OPS Art Workshop took place in February 2013, and it has been running continuously on a drop-in basis every Saturday since then. Because of the complex and chronic nature of the trauma experienced by women who have been survivors of CSE, and because most of these women have experienced it over the course of their lives, generally beginning with early child sex abuse, the way the workshop is organized has contributed to its success as both an entry point to services as well as being a safe therapeutic space for ongoing healing and recovery. The associative nature of the overall experience is powerful for women who have suffered from isolation, marginalization, dissociation, and fragmentation of the self as a result of their being in the life of prostitution. There is the very personal relational nature of the work itself between the artist and herself, along with the relational nature of artmaking in a community providing women with a safe way to connect and relate with other women who are also survivors. Without having to tell her story, she explores a freedom to describe what I frequently hear was, until now, "inexpressible". She experiences what it is to be seen, heard, and validated by her community and also bear witness to another survivor's experience.

The overall structure of the workshop day is consistent from week to week so the women come to know what to expect; they learn to trust the process leading to their taking ownership of the group and of their own unique creative process. The first hour is social time, which includes a home-cooked meal, followed by our circling up to ground through a brief mindfulness practice using breath, and sometimes movement, to share poems, and finally to be introduced to the art project which varies from week to week. Themes that we have recently explored together are protest art, sisterhood, liberation, the color red, bodily integrity, solidarity, fire, masks, vulnerability.

Guest artists sometimes join us to share a particular skill, medium, or to explore a special theme. Maggie Smith, a Bainbridge Island-based clay artist, has been coming once a month to work with us on a theme very close to OPS's heart: remembering, celebrating, and honoring the lives of the Green River Victims. This art workshop serves as a sort of living memorial for the women and girls who were murdered in King County between 1984-1993 by the country's most prolific serial killer, who "hated prostitutes." He knew "they were easy to pick up without being noticed" and that "they would not be reported missing right away and might never be reported." Our hope is to one day create a permanent memorial for the victims. The historical trauma of the killings is acknowledged in the art created here, and the process creating that art gives the women an opportunity to begin to heal as we work together creating art and poems for and about the women and girls who did not make it out of the life alive. Other incredible guest artists have included Seattle's current Civic Poet Anastacia-Reneé, social engagement and installation artist Michelle de la Vega, photographer Sherry Loeser, and community-based arts educator, Caroline Brown.

The remainder of the afternoon is spent making art. When new women arrive, those who have been around for a while welcome them in and model the values of our community. This is their space. The afternoon ends with us circling again to look at the art. Artists are invited to share about their experience, we re-ground, and close. One afternoon during our closing circle, one of the women shared about her art-making experience and she put it into these words: "I am not just looking to cope anymore, I'm looking to transform." Visit *www.seattleops.org.* 📖

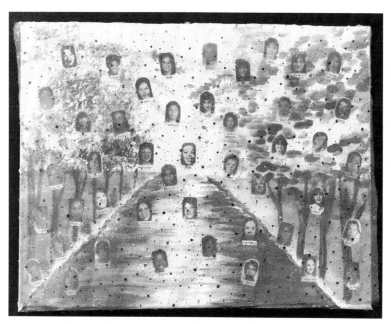

*Precious Jewels*, 2017, Mixed Media, by SMS, survivor

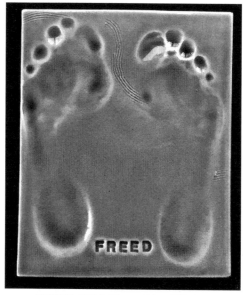

*FREED*, 2018, Green River Victims
Memorial Ceramic Tile, by Survivor

# VII
## FEATURED THEME
## LAST CALL

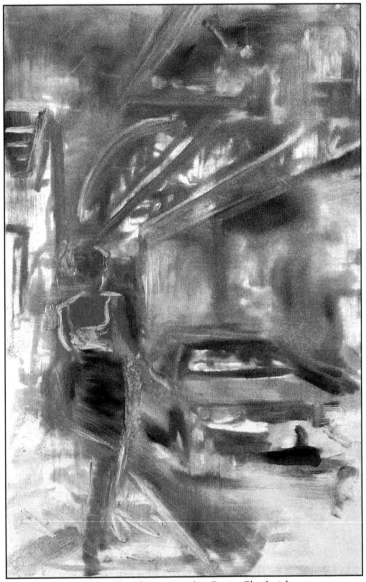

*Under The El*, Painting, by Gregg Chadwick

# Immigration

## Linda Amundson

Let's live in Mexico, where stoplights only work on Sunday,
where the name of the father the son and the holy ghost are
Enrique, Jesus and Luis.
They will sit in faded beach chairs drinking cervazas
and argue the right way to think about everything.

Let it be a place I can say, today I will not wear teeth
only shoes, water droplets and shadows.
On a moonless night we can slip the border like trout,
to find an orange house with hot pink bougainvillea.
We can wander the marketplace finding blue glasses
for our casa, where old dreams collect by the gate,
catch fish, listen to the stars and whales
as we explore both sides of the Sea of Cortez.

Let's eat too much and drink too much and laugh
like we just discovered dancing.
We will think about time travel, and if the place we were when
we first dreamed of Mexico is still the same.
With each sip of morning coffee, we will taste the dreams
of those who went norte as we went sur.

# Decay

## Sara Bailey

She bore her disappointment around her shoulders
Like a lead shawl—cold, heavy, painful.
Resentment burned in her veins and inflamed
Her cheeks, her hope again crushed like a cigarette
Beneath the boot heel of inequity. Giving up was
A privilege not afforded to her as she shuffled along,
Clothed in despair, slouching towards the death of
Another year and the painful, bloody birth of a new one.
"Someday" was the dreamer's drug; "yesterday" was a
Numbing agent for the nostalgic. She lived in the here
And now, rubbed raw from the daily grind. The world
Had grown wicked and warped since she was a youth.
Darkness and depravity had slowly seeped in to every
Crevice, permeated every pore, stained every fiber of
Moral fabric. Innocence had but a brief half-life.

# Ilonka's List

## Anna Bálint

I lonka Sárkozi had no case. This she discovered in the 1950s when there was talk of compensation. She went to the authorities and told them, "I lost everyone, except for a brother already in London and safe, and one cousin, respectable, right here in Budapest, everyone else dead."

"Names?"

"Here. Here are their names."

She had gone prepared. She handed a little gadjo[1] behind a glass partition a list of names written in thin spidery handwriting, not Ilonka's own, for she could neither read nor write, but that of her cousin Tibor, now become so respectable he refused to accompany her on a wild goose chase such as this. Why draw attention to himself? Why invite trouble?

"This one thing then, Tibor, I beg of you. For those who died, write their names on a piece of paper." This much he had agreed to.

The little gadjo sat on a high stool where he could peer down at her. It seemed to Ilonka that the glass was there to protect him from the likes of her. He peered over the tops of his spectacles, and what he saw, she knew. A short, rotund, and sweating Roma woman wearing a big skirt. The sweat was unavoidable, not only because of the heat, but also due to nerves.

The little gadjo's glance shifted to the names on the paper. These were many. Twenty-six in all. He took off his spectacles and polished them with his tie, looked again at the names, then leaned over to compare them with others, these in a book. This took an age. Ilonka continued to sweat. Such a thick book, containing so many thousands of names.

There was in fact no such book.

The little gadjo had looked at nothing at all. With a slight batting of the air with his hand, as if a fly were bothering him in his sleep, he sent Ilonka away.

---

1. Gadjo: Non-Gypsy (man)

"Next."

True, there were many people behind her. All of them had lost somebody. All waited to present their case. The line went out the door and down the corridor. Later, Ilonka remembered them as all being Jews. She had difficulty in recalling exactly how it went. She was sent away, yes. But was that the first time, the second time, or the third? In Budapest or Berlin? Perhaps after all, there had been no one else waiting—no Jews, no Gypsies, no one. The Jews had already been and gone. The Gypsies had not come forward, neither Roma nor Sinti. There were reasons. They did not read newspapers. Had not heard about compensation. Did not trust governments. Had suffered enough. Wanted to forget. Were already dead.

So perhaps Ilonka had been the only one, huffing from her climb up the stairs, standing alone in the third floor office with its polished linoleum. The linoleum stayed polished because so few people found their way there. Most ended up instead in a small room for small people with small problems, with its single desk buried under piles of paper, and a little spectacled gadjo buried behind the desk in a chair so low his face was barely visible. He was hiding. A mere clerk of the court, who never so much as looked in her direction, used his spectacles for nothing. Just handed her a sheath of papers.

"Fill these out, and bring them back."

Was that in Berlin? What had happened to German efficiency?

But Ilonka was not about to be put off so easily. Not after the long train journey, involving two border crossings, armed guards, and frightening memories; also two trams, and three flights of stairs. She reached into the front of her shirt and drew out the carefully folded piece of paper on which Tibor had written the names.

"I have their names," she said. Her voice sounded almost strident. She softened it at once. "Here, here are their names."

The same piece of paper offered. Tibor's handwriting looking uncertain now, insignificant, faded: as if sunlight had bleached the ink. The little gadjo waved the entire list away without so much as a glance.

*Zsuzsa Horváth, Roma survivor of the Holocaust,*
Torony, Hungary, 2009, Photograph, by Anna Bálint

"Bring me the completed forms. Next."

So there had been others, clinging to walls, in shadow, close to the door. It was hot in that room, a furnace. Windows closed, blinds pulled tight, the summer sunshine pressing steadily, relentlessly, mercilessly against the glass, heating up everything inside. Like an oven. Ilonka felt faint. She pulled a handkerchief from her sleeve and mopped her face. Gathering herself together, she stood as tall as she could. This was barely five foot one inch. She puffed out her chest. She would not allow herself to be waved away by a little gadjo in shirtsleeves and dusty spectacles. She trembled but would not leave.

"I have information. Everything that happened, I can tell it." She pointed to the names on the list. "These two shot. This one in the head, he fought over bread. This one my husband, his body flying up against the fence. Still he flies against the fence in my dreams. These two typhus. This one hunger. This one my niece, raped then shot."

She was escorted out.

She found herself beside the tram stop in blazing sunshine. A few yards away a Romani youth was being beaten. Police appeared, slapped handcuffs on the youth, and dragged him away. On the sidewalk were left traces of his blood, but no one seemed to mind and busy people went about their business. With the war a decade behind them, people were happy to live in peaceful and prosperous times. Except in Hungary, where an uprising was going on . . . though Ilonka did not yet know this, and for the moment her troubles were here, in this unfamiliar city, with her brown skin and big skirts. She walked quickly with her head down, autumn leaves swirling about her, relieved that no one seemed to see her, not even the playful young thugs who found sport in beating up Gypsies, and who had now swung themselves onto a passing tram, laughter trailing behind them.

Back in Budapest, soldiers ran through the streets. Tanks rumbled over bridges. The weather turned cold. During that time, Ilonka disappeared from the world, dug herself in, and lost herself in dreams of long ago when snow banked against the sides of her family's tents, and inside was warm with story and song.

In spring she emerged, undertook another long journey and re-entered the building. She waited in line, until she found herself once more in front of the little gadjo's desk.

"Ah, Ilonka Sárkozi!"

Fans whirred overhead, the room busy. So many desks with so much going on, phones ringing, office workers tapping pencils on pads, glancing at watches, clearing throats, straightening ties, pushing paper this way and that, papers stamped with red ink, rollers rolled in red ink pads. Rejected! Approved!

Once more Ilonka presented her list, picking up from where she'd left off. "This one, typhus. This one too. This one's face eaten by sores. This one too. You've heard of Noma? No? Before this I never hear of Noma. The terrible sores inside the mouth, growing and growing, until they eat through the person's face. You have to see it to believe it."

None of this appeared to be of interest to the little gadjo. He yawned, and cleaned under his fingernails with a scrap of paper. So Ilonka entertained him with a brief song and a dance, because she understood that's what he expected of her. That, or to have his wallet stolen. She finished the dance with a swirl of her skirts. A small crowd had gathered. The little gadjo had grown bigger. He sat back in his chair with his feet on his desk, smoking a cigar. He clapped slowly and loudly. His hands sounded hollow.

"Bravo! Bravo!" he said. His enthusiasm was not genuine.

Ilonka leaned on the edge of his desk. Her hands were battered, her fingers misshapen. Carrying rocks will do that to hands. The little gadjo, still swollen to a larger size, twirled his mustache and seemed to notice neither her hands nor her. Ilonka tapped the list of names with a ringed forefinger. Out of the corner of her eye she saw the security guard approaching.

"These two typhus, this one starvation, this one made to drink salt water until he died. These two twin girls, only seven years old . . ." Here her voice faltered.

"Somewhere . . . in a jar are their heads, floating in formaldehyde."

At last she had his attention! He took his feet off the desk and looked at her. For the first time he saw her. His eyes glittered behind his glasses. He put up his hand to halt the approach of the guard. She continued.

"Maybe you've heard of Dr. Mengele, how he loved Gypsy twins? He came into the camp in his white coat and riding boots. Yes, it is true. Sometimes he rode up to the fence on a white horse, and the children ran to him calling, "Uncle, Uncle." He fed them sweets and took them away to his laboratory, where he altered God's creations . . . and then killed them."

At that point she covered her face with her hands, and wept.

"Everyone else was gassed," she whispered.

The phone on the little gadjo's desk began ringing.

He picked it up, and swiveled his chair so that his back was to Ilonka. He talked into the phone. He talked and talked and Ilonka waited.

A week passed.

During that time she camped out in a corner of the office and struck up a friendship with the cleaning lady, who was Sinti. She also sang songs. At night when everyone was gone, she cooked sausages over a match. At the end of the week, the little gadjo, now finished with his phone call, had her forcibly removed from the building. Once more she was deposited on the sidewalk next to the tram stop.

This time it was raining a light summer shower. Ilonka sat on the sidewalk for some time and let the rain run down her face, washing away her tears. People bustled by, not even noticing the heap in big skirts, except for one man, who kicked Ilonka and called her a filthy beggar. When the rain stopped, her tears stopped, and she discovered her hand still clutching the list of names. Wet and wrinkled, but safe at least, she folded it carefully and tucked it back inside her shirt. Then she rode the tram across the city to Tibor's apartment. Or perhaps it was first necessary to convince the authorities at the Hungarian border that her papers were legitimate, and she was in fact a citizen of that country. This may also have involved being detained for several hours, if not days. Though it is possible she later confused things with another occasion. Either way, she rode a train, and another tram, until she found herself back in Budapest, where the trees lining the streets were heavy and green with leaf. She came to the building where Tibor lived and climbed the stairs to his door. Tibor had a sweet, pink wife, who was the only one home.

"Please Ágnes, some different clothes, I beg of you. One of your skirts, a nice blouse."

At five o'clock Tibor arrived home from work to find Ilonka changed. He nodded his approval. Life had taught him it was better to blend in, and he had long since shaved off his mustache, taken off his hat, and took great pains to stay out of the sun.

"You look good, Ilonka. A little tight across the chest, but good."

It was true the buttons of the blouse were straining, but there was nothing to be done about that. That evening, the three of them ate stuffed peppers and drank a little wine. Ilonka shared with

Ágnes and Tibor her ordeal, and Tibor wagged his finger—not unkindly—and said he'd told her so.

"Nonetheless," she said, "I must go back." Yes, back to that place, to the court. For those who died she must return with the forms. Please God, had Tibor completed the forms she had left with him? He had not. But Ilonka's wailed insistence, face in hands, her shoulders heaving, he promised he would.

"Ssh, Ilonka, quiet I insist. Please consider the neighbors."

With a labored sigh he took his fountain pen from his brief-case and stayed up many hours into the night completing the forms. As it turned out, there was much he couldn't make sense of. To make up for the pages he by necessity was obliged to leave blank, he rewrote the list of names on a fresh sheet of paper.

The following morning Ilonka set out in her new costume smelling faintly of lavender water and clutching the sheath of half-completed forms and traveled for what seemed like an eternity. Eventually she arrived at the imposing building where her case was to be heard. Outside a Romani man was being arrested for vagrancy. His eyes as he was dragged away were both angry and pleading. Somewhat unsettled, Ilonka entered the building through its rotating door. Inside were gleaming marble floors and immediately she was startled by echoes. Even whispers became huge. This seemed promising, as if there were no way this time that she would not be heard. Her confidence returned, she made her way up the marble staircase to a familiar room where she reported to the desk of the little gadjo responsible for hearing these cases, who, when he looked up and saw who was standing before him—this time dressed in a rather too small tweed skirt and cotton blouse—stared as if seeing an apparition.

"Ilonka Sárkozi. . . ?"

"Here are the forms," said Ilonka. "Also the list of names, freshly written on a clean piece of paper."

The little gadjo cleared his throat and straightened his tie. The nosepiece of his glasses was now held together with a piece of tape, and he seemed to have shrunk. No doubt this was because Ilonka had grown. Thank you, no, she did not want to sit down.

She stood, undeniably taller in her new costume, one hand on hip, the effect marred only by the row of tattooed numbers, now visible, on her left forearm. Persistence had brought her here, to this moment. To this polished expanse of desk, and to this ashen-complexioned little gadjo in a suit, who pressed his fingertips together and gestured for her to sit down.

"Ilonka Sárkozi, I am happy to inform you I am your court-appointed attorney. Your list of names is here in my briefcase along with your forms." Ilonka's understanding of German was limited, and he spoke neither Hungarian nor Romani, so there followed a long silence during which neither attempted to speak, and Ilonka observed the way the little gadjo's Adam's apple twitched, and she had these thoughts. When the Arrow Cross soldiers arrived at her village that chilly morning in 1944, and rousted her family out of beds, or from wash basins, or from wherever they were—coffee tossed out of mugs, horses and dogs shot, children crying, the barrels of guns thrust between people's shoulder blades, roughly pushing, cursing, guns held to the sides of people's heads—Ilonka had recognized one of them.

"Karoly!" she exclaimed, unable even in those conditions to contain her surprise. There he had been. The innkeeper's son, a scrawny boy of sixteen suddenly turned into a gadjo with a gun. Karoly, a fascist in an Arrow Cross uniform, giving the Nazi salute. What was to say that the little gadjo seated beside her, with her list of names in his briefcase and dandruff on his collar, had not been a fascist too? Maybe he once held a gun to a Gypsy girl's head. Maybe raped her. Then shot her. And now with the war over, had slipped back into respectable society and put on a tie. Perhaps she should leave, now, while there was still time.

Too late. Ilonka Sárkozi's moment had come. She heard her name called, and entered a courtroom full of the echoes of those who had gone before her, many Jews, and a handful of Gypsies. She was surprised they didn't sound louder. As for the judge, something about him reminded her of the little gadjo, though more robust and rosier in complexion, wearing a robe and an eyeglass instead of the familiar spectacles. When he banged his gavel his voice resonated with the authority of his position, and reverberated throughout the echo chamber.

"Ilonka Sárkozi, the names you have given us do not match any on the official lists. What names were your relatives registered under?"

Someone translated. Somehow the words reached her in a language she understood, though faintly, as if but the tail end of an echo.

What could she do but shrug? How was she to know what names the Germans had written in their books? Or what names the various members of her family had given? For as long as she could remember names were changed to suit the occasion, to slip over borders, to blend in, to satisfy the authorities, to escape persecution.

"There. The names on that list, those are their names. The names they answered to."

"As far as our records go, such people did not exist."

"But they did. They were my father, my granny, my niece, my husband ... my children ..."

"Ah, your husband. Where is your certificate of marriage, Ilonka Sárkozi? Do you have a certificate of marriage to present to this court?"

Ilonka was confused. Why would she have a thing such as that? What did paper have to do with marriage? The little gadjo lawyer at her side cleared his throat and waved his hands as if preparing to speak, then deserted her, scuttling out of the room. The judge's questions continued.

"Is your name in fact Ilonka Sárkozi? What name were you registered under when you entered the Gypsy Family Camp in the spring of '43?"

How was Ilonka to know what name the Germans had written down? She could not read. Besides conditions were such that you couldn't exactly look over their shoulder to see what they wrote. Someone pulling you this way and cutting off your hair. Someone pulling you that way and ordering you to take off your clothes. The shame of being naked in front of men. Delousing powder thrown over your head, someone else grabbing your arm and marking it Z for Zigeuner followed by four numbers. What mattered the name? All that mattered in that place was the number.

"Here, here it is. The number on my arm."

Her arm was presented to the bench. The number noted. There followed a huddle, several small gadjos in glasses and dark suits, gathered about the bench, talking in whispers so small not even the echoes could decipher what was being said.

"It appears Ilonka Sárkozi, that the number on your arm was not registered to Ilonka Sárkozi. Either you are currently a fraud, or fraudulent information was given at the time of registration. In addition, it appears that you have no permanent address and are in fact a vagrant. Case dismissed."

Back in Budapest, Tibor could only say that he had warned her, and offer her a glass of schnapps. Ágnes told her she could keep the blouse if she liked, to which Ilonka said thank you, but no, nothing with short sleeves.

From that time forth the number tattooed on her arm remained forever hidden under the long sleeves of her clothing. Hence it was not there. As for the scar on her abdomen—which through the entire proceedings she never mentioned due to the shame of it—this she kept well-hidden under the big skirts she returned to wearing. Hence the scar too, was not there. Never had she been under those lights, or that knife, slicing away the chance of her ever again bearing children. With her daughters' sweet faces floating in jars, their father shot, what had she needed of more children? Never had she mentioned at any time that the twins had been hers. That had been too much to speak.

The Sixties arrived. Rations had long been lifted. Blessed the abundance in the home of Ilonka's cousin and his wife. Blessed the bonbons, pastries, and chocolates with crème fillings that graced their table. Blessed too the magnificent blossoming of Ilonka's abdomen, to such proportions that the hateful scar was hidden even from her own view.

And so it came to pass that what happened, never happened. For memories can be buried. Like burying the dead, it is important to bury them deep, otherwise hard rains and animals will uncover them, and they will have to be buried all over again, deeper than before. Always deeper, deeper.

Time helps.

Time is the dirt thrown in to cover the coffin so that people who once were on this earth and no longer are—husband, twin girls, niece, brother, cousins, Granny—can rest at last, so long as their names are not spoken. Yet, still, to this day, hidden inside her shirt next to her heart, Ilonka Sárkozi carries the list of names, on folded paper worn thin by time. 📖

# And Then On To Palookaville

## Paul Bamberger

i see you bought a one way ticket welcome to hotel
palookaville come on in we're always open come we
have seven fine days set aside under your name your
weary travels are over and as for night well that's just
rumor and don't concern yourself with whispers come
relax we're stress free here at hotel palookaville best
rates in town
what hard scrabble it must have been   your trip to
palookaville  all those jackhammer ravings of a mad
language those half truth inhibitions the unforgiving
wounds  we here at hotel palookaville take no pleasure
in  say aren't you that fellow the north bound traveler
everybody's talking about  you'll find we make no
mockery of wannabes here at hotel palookaville come
on in  heady days ahead

*Tipi Sunrise*, Photograph, by Theodore C. Van Alst, Jr.

# Emerald Princess

## Jane Blanchard

I serve a lot of divas every trip.
None but that one has ever let it rip
so bad. Yeah, she was nasty drunk before
we even reached three miles off shore, drank more
each hour. Win or lose, at slots or dice,
roulette or blackjack, she was never nice
to nobody, especially not her hus-
band. Sure, he staked her play all night because
he had some manners. Her? She threw a fit
when he suggested she slow down a bit.
He just laughed. Well, she got so mad, my Lord,
she ran out on the deck, jumped overboard!
A shrimper saw her, picked her up, and called
the ship. The captain searched. Her husband stalled,
then said, "Keep her. Or leave her at the dock."
I still have not recovered from the shock.

# Salvage

## Barbara Bloom

*Nothing left to save*, is how it felt,
as I drove to the new house,
the backseat of my car
piled with the last belongings from the old place,
not even in boxes, just thrown in hastily—
a tea kettle, some shoes, books, t-shirts,
a stuffed elephant from my daughter's room.

How could a marriage die so quietly?
No struggle, just a flattening out of hope,
of desire.

Halfway there, at the corner of Clares Street and Capitola Road,
where a shopping mall was being built
on the old bulb farm,
was a rose bush, leaning on a cyclone fence,
in full bloom. I pulled over to look—
the pink flowers: wide open,
a scent like pepper and honey
when I leaned into them,
and, behind, a bulldozer, looming, idle,
the blade resting on the ground.

So I picked as many of the flowers as I could—
the bush would be gone in a day or two,
making way for the parking lot.
The afternoon traffic rushed by
as I bent the stalks back
to break them off, trying to avoid the thorns,
and once home, I put them in water,
but the petals slipped off, one by one.
They couldn't hold themselves together.

The color was like the inside of a seashell,
I thought, and tried to be glad
I'd picked the flowers, even if
they were falling apart.
Tried to think I'd saved them
from what was coming.

# Flame

## Judith Borenin

You used to snatch small birds that lit for a breath
in low shrubs with your young agile fingers when
you were a boy in your grandparent's back yard.
A lizard's covert crawl was not secretive enough
to evade your raptor reach & clutch. At the beach
you became a crab squatting sideways on the
scathing sand—inching dipping along-fingers splayed
and pinching—turning over rock after rock to expose
their hidden habitats. On our weekly walks to the
post office with your guileless grin you deposited
a curled sow bug or two as a prize to be discovered
in the emptied box. At Lake Havasu your brother
and I cast out lines and looks—mincing our reluctant
fingers down inside the bait-filled jar with its gooey
occupants to impale upon our hooks. You just dipped
tanned arms in the lake with netless hands—a second
thought and lifted out a trout.

This morning I saw a Sharp Shinned Hawk composed
in its reflections perched upon the curved rail top
of the floating dock—its pupils fixed in concentration
within the amber liquid of its eyes. I stood way back
not wanting to disturb its absorbtion
in the moment and became a motionless
black cloud stalled in the wind's circumference.
It flew closer—its flight a wonderment of wingspan—
black and white stripes vivid against the grey sky—
tail of black strokes brushed upon white feathers.
Breast down smattered with soft brown dashes—
it beat a mysterious alphabet—wind lifting
each soft feather of the downy braille.

I waited there on the dock in my black shroud
of hoodie and sweats and wondered if it was
you perched on the piling bringing me a message
from another world. I have looked for signs
everywhere since your death. I used to believe
in sudden transformations—a key that would unlock
the secrets of life—had a child's innocent belief
that a moment—a bird—a cloud—a word—would be
followed by an answer or an end to blackest
of black nights. So—for a moment-as I watched
the hawk vanish from sight—I willed it to return
with a message that you still lived in some form—this
hawk—in some flicker of light—in a flame that—once
resurrected—would not consume but only burn.

# Small Fry

## Jessica Brown

She watched from the window. One leg perched on the chipped ledge, the other outstretched, her hot foot pulsing in a black pump and hovering above the tiled floor. She saw a woman gather a handful of children under her arms, glide past a baby screaming into a breast and offer a smile the new mother would muster in the dead of night.

Two grunts: fish and chips. She did what she was paid for, watching impatient fingers wrap around sticky sauce bottles, pushed into salt-hungry lips before offering a greasy tip. Crisp flaps of paint flattened under her thigh as she returned to her vantage point to watch people smear the streets with the things they thought they kept secret.

The city became a cacophony of life and lights whenever it rained, and with every drop another world floated closer to the surface, contained in the smudges of expanding puddles until she didn't know where the lies bled and the truth began. Men held umbrellas over the heads of their women, hiding in double page spreads filled with airbrushed legs. Suited commuters, ordinarily curled around desks with hunched shoulders and sore necks, spread their bodies and glided to the puddle's end.

And when the daylight began to fade she watched eyes open up like sun-starved wildflowers at the suggestion of spontaneous after-date drinks. Women with structured shoulders talking into one phone and texting on a second, air-kissing friends into restaurants and emerging three hours later as red wine stained-lipped sisters who belonged to a world where technology didn't exist.

Her shoulders dug into the wall, weighed down by an absence of pleases and of people to please, though they were as similar in weight as milk and cheese. She took sips from a can of coke through a straw, and jumped up whenever she was required to listen to lonely stomachs tilting their heads back and roaring for some warm company for the night.

She recited the day's two-for-one deal over angry batter as bits of hands brushed the window, carrying portfolios, poems, lipsticks, and guitars pointed towards stadiums. A girl who couldn't bear to hear something as funny as whatever she'd just heard turned her head away from the city, lifted her closed eyes and open mouth to the window with flared nostrils and hair dancing across her face like the dirty napkin sitting in the fan's line of fire. Sometimes, someone looked at her looking, and she felt satisfied that they, too, took her home and wrote her story.

But they, the real ones, they always returned. She knew their faces, their orders, and how they poured change onto her hand. Those who counted coins out loud as they fell from fingers were the same ones who ate their chips one at a time. She watched them hug their food like wrapped-up babies, rocking it home and eating with teary eyes; one day they'll put on less vinegar, she thought, and maybe one day I'll be too busy to worry about people's clumsy hands.

Just as steadily as life continued under the thirty-year-old menu harbouring aged and changeless routines of fish supper on Fridays, a flash at the window would freeze in her mind; good news falling on nervous ears and unfolding worried wrinkles, a fight spilling out of the pub and sending an eruption of empty chants down the road.

With every handshake and punch and kiss and donated cigarette, every bag of vegetables spinning in the air as it moved from market stall to handbag, she felt a million micro connections break down and build up like the flux of the city itself, moving people around above and underground, putting them in place for another day of exchanges.

Another customer filled the sad silence of fish being fried with mock outrage at the weather as she longed to sit back down and watch furrowed brows and thin lips hail taxis and discuss the economy. Every day was a parade of design and architecture, carved by the same hands as those closing in on the wooden forks in front of her.

She watched from the window, looking past her reflection at the one-armed hugs and fake goodbyes, ugly, naked laughs, and children gathered under warm wings; to the blurry city staring up from wet ground, and, finally, back inside, to outstretched, hungry hands, pointing towards the woman with the vinegar eyes. 📖

# Man: Made

### C.W. Buckley

Even before you find your sleeping words
I am there with you
Hand on your sweating head

Something about faces too much like our own
The uncanny valley beckons
We cannot back away

I stand guard against those australopithecenes
Fevering your dreams
Brows furrowed like yours

Upright, becoming, hot-blooded like you
They too feared in the dark
Brains folded just enough to dream

But rest easy my son, your monster was real
That great mother I once saw dreaming under glass
She's awake in your eyes tonight

# In Hiding

## Thomas Brush

October, looking out
As the light begins to fail but it should be enough
To see what's written on the side of the building
Where I live—I was here but you'll never find me.—Heroes
For Hire—scrawled on garbage
Cans just down the street, and the red and blue faces of strangers
Staring at me from the inked flesh of the bartender
As she mixes another Tequila and lime.
                    So many messages
To consider and try to understand give me stories
To tell, things to do.
                    Lord, let me do them,
In spite of the cold trail midnight sprays across the night sky,
Or the homeless howls half-eaten by their separate
Prayers, their familiar voices and deaths
To come.
                    A poor man's choice,
Hoping for what can still be found, that should last longer
Than a lifetime, out of the ruined fields
Of Antietam, out of what's left
Of Fallujah.
                    Out of Blue Earth, Minnesota, and Squirrel Run,
Arkansas, towns I passed through growing up and will visit
Again, I keep telling myself, hiding out, staying close
To home, a block to the park, the bar
The other way, both useful and necessary
As the silence drifting toward me and why
The hell
Not.

# Departing the House of My Former Life

### T. Clear

Once I close the door, hear the click
of the latch, there's no going back.
I may run circles around it, peer

into each window as long as desired,
but entry is impossible. The single key is,
from this day forward, forever lost.

Best to gather the few remaining flowers
before the garden lapses into ruin,
fill my pockets with apples.

Disavow all I've abandoned
inside this lathe and plaster fortress,
every root still clutching a fist of soil.

Better to leave and not return,
not recall the accumulation of broken beds,
the last unshattered cup, the wedding china.

And a rock thrown at a pane makes bad luck.
I'll unpin the solitary dress hung ragged
on the line, yank the numbers

from the siding, check the mailbox.
No curtain wavers; every candle's a stub.
Not a soul to wave me on but my own.

*Horses and Dust*, Photograph, by Theodore C. Van Alst, Jr.

# Seven Things To Do in the Sandhills of Nebraska

## Terri Cohlene

1. Drive and drive and drive
from highway to aggregate
to rutted, grassy roads.
Marvel at clouds
embracing their tornados.
Note the diminishing traffic—
houses, barns, buildings of any kind.

2. Stop in the middle of nowhere.
Except this is not *nowhere*, exactly—
this is the homestead
of your great-grandfather,
640 acres claimed in 1904—
land that barely fed the livestock
and his growing family.

3. Follow the line of your cousins,
crawl under barbed wire
held up by your uncle—
one of your mother's three brothers
estranged from you
these past fifty-eight years.

4. Watch Cousin Lee,
the only cowboy in the bunch,
scrape prairie burrs
from his pant-leg.
Feel overwhelmed
by the sky.

5. Stand around, scratch your head
at the stories:
*The house was over there.*
*Can't be. There's a big tree.*
*It grew after. That was a long time ago.*
*Here's where the garbage was.*

6. *Look at old, glass bottles,*
wonder who drove
the Model A—source
of that rusty, old gear with the filigree knob—
worry how you are going to get
it past security at the airport.

7. Breathe. Take in
the Nebraska air
your lungs crave.
*Space is not the final frontier,*
your uncle declares. *It's here.*
*No one wants the Sandhills.*

But, you want them—
know you are only
one generation away
from belonging
to this useless, stunning place.

# Sunday Pork Chops

## Minnie A. Collins

The last smothered pork chop stared at me. It oozed black pepper pan juices and wafted onions browned in Crisco up my nose. My eyes and mouth watered for dinner to be over. It meant that our stomachs were satisfied with Grandma's Sunday dinner. Visiting my grandma this week was my New York aunt and her husband who always came during their summer vacation to see her mother. I was the oldest of four Grandchildren who lived with my arthritic grandmother so that Grandchildren could take care of her.

When Grandma's children, who had migrated north or west came to visit the South, we had to give up the front room where sat a sofa with a fold out bed and an oil heating stove. We also gave up the only radio and record player in the house. We ironed sheets and pillow cases, beat dust from the rugs, and passed the finger test for a dust-free house. Grandchildren were forewarned that visitors had "first turns" in the one-bathroom house. We catered to all of their uppity pseudo ways. When Grandma called out that the bathroom was free, we often had to wait until the basement water tank reheated. Or we had to heat water on the stove and pour it into a galvanized tin tub that sat next to the kitchen stove.

We catered to all of their needs and desires. One wish before their going back to New York was dinner on Sunday after church, with fresh meat, the best cuts. My grandmother told me to go with my aunt to the uptown butcher on Saturday morning. I could not wait to take a bath. At twelve years old, who needs a bath, I thought. I splashed water on my face, parted my hair down the middle, plaited two tight-crooked braids, and tied them with two stiff, old, rumpled red ribbons. I was going uptown.

Walking uptown was not an easy jaunt. We avoided stares and raised eyebrows. My aunt looked ahead and asked, "How many streets to go?" I did not mind the walk. My grandmother had sent me on many errands to the neighborhood black-owned store and I was happy to go because I would get one Mary Jane surprise for helping. But this time my aunt walked with me. My grandmother had given me, not my aunt, a written notice to give to the butcher. After we walked uptown to the white neighborhood, we entered the butcher shop at opening time before other customers arrived. We needed to avoid any strange looks or questions.

"My grandma sent you this note." I handed the note to the butcher.

"Yeah, I remember your grandma; she sent you here before." He stared at me and opened it. "OK, but tell her that she needs to send some money; I can't continue to put stuff on credit."

I was embarrassed because Grandma had always given me money to shop for canned goods at the neighborhood grocery store. Perhaps she thought that my New York aunt would pay for it. My aunt scanned the meat case and pointed to the pork chops. The butcher pulled out her choice: one-inch rib pork chops, the size of my palm. She wanted something special for Lincoln, her train porter husband, before they returned to New York on Sunday on the train. My aunt treated him like he was a paying passenger on the train. The most important person in Grandma's house.

At Sunday dinner, we all sat down—children on one side, adults on the opposite. The platter of fried chops was center stage. My aunt served Lincoln the biggest chop, she took second choice; my grandma reached for her helping. Soon a chorus of "delicious, yummy" and bone sucks filled the table. I stared at the last chop, glanced sideways out of the corner of my eyes to see if anyone would reach out and stick their fork in to pierce it for their plate. I knew better than to take the last one, but I did not have the first, second, or third. Not even asked if I wanted one. My aunt served Grandchildren chicken from the backyard hen house where my grandmother raised chickens. Earlier that day, I had helped chop off the chicken head: pulled and held its neck over an old tree stump, then jumped back as the headless chicken took flight in a splatter of blood across the yard. I had even doused the headless chicken into a boiling pot of water and plucked off the feathers one by one. I did not mind because I looked forward to an uptown butcher's center chop as my surprise. It was worth the price of a Sunday pork chop dinner.

When I slowly inched my right hand forward, and stuck out my fork toward the platter, "No. You cannot have it. You have had dinner. That's going to be Lincoln's pork chop sandwich for the train ride home on Sunday."

I dropped my head; anger flooded from my feet to my head. Bewildered, I stood up without excusing myself, picked up all of the dinner plates, slouched to the kitchen sink, and scraped the plates for someone else to wash, and cleared the scraps and bones into a paper napkin. With hands cupped around scraps, I tramped outside, where I flopped on the back porch steps and shared the bones and leftover pork fat with the family dog. 📖

# Ordinary Signs

## Linda Conroy

At ten to four, I sidestep kids freed
from the middle school, laughing, taunting
one another, tossing jokes and backpacks.

Markers point north across the bridge
to where young men sort alpine gear. Sweat,
mud and backache cling as though still

on a mountain track, as if the counting of supplies
might grant another chance. A playing card,
the jack of hearts, lies abandoned on the ground.

*Improperly parked vehicles will be impounded,*
the notice says, where lights flash on a van,
left by a driver limping in for urgent care.

The crosswalk safety sign counts off
my time. Clouds mock the bright horizon line,
a distant, soundless blood-red slash.

Two blackbirds pecking winter berries
threaded through a hedge, fly low as I pass, eyes
blinking in a mastery of knowledge I don't have.

# The Second to Last Hookup

## Cathy Cook

His body was the blanket
I strangled myself with
in my sadness, in my own
sorrow. His hands were
the rope I strangled myself
with in his bed in my own
sorrow. The names he called
me, that I asked for, the stones
I piled on my own grave.

The slap across my face, I didn't
ask for. Broke something open
in me. Something unholy
about his body in my body
about the dark pits we've
made of ourselves and the flesh
we fill it with. Something unholy
about fucking through tears.
His body was the blanket
I smothered myself with.

# Post Apocalypse

## Mary Crane

After the apocalypse
came warm rain

a hole of light
hazy in the dark sky.

Can you feel the  end
of the long deep breath

like kelp suspended?

The smell of damp earth
falling in the arms

of a lover
returning from the war

trying to remember
how to weep?

# The Virgin Knife

## Michael Daley

*—for Art Goodtimes*

I was always just a cabaret singer off the street
in my loose chemise of tribal songs.
My dog shakes seawater, snout to tail,
and sprays the Muses over you.
Effortless as a silken tent in the breeze,
we'll howl you this greasy dirge.

I once knew a master
of the art of chanterelle
who dropped a sack of dirt
tendered by some tree roots
on my blue-lined foolscap,
forest meat soiled under hunter thumbprint.

You'd never complain of such dinner.
He followed no trail you could forage—
not-so-soaked mud, shade of old growth.
Sunlight slant, fallen orange needles
sprout their clusters' delicate wiggle,
good with fish.

Long after I drop into this valley
"like a high fly ball,"
let the rainbow buses hide behind posts,
city freaks slither under barbwire,
their sandals in muck cowplops
where the psychedelics grow.

But the only true mushroom spy I know,
sworn to secrecy, hunted off trail.

Pickup in camo cedar boughs,
he snaked beneath outposts,
slinked passed duck hunts.

Kept hidden where chanterelles grow,
his feet up on a workbench,
while a greenhouse lean-to transistor
hummed: "Mariners fry the Red Sox"—

*"Can't show you*
*I'd like to, but I won't*
*Find your own*
*Here's a bucketful*
*Don't overdo the butter"*

Olive beret, a trek through the high grass
where no one goes, a last look over the primal shoulder:
*"Apres moi le deluge,"* he lisped the kingly joke.
Responsible for the world, he finally
wanted to tell, but—incoherent
on his last directions—the trove still thrives,
thrives in the sump of aching.

I can hardly keep from dropping a word of praise here—
sharp folds of our ersatz maps
crinkle across steering wheels
on his, or any such, hillside pullout.

When I unsheathe my pure blade,
having come so far
only to shed everything I've witnessed,
highways burn yet another detour,
plunge wild up the Yukon,
crossroad Devils trade guitar licks
where we scurry down a monk's deer trail
into deeper Kentucky, lost in the crowd.

Praise those, sans teeth sans eyes,
waltzing past me on the stage,
sweet imbeciles
who rumble onto raw untrained road
with or without the gear
they know they better have on board
for the inevitable breakdown.


# I Drive Myself at Night
# to Dinner

## Lauren Davis

& pay at the window for fries.
Turn down an unfamiliar road.
No one to tell me go home.
Me & the man on the radio.
He's talking of cloud cover & rain.
Listening to him, I think
we could be friends.

# Our Bodies Were Dazzling

## Risa Denenberg

Our bodies were dazzling in their moment,
our tresses curled like spirulina. It served us
    at the time to hold out cupped hands
to accept our trophies. Now our sons
    have bald spots, our daughters' hairs
have grayed. We can't stop staring at photos
    from those scarce perfect days.

    Last night, I dreamt a dozen men forced
entry into my body. That sequence crashed
    into a panic over remains I can't remember.
Here are the barbs you left in me, my helpless
    tears, a longing to stay in bed forever, hunger
for more gadgets to blur the memory
    of your hands at my neck.

    I've been fired again. They're saying
I'm troubled. They're claiming I'm trouble.
    Let them. I know this feeling, a sudden hollowed-
out abyss in my solar plexus. But I've learned
    to put thoughts of suicide aside rather quickly.
I will not kill myself. I will give an account as I see it,
    and carry on.

    No one lives in the present. Every action
takes parsecs to light up neurons. You'll never
    know if something you think
is your own thought or someone else's, the memory
    of a face or a photo. Pure joy is life's
rarest commodity, unlike fictions stored serenely
    in false memory cells.

In the crush of regret subject and object
exchange garments. Time is a notion too liminal
         to survive. If you're willing to amend, there may be
hope. For a moment, the stricken sparrow's shivering heart
         still beats. It's time to loosen the strangling cord
that binds us so painfully to one another
         and consider freedom.

*Flight*, Photograph, by Alfredo Arreguín

# 1957

## DC Diamondopolous

Welcome to The Shady Lady, a queer bar in San Pedro, California, across the railroad tracks, near the docks, in a back alley off Harbor Street. It's a raunchy hole in the wall dive where dykes and drag queens hang. So you didn't think they mixed? Well, think again Daddy-O. Over there, slouched against the juke box, listening to Gogi Grant croon "The Wayward Wind," is Stormy, a big broad-shouldered butch who flirts with anyone who has tits and a pussy. Cigarette clamped to the side of her pouty James Dean lips, she can talk, play pool, and switch-blade her way out of a fight, and the L&M never moves a lick. Her hair is greased with pomade and combed up on the sides with a pompadour rising like a tidal wave from her forehead. On the outside Stormy appears cool, but on the inside her stomach is doing wheelies. You see, a bust is about to happen, and she knows it.

Stormy yanks the jukebox plug from the wall. "It's the fuzz!" she shouts.

The teeny-weeny dance floor empties. The pool table is abandoned. Everyone scatters to small wooden tables and bar stools.

Stormy struts to the center of the room. "If the man rounds us up, fight back, you dig?"

"No sweat," someone answers.

Across the room, under the exit sign, meet VaVoom, a six-foot-five drag queen in stiletto heels raising her height to a near sky-scraping altitude. She wears a floral skirt with mesh petticoats, a black low-cut blouse, and a choker of fake pearls just below her Adams apple. Her short, Italian-styled wig is from Max Factor of Hollywood, and her layers of false eyelashes from Ohrbach's. She holds a cue stick like a ball bat. No way is VaVoom going to let Johnny Law give her the royal shaft.

Blue and maroon vice cars surround the seedy bar. Parked outside the lonely hideaway, the Black Mariah waits to haul off the sickos.

A gust of fish and gasoline swooshes in through the entrance. It's another night in the city where the heat gets their kicks hassling stompers, fems, and swishes.

"Okay motherfuckers, let's go. The freak show's over and the paddy's outside," a cop shouts.

"Didn't you get your pay-off?" a queen with a falsetto voice asks.

"Shut-up."

VaVoom hits the breakers. Blackout!

*Crash! Boom! Bam! Pop!*

The Shady Lady turns into a blind noise of sticks swooshing, pool balls cracking, and feet scuffling. A flashlight cuts across the ceiling like a search-light at a movie premiere, but this ain't no movie. This is where dreams turn to pulp.

A fist slams Stormy in the back. "Ohh," she moans. A stick strikes a skull.

A scream freeze-frames the moment.

It's our heroine VaVoom, holding the bloody cue. She shoves open the back door, swings the pole across the face of the cop guarding the exit and knocks him to the ground.

"Ahh," he cries and covers his broken nose. VaVoom grabs Stormy. "Follow me."

"Where to?" Stormy asks.

"Hush-hush," Vavoom says. "It's very confidential." She pulls off her heels and sprints down the back street like Elroy "Crazylegs" Hirsch.

Stormy grips her cigarette between thumb and forefinger and flicks it away. She bolts after VaVoom.

Under a full moon, they run past cargo crates and pallets. The stink of diesel and garbage hangs in the air. The two escapees turn the corner at a cannery and dart alongside the Port of Los Angeles. Lights from Terminal Island flicker across the harbor. To the south, oil derricks and wells pump in an urban field of dinosaur spiders in 3-D. They both know what happens if caught—booked, fingerprinted, their names listed in the *Daily Breeze* under perverts. Lives ruined.

Stormy catches up to the towering drag queen. "Where the hell are we going?"

"To my boat," she says in a high-pitched breathy pant. "It's fabulous."

"You have a boat?"

"I dock in Long Beach," the transvestite says, gulping air. Her wig slips. She tugs it forward with one hand while dangling the straps of her heels with the other. "And sail here." She hurries toward the wharf.

Stormy charges after.

VaVoom runs down the pier to a small wooden cabin cruiser and unties the rope. She lifts her skirt and long legs over the edge and steps into the boat. It rocks. Water ripples and gurgles. She opens the door to the cabin and disappears inside.

Stormy climbs into the boat. The cruiser laps from side to side. The door creaks back and forth.

"C'mon. Let's split." VaVoom's voice dips an octave. She fires up the engine.

Stormy swings open the cabin door and steps inside. The crossdresser sits at the helm with her back to her. The queen's wig and stilettos are on the table. She runs a large hand over her crewcut, then peels off the blanket of eyelashes.

The big butch sits beside her partner in crime and lights a cigarette.

VaVoom powers the craft away from the dock and heads toward Long Beach.

"Thanks," Stormy says around the filter of her L&M.
VaVoom wipes her lipstick off with a tissue. She turns.

Stormy's cigarette falls to her lap. "Mr. Hazzelrigg!" she says,
staring into the face of her tenth grade math teacher.
"It's good to see you again, Mary Louise." 📖


# Not the Time

## Patrick Dixon

He balanced himself behind his walker
on the sidewalk in the spring sun,
and smiled as he shook his head.
*I didn't get to do all the things I wanted.*
He looked up at the bright blue sky
empty of clouds. *I have all the money I need.*
*Just not the time.*

You didn't know what to say.
*None of us do,* rattled hard against your skull.
Your stance wobbled in the glare
as a soft spring day turned hard inside his words.
You felt concrete press against the soles of your feet
and the vast immensity of sky stretch
above your head.

*Don't matter now,* his hand waved away the thought
brushing at something that had flown too close,
and he shuffled on, leaving you standing there
bathed in blue and yellow, watching pink petals
of a flowering plum drift in the breeze.

# Suquamish, Washington, 1959:
# Burial Place of Chief Seattle

## Mike Dillon

She was just a mom but as Cub Scout den mother
she stood us in the November cold and rain
before a cement cross footed with clamshells.
I wanted to go home, to be warm and dry,
but I kept in line with the rest of my friends
to maintain our den's simulacrum of reverence.

As if nothing had happened we climbed back
into her car, yet something followed me home
from that graveyard where the dead
remained the same. When my den mother opened
a cemetery gate in the rain I stepped
from one world into another.

Months later my parents held a party.
One man's joke about bows and arrows,
fire water and fire crackers triggered such gales
of laughter the ice in their highballs tinkled.
I looked up to a room full of familiar strangers.
Where my den mother would never be.

*Indians Allowed,* Photograph, by Theodore C. Van Alst, Jr.

# The Blood on Your Fingers

## Chris Espenshade

The blood on your fingers is not red, white, and blue. It is the graphite, silver gray of burnt powder clinging to the barrel twists of yet another military-grade weapon, fired recently, fired rapidly. Yet another student clings to life.

The blood on your fingers is not red, white, and blue. It is the green of American cash, the green of the cemetery lawn. Here envy has surrendered its favorite color to greed, at gunpoint. The American graveyard is greedy for more bodies. The American politician holds up his sign "Will Pimp for Death."

The blood on your fingers is not red, white, and blue. It is colorless in its transparency, so that even the high school freshmen, days after burying classmates, can see why you really do nothing. It is as transparent as your trite sayings and bastardization of American Tradition

The blood on your fingers is not red, white, and blue. It is instead the chilling, translucent white of the frozen waterfall recalling your slippery slope argument against sensible gun control. Have the inspection and licensing of all cars led to Big Government taking away our autos?

The blood on your fingers is not red, white, and blue. It is bordered in gold and black like your sacred texts, the same tomes so readily tossed aside when you sold your soul to the highest bidder. You rationalized that it is better to re-elect a Right-thinking man than a good man.

The blood on your fingers is not red, white, and blue. It is the dull grey of granite, the same stone in which, by NRA rule, the Constitution and Second Amendment are written, never to evolve. In Biblical times, cobbles of granite would have been used to stone a hypocrite such as you. Stones don't kill people. . . .

The blood on your fingers is not red, white, and blue. It is the flashing polychrome of mass paranoia, nurtured for years by the Right, Fox News, your buddies, and you. The public must be ready to protect themselves. The public must fear blacks, must fear Muslims, must fear Mexican rapists, and must fear Salvadoran gangs coming for Americans. The public must fear government overreach coming for our guns.

The blood on your fingers is not red, white, and blue. It is the shiny copper of the thirty AR-15 rounds in each magazine engineered solely to take human lives. It is the shiny copper of the strap-on metallic spine, a miserable replacement for that which you surrendered when you cashed that first check.

The blood on your fingers is not red, white, and blue. Oh, the blood is red after all. It is the beacon shine of the red-light district, as gun makers and the NRA wait their turn to demean the whore that is you. It is the dark red of caked human blood, badge of life lost. It is a stain not easily removed—out, out damn spot—with public statements of hopes and prayers.

The blood on your fingers is not red, white, and blue. We see the stains even if you choose not to. We will remember those stains when we next mark the ballot in hopes of sending you home to consider what terrible things you have done, by doing nothing at all. 📖

# Line of Best Fit

## Alex Everette

The idea was always to meet certain points
on a hypothetical map they'd drawn out for
us. I assume it looks a little like the map of states
we had to memorize in fourth grade, since they call it
The American Dream.
The early points they'd walk us to, like learning to
ride a bike and our first days of school,
but then we were meant to find girls and boys pretty
without getting them mixed up. They left us
to learn the social rules in school, showed us only
cartoons and themselves, expected Lord of the Flies
and got socialists. We killed dying markets
out of mercy and created a hundred and one ways
to give each other money and share
our cars, homes, and minds.
They point at marriage and purchased land, we
point at pipelines and divorce rates
shout loud about rushing into the very things
that destroyed them until they yell back. They
yell and scream, raising their voices in hopes we hear
their argument for the hundredth time.
We point back to cartoons, how we learned from
villains and heroes and each other, how we
learned they sound more like the villains they wrote.
We hold up the screens they sat us in front of, hoping
against all hope they work as well as mirrors.

# The Roses that Bloom at the End of the World

## Catherine Fahey

are $5.99 at Trader Joe's.
They come wrapped in cellophane, surrounded
by ferns, with a futile packet of plant food.

I place the roses in a milk glass vase on the windowsill
behind the sofa, so the cat can enjoy them, too.
It's not her fault the world is ending.

The roses that bloom at the end of the world
are hybrid—all vibrant colors,
perfect petals, no scent. I'm not worried
about the cat swallowing a thorn,
or the vet bill. Useless pet insurance.

I place the vase on the windowsill,
framed by the curtains, so the neighbors
can see it, too. They should enjoy this
last chance for gossip while
they can. Busybodies to the end.

The roses that bloom at the end of the world
last long enough. It's their job—to stay
with us. To watch, to wait
to witness. To say
yes there was a world
and yes there was a life
and yes that is over now and

# The Battle Cry of the Survivor

## Rebeka Fergusson-Lutz

I was six years old the first time I was sexually assaulted, and for years I never said anything to anyone because I lived in such crippling shame that I couldn't even admit this to myself.

On a cognitive level, I had it all together. I read all the books and listened to the experts. I publicly inveighed against those who committed sexual violence against others and to systems that perpetuated society's casual acceptance of such violence. As a feisty feminist, I spewed vitriol when I read headlines about gang rape and human trafficking, at home and around the globe. I devoted years of my life to advocating for women and the creation of criminal justice, public health, social welfare, and educational systems that protect their God-given rights.

And it's not that my fiery sentiments were in any way insincere—but they were only half of the picture. As with many such things in life, there exists an enormous chasm between the intellectual and the emotional, between the head and the heart. I had railed because I knew on an instinctive and academic level that sexual violence is the worst kind of offense against another human being. I just had been in massive, pathological denial about the way that the issue touched me on a personal level.

For years I buried my first assault so deeply in my subconscious that even I forgot that those memories existed. If you had asked me, even up until my early thirties, if I had been the victim of childhood sexual molestation, I would have denied it—because I literally could not remember it. The mind has an incredibly powerful way of healing itself and recovering from traumatic events: forgetting. I think that those memories stayed hidden for twenty-five years in the deepest crevices of my neural receptors because I simply didn't have the wherewithal (in terms of emotional or personal strength) to cope with those memories. But over the past few years, snippets of memory slowly came back to me. At first I got back two of three just seconds video clips, fuzzy images replaying again and again. The images were just fuzzy shapes at first, then began to gather color and definition and texture, and eventually sound. All the ephemera began to rematerialize. And once I had those memories back, I couldn't deny it anymore—to myself or anyone else.

Once I admitted it to myself, there was a moment of sweet release, because I realized that so much of the insecurity and self-doubt that I've carried with me for years wasn't just a cruel monster of my own creation. My pain had a source, an origination. All the years that I spent tormenting myself about my weight; all the years that I tortured myself about not feeling smart enough, pretty enough, funny enough—it was a way of illogically punishing myself for the experiences that I endured.

It wasn't until a few years ago that I could finally be honest with the people I love because, as Maya Angelou wrote, "There is no greater agony than bearing an untold story inside you." At first I worried that telling my friends and family—and the broader world—would make me too vulnerable. I worried that I'd have to spend too much time reliving and retelling those experiences. I was afraid that the people I love would smother me with their sympathies. I was concerned that people would speculate, would take on the roles of "armchair psychiatrists." But I know all about vulnerability. For most of my life I've been vulnerable, and it hasn't ruined me. In fact, those experiences have compelled me to walk into difficult situations, take on challenges, and expand my literal and figurative horizons. The psychological burden of the assaults made me at times irrational and unstable, but it also made me empathetic.

I am "over" my own trauma; I have made peace with my past and have learned to sublimate all that pain into something useful and even beautiful. But when I go to social media and news sites and see the face of a known sexual predator—a man who has repeatedly faced insidious accusations that have quietly and mysteriously disappeared for reasons that should be obvious to all—I feel a pang every time. My heart beats a bit faster and my throat catches. I have to take a few deep breaths. I feel an acidic flop in my stomach. It's not just that I disagree with the man's fiscal, foreign, education, health care, and environmental policies. It's not just that I find his rhetorical habits abhorrent. I am literally re-traumatized every time that I am reminded that Donald J. Trump—a brazen and unabashed sexual predator—is serving as our nation's Chief Executive. I am reminded that there is very rarely justice (in or outside the court system) for perpetrators of sexual violence. I am reminded that there are millions of people who think sexual assault is just not a big deal. I am reminded of all the shame that I spent years attempting to bury.

I don't need anyone's pity. I don't want anyone's opinion on how I may or may not be coping with my personal trauma. What I do need is for everyone to fight to politically enfeeble and eventually impeach the known sexual predator who took office in January 2017. No matter how you may have voted in the election, this is the time to take a moral and ethical stand against sexual assault and those who commit it. Start with him. 📖

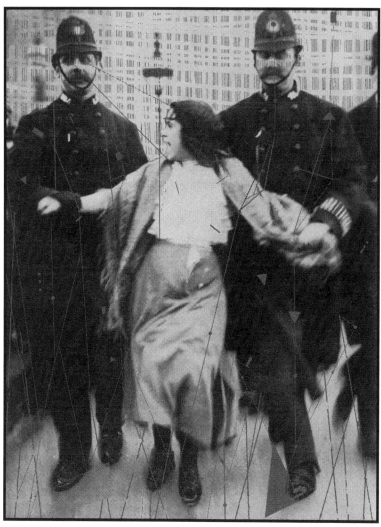

*The Civil Rights Activist, Edition 4,* Photograph, by Julia Justo

# A Good Life

## Anne Frantilla

What was my position on feeding tubes? Leaves glistened in the sun outside the window. My dad slept. We sat beside him, in the bedroom of his care facility: the visiting doctor, the nurse, and me. They couldn't decide if my father should be in hospice or palliative care. Hospice provided comfort care for those with terminal illnesses within six months of death; palliative care provided comfort care at any stage of an illness.

My dad startled with a snore and almost woke up.

"Even if the caregiver has to call 911 by law, you can request on the telephone they not transport him," the doctor explained. I could tell she was trying to be helpful. "We'll redo the Physician's Orders for Life Sustaining Treatment (POLST) form to make that clear." She paused, typed some notes into her laptop, and then looked up. "Do you think that's what he would have wanted? Did he ever talk to you about it? Would your sister agree?"

My sister was far away, in England where she lived. I wished she were here.

"I want the end to be peaceful for him and for him to be as comfortable as possible . . ." I started. But I couldn't continue in intelligible words. They both looked at me, concerned. I got up to get Kleenex. They decided on palliative care.

We all disappear from this earth I told myself as I drove back to work. He's had a good life, I told myself on my early morning run the next day. He's comfortable now, I told myself on the bus on the way to work.

More than the man asleep by the window, my father is the little boy from Lead, South Dakota who grew up in Port Orchard, Washington. The boy with a father born in Finland and a Finnish mother born in South Dakota. The black-and-white photograph of the little boy in a snowsuit on a porch must have been taken in South Dakota. And the photograph of the older boy who stood beside his father and a team of horses could have been taken in South Dakota also. In any case, it was taken before the grandfather I never met lost his farm in the Depression. Dad never talked about horses or gave any clue he knew how to handle horses.

There are no pictures of my seven-year-old father in the hospital with empyema but we know it happened because he has a huge scar on his chest and he told us about how pus shot up to the ceiling when they opened him up. Empyema is also called pyothorax or purulent pleuritis. Pus gathers in the area between the lungs and the inner surface of the chest wall. It usually develops after pneumonia. We never got the feeling his dad was tender to him but he told us that after the empyema his dad made sure he got lots of exercise. Why didn't anyone notice he had pneumonia before the empyema? Where was his mother? She stands beside him in the photograph of the young man in a Navy uniform. She is laughing and wearing a cotton print dress. His father also stands beside him, tall and thin and not laughing. His father served in World War I. My dad was part of the Navy Seabee band during World War II, and played the saxophone. He said the band saved him from being killed. In the photo album of his Seabee years, he's swinging his saxophone high, hamming it up as part of the big band.

"There are many kinds of dementia," the doctor said.

"Yes," I said, "I know."

"This could be vascular dementia."

"Yes," I said, "that's what I thought." I wondered if she'd read his chart and knew he'd had a stroke about fifteen years ago.

"Vascular dementia is like a hardening of the arteries of the brain," she explained. I winced inside and told myself the doctor was trying to be clear and concise. I didn't tell her I'd taken an online class on dementia four years ago, thinking there must be a way to help my dad, to slow the hardening. I knew he did not have Alzheimer's, which accounts for about eighty percent of all dementia diagnoses. I also didn't think he had frontotemporal dementia, Huntington's disease, Creutzfeldt-Jakob disease, or the other kinds of dementia. Vascular dementia fit him best. With vascular dementia, changes in thinking skills follow strokes that block major brain blood vessels. Thinking problems may begin as mild changes that worsen gradually as a result of multiple minor strokes or other conditions that affect smaller blood vessels, leading to cumulative damage. The term "vascular cognitive impairment (VCI)" is preferred over "vascular dementia" because it better expresses the concept that vascular thinking changes can range from mild to severe. But in the end I decided my Coursera class was useless. The mini mental state exam or MMSE the doctor conducted was not helpful either. Once my dad received a score telling the doctor he definitely had a dementia diagnosis, I didn't take him back. It didn't matter what you called it. It didn't matter what his score was. My dad was losing things.

Before I knew he was losing things, he lost the skill of starting a weed whipper. He lost the ability to drive, forgetting to take the car out of reverse in the alley behind the house and backing into a neighbor's car. Then he lost the ability to say no. He could not say no to the myriad of organizations that called him: Oglala Lakota College, Help Me See, the Gabby Giffords, the Sioux Nation Relief Fund, the Memorial Sloan Kettering Cancer Center, the Southern Indian Relief Council, the Salvation Army Planned Giving, the National Committee to Preserve Social Security and Medicare, National Association of Chiefs of Police, the American Indian Relief Council, or CARE. Putting him on the do not call list was a stopgap measure. He received more mail than I thought possible: The Sierra Club, the Democratic Party, Children without Hair, or the Red Cross of King County, Boys and Girls Club of America, UNICEF, Catholic Community Services.

He lost more than I thought was possible to lose. How to recognize his friends, how to recognize his family. How to sign his name. At first he forgot the flourishes on the W for William and on the F in Frantilla, and then he started signing his name on a downhill slope. The last time I asked him to sign something, he fell asleep halfway through the signature. He forgot how to dress himself, to put on the belt he always wore, to place his wallet in his back pocket. He is forgetting how to use the bathroom. He will forget how to swallow or how to put one foot in front of the other.

In the early 1970s, my friend Juli and I saved money from babysitting and other odd jobs to buy our first pair of running shoes. We were sure our new running shoes would make us the fastest runners around Green Lake. My dad drove us to REI on Capitol Hill, walked with us across the creaky floors, and watched us buy our Adidas with the three red stripes. He just smiled. He didn't contradict us or dampen our enthusiasm. After he drove us home, he watched us change our shoes and go off to run Green Lake. The shoes didn't make us run faster but we still loved them. And I loved my dad for not pricking our excitement, for letting us discover what made runners fast.

Our dad was the positive person in the family and our mom the difficult one. Dad made games out of getting dressed in the morning when Mom wasn't speaking for reasons that eluded me. Later, when my sister and I ranted about our mother, he would remind us that she never had a mother. She had overcome a lot in her life. Compassion was a good thing. He never gave up the hope of making her happy. Ever. After they moved into their assisted living facility, I refused to go to the liquor store to buy the Greek brandy, Metaxa, my mom wanted. The doctor told her when she left the hospital that she should never ever have a drop of alcohol again. Metaxa has an alcohol content of over eighty percent. One day, my husband was driving down the street near where they were living and saw my dad walking the other way. He stopped to give him a ride. My dad was walking home from the liquor store with a bottle of Metaxa.

Growing up, one of the discussions I hated having with my dad was the goals discussion. He'd ask me if I had time to talk. I could put it off for awhile but eventually I had to sit down with him. "I'm just curious," he'd start, "what are your goals right now?" In my high school and college days I had no idea what my goals were; I just wanted to fit in, pass my classes and get away from home. I'd make something up and he'd be pacified for the time being. Making a difference was never part of the out loud goal making he asked about. But looking back I see how he made goals. He fought to make a difference. He talked about visual pollution when McDonald's started being built. He went along with my mom's denouncement of Disney and the appropriation or rather destruction of children's literature. But the biggest fight he took on was against the proposed "Empire Expressway," or R. H. Thomson Expressway, that our city, Seattle, and Washington State highway engineers planned to build from south to north right through our neighborhood and the Arboretum. He became president of the Ravenna Bryant Community Association. He went to city council meetings. And more meetings. He took me leafleting on Saturdays and the green flyers I placed between screen doors in Green Lake and Wallingford neighborhoods were probably my first activist action. The flyers talked about meetings, public hearings, and eventually asked people to vote on a ballot measure that defeated the freeway. Figuring out what the right thing was and fighting for it was how my dad established his goals. My mom said he lost his job at the Applied Physics Lab because he spent too much time at meetings. But the freeway was defeated.

In every photo of my dad and his youngest sister Erma, the two of them are laughing. In his Navy uniform with Erma in the 40s, he's holding her as she leans back and they are both laughing. Forty years later, in the photograph of Erma with my dad on his sailboat, she's got her hands on his shoulders and they're still laughing. At my wedding, even though Erma was sick with multiple myeloma and would die within two years, Erma is the only one laughing with my dad in the photograph of him with his three sisters. I imagine Erma to be like the grandmother, Lydia, who I never met. I imagine Lydia sitting on the porch in Port Orchard in the summertime, offering a cup of coffee to her neighbors, and laughing the way Erma did. Her laughter sounds like my dad's, sincere and heartfelt.

When my dad went in for surgery on an artery close to his heart at age eighty-nine, they read him the risks and everything bad that might happen, including death. I walked with him to the surgery door. Lying on the gurney, he looked relaxed as I tried to hold back tears. I've had a good life, he told me. I love you Dad, I told him, and turned away as they wheeled him through the door. After his transfer to an adult family home, before he lost his words, he would tell me every time I visited how lucky he was. So lucky to have had such a good life, a life with hiking, with two children doing well, to have had friends and travel. He was grateful to be living in such a good place with such caring people. I'm grateful too, I'd tell him. I'm grateful to have you for my dad.

My dad brought his love of the mountains to his family. My mom made sure we all got backpacks, planned out overnight trips and weeklong trips in the Cascades and the Olympics. She loved the exercise and often hiked ahead so she could hike faster. My dad hiked with my sister and me, his red REI backpack piled high with two sleeping bags, pots and pans tied to the outside. He made games out of what was around the next corner. He found logs near streams so we could sit and snack on gorp and watch the glacier water run over the green mossy rocks. He put up the blue tent at our campsite. When he took up rock climbing and climbed Mt. Rainier, he told my sister and I that climbing a mountain wasn't hard. It was just a matter of putting one foot in front of the other.

Today, I watch the man who climbed mountains grip his walker and put one foot in front of the other. I follow him outside and we sit in the afternoon sun, watching the leaves glitter as a soft wind blows through the trees. I reach over to put my hand on top of his and he looks at me, his blue eyes smiling, a blue I will always carry with me. 📖

# Straw and Tin

## Rich Furman

The Scarecrow and Tin Man in the Wizard of Oz—they both walked so stiffly. Knees would not function well made of either straw or tin. There are days when they feel like the former, dried out reeds that bend under my weight, sway in the slightest breeze, or from the gentle touch of a twelve-pound dog, or the slightest glance of passing child. Even worse, however, are the days when they are corroded and deformed metal, thinned by time and chance, barely able to support me standing, parts meeting parts that were never designed to meet.

# Without Supervision

## Rich Furman

Waiting for my knees to come out. Not today, but soon. I will be incapacitated—placed under anesthesia—and a man that I barely know will cut into my flesh, scoop out from behind my patella the damaged soft tissue that has failed, saw my femur smooth, screw a metal plate into it, and attach metal hinges and bolts that will then become me. I will allow him to do this, and other things I am only beginning to understand. I, who normally does not even let anyone wash my t-shirts without intensive supervision.

# Searching for My Name

## Sharon Goldberg

### Family Name

My family name, Goldberg, was pilfered from a crumbling, untended gravestone in a Jewish cemetery in Ponevezh, Lithuania. My great-great-grandfather, Feival Margolis-Gordon, chose Goldberg along with three other names for his four younger sons. To save their lives. Only his eldest son kept the original family name.

In the 1800s, in the Russian Empire, Czar Nicholas I, at war with Polish dukes to the west and Japanese warlords in the Far East, demanded soldiers to fill the rank and file of his army. While Christian peasants were eligible at ages eighteen to thirty-five, Jews were drafted at ages twelve to twenty-five, a policy aimed at converting the young and susceptible to Christianity. Each Jewish community had its quota. But there was a loophole. "Only sons" were exempt from the draft. My great-great-grandfather registered his sons with Jewish authorities who were savvy and accepted bribes. His firstborn was named Zalman Shlomo Margolis-Gordon, and his sons with fake names were Avraham Druskkovitz, Hanoch Giddish, Meir Schochat, and Yehudah Goldberg, my great-grandfather. And so our family tree with its grafts survived.

Yehudah and his brothers evaded the army and with my great-grandmother, Hinda, he had six children. The youngest, my grandfather Feival, married Rivka, his second cousin, whose last name was also Goldberg. But his generation faced more persecution. The 1882 May Laws further restricted where Jews could live, where they could own or lease property, and when they could conduct business. Worse, the government sanctioned pogroms.

On a winter night in 1920, a pack of men invaded the home where my grandfather, pregnant grandmother, and their five young children lived. One man pulled a gun. Another beat up Grandpa.

A third man threw the crying youngest child on the dirt floor. The men ransacked the house searching for money and other valuables. Finally they left. My grandparents no longer felt safe. With the children, they fled the country. Like nearly 160,000 other Lithuanian Jews, they immigrated to America. On February 3, 1921, my family arrived at Ellis Island and were welcomed by Sol Goldberg, Grandma's brother. They settled in Lorain, Ohio, a small city on the shores of Lake Erie, where Grandma's older sister and her husband lived. They adopted the English names Phillip and Rebecca. They gave their children English names. Later that year my father Hyman was born. His Hebrew name, Chaim, means life. Twenty-nine years after that, in 1950, in St. Luke's Hospital in Cleveland, my mother gave birth to me.

## Hebrew Name

Jewish parents traditionally give their children Hebrew names as well as names in the language of their native country. My Hebrew name is Sheindel Sora. I am named after my maternal grandmother's two sisters, my great aunts, who lived in Romania, who did not immigrate to America, whom I never met, whom my mother never met, who were rounded up by Nazis, who were packed like cattle in a one-way train to Auschwitz, who took their last breaths in a gas chamber.

## Given Name

My parents chose my English name, Sharon Sue, because it sounded similar to my Hebrew name. Sharon is of an era. Sharon is a Baby Boomer name. Sharon first became popular in the late 1940s. In 1950, the year I was born, Sharon was the eleventh most popular baby girl name after Linda, Mary, Patricia, Barbara, Susan, Nancy, Deborah, Sandra, Carol, and Kathleen. In 1960, Sharon dropped to number sixteen; in 1970 number thirty-seven; in 1980 number 129. In 1990, "Sharon" didn't make the top 200. My name telegraphs my age. It dates me like the rings of a tree.

Sharon is a biblical name originating in the Old Testament. But Sharon is not the name of a person. It is a place name meaning "plain" and refers to two different regions: a pasture land east of the Jordan River occupied by the sons of Gad (*Chronicles 27-29*) and a fertile plain that covered much of the north coast of Israel (*Chronicles 5:16*). I've never been to Israel but many members of the Goldberg clan have sojourned there: my parents, my brother Howard, many aunts and uncles and cousins. My nephew Jeremy and twin nieces Allison and Rebecca, my brother Sherwin's children, spent their first year of college in Israel. The many visitors were welcomed by relatives from various branches of the family tree, the offspring of my great-great-grandfather's fake-named sons who immigrated to the country established as a Jewish homeland.

I have not visited Israel and I feel Jewish guilt. Other destinations have drawn me more: France, Italy, New Zealand, Costa Rica, Viet Nam, Thailand. Why have I neglected the country so deeply rooted in my Jewish heritage? Perhaps because I am a completely secular Jew. Perhaps because I've been reluctant to dredge up reminders of persecution. Perhaps because I've resented family expectations.

Now, at sixty-seven, I feel the pull. I want to see the archaeological sites of Masada, Caesarea, Tiberius. I want to visit the Wailing Wall, the remains of the second Jewish Holy Temple which dates back to 516 B.C. Maybe even leave a prayer note in one of its crevices. And I want to visit Yad Vashem, The World Holocaust Remembrance Center, where the names of 4.5 million Holocaust victims are recorded. Including the names of my great aunts.

Jewish Name

Goldberg is an Ashkenazi Jewish name—a name of German or Yiddish origin—meaning "gold mountain." As a child, I didn't realize Goldberg was a common Jewish name. Perhaps the quintessential Jewish name. Only 300 Jewish families lived in Lorain, Ohio (population 80,000). They attended the city's one synagogue, Agudath B'nai Israel. Everyone in Lorain named Goldberg was my close relative: grandma, parent, brother, aunt, uncle, first cousin, including Meyer Goldberg, my uncle whose name appeared in giant letters on five Lorain-area supermarkets. Not until I scanned big city phone books—Cleveland, Chicago, New York—did I learn how plentiful we Goldbergs are. In the Seattle area, where I now live, there are about 63,400 Jews, of which *anywho.com* lists fifty-eight Goldbergs. None are related to me. Nor am I related to Bill Goldberg, the wrestler, Arthur Goldberg, the former Supreme Court Justice, or Whoopi Goldberg, the actress and comic, who changed her name from Caryn Elaine Johnson.

Two TV shows have been named *The Goldbergs*. The first, a comedy-drama which ran from January 1949 to June 1961, starred Gertrude Berg as Molly Goldberg, and told the story of a family from the Bronx complete with ethnic humor and Yiddish accents. During the final season, the Goldbergs "immigrated" to Connecticut. The current sitcom, *The Goldbergs*, is set in the 1980s and loosely based on the childhood of its creator Adam F. Goldberg. It features a family with three kids, a grandfather, an overprotective mother, and a hot-tempered father who screams a lot. The ABC network describes it as a show about a loving family like any other—just with a lot more yelling.

I watched the first episode and never watched again. I don't like my name associated with those annoying TV characters. I worry that negative depictions of "Goldbergs" might reflect poorly on me. Or worse, on Jewish people in general. Though seven decades have passed since World War II, I still fear anti-Semitism. In the United States, the Alt-Right spews white supremacist, Nazi, and fascist hate. In Hungary, anti-Semitism resurged with the success of Jobbik, a radical nationalist party that preaches anti-Jewish and anti-Gypsy rhetoric.

In 1991, my then-husband Steve and I traveled with our friends, Tony and Linda, to Germany. In Bavaria, in Garmisch-Partenkirchen, we stayed at a lovely inn complete with Hansel and Gretel furniture, fluffy down comforters and pillows, and a restaurant that served traditional German food. As we dined on schnitzel, spaetzli, and dumplings heavy as grapefruits, a family, maybe eight people, sat down in the booth in front of us. The men wore lederhosen, suspenders, knee socks, forest green felt hats with feathers. Did the women wear dirndl skirts and puffed-sleeve blouses? I don't remember. A band entertained; one man played spoons, another performed a Bavarian slap dance. The family locked arms, swayed back and forth, and sang along to German folk songs.

For me, it was a Holocaust moment. The Nazi movement was born in Bavaria. Some of the people in the booth were, no doubt, alive during World War II. I flashed on the scene in *Cabaret* where a young, rosy-cheeked Hitler Youth rose at an outdoor café and sang "Tomorrow Belongs to Me." I felt unwelcome. Unsafe. I did not belong. Could they tell I was Jewish?

With a name like Goldberg, I can't hide.

## Nicknames

My Grandma Rebecca, my bubbe, called me Sharila. My father sometimes called me Susie Q. When I argued with my parents, stomped to my bedroom, and slammed the door, they called me "The Ostrich." At one point in elementary school, I signed my name as "Sharon Sue Shari Crackers Goldberg." My high school friend Dia calls me Shari-Poo as if I was still seventeen instead of sixty-seven. My life partner Arnie just calls me Sweetie.

## Stage Name

At the age of thirteen, I decided I wanted to be an actress. I needed a stage name. A name more dramatic and compelling and memorable than Sharon Goldberg. A name less ethnic. I considered Ricki Van Ronson, a Waspish mash up of Ricky Nelson, one of my heartthrobs, and Randy Van Ronson, a character in *Katy Keene* Comic Books. I liked the alliterative sound. But I did not look like a Ricky Van Anybody. I settled on a shorter, cuter version of my own name: "Shari Gold." That name, I fantasized, would eventually star in Playbills, flash in neon lights, and glow on my "Best Actress" Oscar statuette. I never officially adopted Shari Gold, but I did morph my name in various ways.

When I escaped Lorain, when I escaped Ohio, when I arrived at Northwestern University in Evanston, Illinois, a theater major, I seized the opportunity to create a new identity. In Allison Hall, my dorm; in Annie May Swift Hall, home to the theater department; at the Sigma Delta Tau sorority house, a Jewish sorority—I introduced myself as "Shari." But Shari never really felt like me. Was it too perky? Too bright? Too girly?

After two years, I transferred to Bowling Green State University. A school in Ohio. A school just two hours from Lorain. A school that several of my high school friends attended. But I was a theater person, and our paths rarely crossed. They didn't know I was "Shari."

I became Sharon again in graduate school. I'd outgrown "Shari" and my identity felt fractured. Two years later, I moved to Los Angeles to pursue my boyfriend and an acting career. I lived down the street from the Hollywood Sign. I studied acting. I auditioned. Rehearsed. Performed. Mostly in plays. And I remained Sharon Goldberg for eight more years.

### Jewish Nose

By the time I reached high school, my facial features had reached maturity. My nose was long. Bumpy. Big. With my looks reinforced by my Jewish name, I feared I'd be typecast, pigeonholed, stuck, overlooked, passed over, limited, restricted, and relegated to mostly ethnic roles. I believed I'd be prettier, less "character," and more likely to be cast with a smaller schnoz. At thirty-one, I got a nose job. And I changed my name. Again. I chose a less ethnic name to match the new nose. I did not choose Shari Gold as I'd planned at thirteen. I was done with "Shari." I opted for Sharon Gardner, generic enough but distinctive enough. And there was a family precedent. The playwright Herb Gardner, author of *A Thousand Clowns* and *Conversations with My Father*, was my father's first cousin once removed, the grandson of Sol Goldberg, who met the family at Ellis Island. Like so many other Jews in theatre, film, and comedy, Herbert Goldberg anglicized his name.

Like Allan Stewart Konigsberg who became Woody Allen, Jerome Silberman who became Gene Wilder. Bobby Zimmerman who became Bob Dylan, Joyce Penelope Frankenberg, who became Jane Seymour, Jonathan Stuart Leibowitz who became Jon Stewart. Jonah Hill Feldstein who became Jonah Hill, Winona Laura Horowitz who became Winona Ryder. They chose shorter names, easier-to-pronounce names less likely to stir prejudice or assumptions or stereotypes. On the other hand, Barbra Streisand kept her name and her nose. And Whoopi adopted "Goldberg" because her mother thought a Jewish-sounding name would help to advance her career.

## Married Name

When I got married in 1986, I did not change my name to Isaac, a German-Jewish name, although if spelled "Isaak," it's not a Jewish name. I did not want to be Mrs. Anyone. My consciousness had been raised by the Women's Lib movement. I was not property. I would not capitulate to the patriarchy. Okay, my name was my father's name but it was also my grandmother's birth name and it had been mine for thirty-five years. I did not wish to be Sharon Goldberg Hyphen Isaac either. To my surprise, my husband-to-be, who was seven years my junior, who was modern and forward-thinking, who was no "Macho Man," believed I should change my name to his. Steve claimed he did not care about carrying on his family name, but he believed all nuclear family members should have the same one. I suggested he change his name to Goldberg. No. For a while, we joked about choosing a new name for both of us—Blueberry, perhaps—but neither of us really intended to relinquish our own name. What about our future children? Steve feared multiple parental names would cause confusion for schools, for hospitals, on forms of all sorts. I suggested our children use Isaac-Goldberg. Or Goldberg-Isaac. Or they could have his name. But my name would remain Goldberg.

We had no children. After eighteen years of marriage, we divorced.

My nieces, Allison and Rebecca (named after my two grand-mothers), both kept "Goldberg" when they got married. I'm glad, especially since I have no children of my own. I feel a strong connection to them as well as to my nephew, their brother Jeremy. I like the family name chain and so do they. Another generation removed from The Holocaust, they don't share my fears, although they acknowledge some concerns about travel in the Mideast. As Allison said, "I have always felt very proud of my last name and it being so obviously Jewish. Dad and Grandma and Grandpa definitely instilled in us a pride of not only being Jewish, but being part of the Goldberg family." Jeremy felt he was "anointed" in the Lorain Jewish Community as one of the next Goldberg genera-tion with high expectations to carry on the family name. He and his wife Vanessa named their son Marco Bilanceri (Vanessa's last name) Goldberg.

In the Salem Jewish Cemetery in Lorain where many Gold-bergs are buried, gleaming black granite headstones honor my grandparents; a joint black granite stone honors my parents. On all three, the names are engraved in English and Hebrew.

Pen Name

My pen name is my birth name—Sharon Goldberg. I wonder if I should choose a more dazzling name. A name that pops on a book jacket. Perhaps "Sharona," a Hebrew name and alternate form of Sharon immortalized in the song "My Sharona" by The Knack. Should I play up ethnicity and use my real Hebrew name, Sheindel Sora? Would add-ing my middle name add more impact? Should I anglicize my name again? Pick a name with more gravitas or melody? Adopt a man's name? Or perhaps consider the initial-only approach and conceal my gender?

No. None of the above. What matters is not an author's name, but the quality of her writing, the power of her words, the clarity of her thoughts. I'll continue to examine, mull over, rework, refine, revise, revise, revise my words as long as I'm able to compose a sentence. And I'm done changing my name. I've finally embraced it. 📖

*National Memorial for Peace and Justice*, Montgomery, Alabama, 2018, Photograph, by Anna Bálint

*Willow and Birds*, Painting, by Katsushika Hokusai

# One Way of Looking
# at Thirteen Blackbirds

Rafael Jesús González

Willow in a storm
and thirteen flying blackbirds
turning in the wind—
kerchiefs snatched from women's heads
bowed at a friend's funeral.


# Un modo de ver
# trece pájaros negros

Rafael Jesús González

Sauces en una tormenta
y trece pájaros negros volando,
volteando en el viento—
paños arrebatados de las cabezas de mujeres
inclinadas en el funeral de una amiga.

# In the Break of Time

## James Grabill

Anyone entering a room
has already stepped
through a threshold.
Anyone who lives between walls
has grown out of a tiniest origin.
Where you have being,
you have an extended moment
of being born. Everything happens
to exist in the only place it could be.
Now everything's changed.
Any person picturing a person
is alive on a planet in the cosmos.
The mind shows documentary
footage, as the brain entertains
presence. In the split second,
plants assist the planet undergoing
utter mitosis. Erasing long-term
indivisibility while embracing it,
the mind survives what the brain is
serving under the only tent in the sky.
Like the moon, longevity orbits
whales and the ants, gray squirrels
and the swift gold-brown foxes
of the foothills where being's born.
Whatever happens, whatever
has been working through presence
knows being blooms here and flies
as it swims. In the break
of time, a person's a prism
in the making of color
received from the root-pulse
spectrum within being quick.

# The End of Conversation

## John Grey

We talk a lot about
why we don't talk any more.
Then sex enters the picture.
More like a default than a passion.
But instead of tearing our clothes off,
we both potter about after something
we might have in common.
After all, we're a couple.
Surely there's something
besides sharing a bed.
We circle around a non-existent subject.
Then we just hug.
It feels like conversation
when nothing else does,

But our mouths are mute.
Our imaginations likewise.
Maybe we really have said
all we're ever going to say to each other.
So we sit in silence.
But, after all these years,
it's a comfortable silence.
It has a lot to say
even if we don't.

# Blues for John T. Williams

## Steve Griggs

"Hey! Hey! HEY!" the cop shouted. "Put the knife down! Put the knife down! PUT THE KNIFE DOWN!" The old Indian, walking along the sidewalk, lifted his gaze from his carving and looked over his right shoulder toward the young, white lawman nine feet behind him. The officer jerked the trigger of his sidearm five times. The Indian fell to the sidewalk, dead. It was just past 4 p.m. on August 30, 2010, at the corner of Boren and Howell. The sky was blue. The air was still. The Seattle Police Officer's name was Ian Birk. The Indian's name was John T. Williams.

Deliberate and unlawful killing of one person by another is homicide. The officer's shooting was ruled as "unjustified," but the officer was not charged with homicide. The killing was awful but lawful.

Why can police legally kill, even when unjustified? I had to know the answer. John T. Williams was an artist, born in 1960, just twenty-eight days before me. It is my responsibility as a fellow artist to witness and try to understand this injustice.

Following the killing, the relationship between the victim's family and police worsened. John's brother, Rick, took on the role of spokesperson, and through his grief and anger, spoke of the wisdom of his ancestors. "I must be a warrior for peace."

Two weeks after John's death, a lawyer on behalf of his family convened a Restorative Circle at the Chief Seattle Club. The club served as a sacred healing space where those linked by this shared tragedy could express themselves, seek understanding, and connect. Afterward, Rick said, "What we need are more opportunities for safe, direct communications like those we had."

Within days of the restorative circle, drummers, elders, and protest marchers chanted tribal thunder in City Hall. The protesters raised their voices and a city councilman raised his hands.

"I'm going to ask that we try to look at this event through the eyes and the lens of Officer Birk," the council member said.

"And I will tell you why—because if we can do that, we can then say with a heightened sense of strength and courage and conviction that you must see this incident through the eyes of John T. Williams. From any perspective other than your own . . . this is the challenge of fighting institutional racism."

The eyes of Officer Ian Birk—what did they see? Were his eyes blinded behind the one-way lenses of racism? And the eyes of John T. Williams? Did a beer buzz cloud a vision that this was how his days would end? And me. Can I see this from any perspective other than my own? Probably not, but I will try. I invite you to try.

Four days after the shooting that took Williams' life, officer Birk recounted the events for the Firearms Review Board. The light turned red at the corner of Boren and Howell. Birk stopped his patrol car. The sun was shining and a man shuffled in front of Birk's car. The man was stabbing and scraping a piece of wood with a knife. The man appeared to be mentally impaired and oblivious of the presence of a police officer.

What was Birk thinking? Unless he tells us, we may never know. Police hide their thoughts from the public. But as a twenty-seven-year-old officer with merely two years on the job, Birk likely had thoughts similar to another fresh white recruit who killed his first civilian and wrote about it, Norm Stamper. In his book *Breaking Rank,* Stamper shares his experience with the rampant racist fears of white officers. He wrote, "Why am I so certain that white cops are afraid of black men? Because I was a white cop. In a world of white cops. For thirty-four years."

Stamper goes on to recount his early police academy training which taught, "that of all the people we'd encounter on the streets, those most dangerous to our safety, to our survival, were black men." Specifically, black Muslims "will kill any police officer when the opportunity presents itself, regardless of the circumstances or outcome." I don't have any quotes from white officers about indigenous people, so I am going to take the liberty to suggest that Stamper's quote refers to all non-white people and that the police academy trains new police to see the community as a war zone.

Stamper's racist academy training was reinforced by racist field training. Stamper was ordered to take his police baton, referred to as a "nigger knocker," into a bar and arrest the "biggest, blackest, meanest motherfucking nigger in the place." Halfway to the door, Stamper was called back. The field trainer was laughing. Stamper stopped shaking five minutes later. Field training emphasizes aggressive warrior tactics.

Soon after this hazing, Stamper watched a different white officer interact with blacks in a "respectful, transparently fearless approach." This contrast in styles of white/black contact helped Stamper recognize his own "panicky, impulsive" approach. Stamper went on to confess, "I was hardly your ideal cop candidate. Like many other screwed-up kids who go on to become police officers, I used the job, or it used me, to work out all kinds of developmental and emotional challenges. I figure upwards of a hundred San Diegans paid a price for my on-the-job 'therapy' during my rookie year alone."

So what were Ian Birk's developmental and emotional challenges? How had he been trained to see indigenous people? Would Williams have to pay the price of Birk's on-the-job therapy?

Unknown to Birk, Williams descended from the Ditidaht Tribe, from the Nuu-cha-nulth Nation of western Vancouver Island. For centuries, these tribes have transformed tree trunks into effigies of spirit characters from their stories—eagles, orcas, frogs, beavers, wolves, minks. The stories provide lessons from connections between nature and humans. Stories that entertain. Stories that instruct. Stories that preserve a culture of this place, from ancient history to the present. Carved wood from the Williams family reference these vital stories. While John's brother Rick carved, he told a reporter for *Seattle Met* magazine, "I'm not whittling here. I'm telling stories without talking."

In the book, *A Totem Pole History*, Michael Pavel writes, "Every Coast Salish community needs artists to record our history in the pieces we bring to life. In doing so, we did what our ancestors did: we carry forth a profound and beautiful way of life."

Birk also did not know that John T. Williams was only one of a large family of carvers living in Seattle for generations. John's older brother Harvey had been the subject of a 1965 *Seattle Times* full-page story, "Victoria's Boy Totem-Carver." The article includes a picture of Harvey carving while his parents and five siblings, including John, watched. Even though Harvey received this public recognition, carving four totems a day, later he acknowledged John's superior talent saying, "Some of his carvings made me feel like an amateur."

John and his siblings had learned carving traditions from Ray, their father, who had learned from Sam, his grandfather, who had learned from a lineage stretching back four generations before. "We're really proud people as carvers," Rick told *Seattle Met.*, "It's who I am. I'm in my element when I'm carving." And the reputation of the Williams family of carvers was wide. "North, south, east and west. Dad, Sam, John, Dave, Eric and I were in different points of Seattle," Rick said. "Everybody knew who we were in those days."

John's grandfather Sam came to Seattle back in 1901, and carved totems for sale at Ye Olde Curiosity Shop. The book *,1001 Curious Things: Ye Olde Curiosity Shop and Native American Art* (2001), contains many pictures and stories of Sam and his work, including a three-and-a-half-story-tall totem purchased by Robert Ripley in 1936. Ripley, famous for the *Believe It or Not!* franchise, also purchased Sam's ten-foot-tall carving *Potlatch Man*. Ripley displayed *Potlatch Man* at the 1939 New York World's Fair.

Ripley was not the only person to purchase a Williams totem. Of all the totem poles sold at Ye Olde Curiosity Shop since it opened in 1899, one estimate is that over seventy percent of them were carved by a Williams family member. Art by generations of the Williams family can be admired together on the shelves today. They were on display the day Ian Birk encountered John T. Williams. Before John was shot, he was likely carving something that would stand on the shelves next to the other family pieces.

Unbeknownst to Birk, Williams was transforming the chunk of scrap lumber into his favorite spirit animal, the eagle. The eagle flies on high, with a wide perspective, seeing the larger view beyond the details. Williams guided his small blade into the grain with skilled sculptor's vision, unaided by an outline of pencil marks.

Birk, from his limited perspective, did not see that the knife was only three inches long—half an inch less than the minimum necessary to meet the definition of "dangerous knife" in the Seattle Municipal code—the laws Birk was sworn to enforce. Birk did not see that Williams was walking from his room on Eastlake to Victor Steinbrueck Park, where he and his brothers would carve under the fifty-foot totems.

While we can't enter Birk's mind, we can observe what he did, and didn't do. Birk had seen a knife. His duty as a police officer was to initiate contact to determine if there was a crime or a threat to the public. He activated the revolving cruiser emergency lights, reported to the dispatcher his contact with a suspect, rocked out of his vehicle, reached for his holster, and released his sidearm.

Here, Birk's misstep strayed from policies and training. He didn't provide the dispatcher with any details about the suspect. He didn't mention the knife. He didn't say where Williams was or which direction the suspect was walking. He didn't call for backup, even though there were officers with Tasers within twenty seconds of his location. Birk justified his deviation with a strange personal belief, not one supported by polices or training—he expected that other police listening to their department radios would rely on a "sixth sense" to intuit the specifics of his encounter.

Perhaps Birk thought the officers would just understand that this was just another chapter in the frequent mistreatment of indigenous people by the police. Maybe Birk bought into the idea that downtown Seattle on a summer afternoon was a war zone where his actions on camera would show he was a bad ass.

Approaching Williams from behind, Birk shouted, "Hey!" three times and "Put the knife down!" three times. He did not identify himself as a Police Officer and he did not warn that he would shoot.

Birk left the protective cover of his vehicle and closed the distance between himself and a man with a knife. But why? Police are trained to maintain at least twenty-one feet distance from a knife-wielding suspect to allow enough time to draw a sidearm and shoot twice at the center of body mass.

Williams turned his head toward Birk. Birk saw a "very stern, very serious, very confrontational look on his face." Birk testified, "His brow was furrowed, eyes were fixed in a thousand-yard stare. His jaw was set. He had the knife raised up."

What could Williams' face have been saying? Williams' skin, darkened by years on the street, may have triggered a fear of the "other" in Birk. Williams could have furrowed his brow, perhaps struggling to understand the voice behind him through his impaired hearing. Williams likely widened his eyes, snapped out of his concentration on carving. Imagine the focus and coordination required to walk and carve at the same time. Williams clenched his jaw, disgruntled at being detained from meeting his brothers. If Williams frowned, perhaps he was recalling his one hundred misdemeanor arrests over the previous twenty-five years and wondering if the recent beer he drank would again lead to jail. Williams raised the knife, maybe to show that it was small and he was closing the blade.

"Knowing that he could attack at any moment," Birk testified, "that he had failed to comply with my lawful orders, and that he was so close that he could attack me before I could react, I made the decision to fire." The first officer responding to the report of shots fired told Birk, "Good job."

At the King County inquest, Birk explained, "The concern was basically immediate, and I needed to respond as fast as possible. . . . There was no intent on my part to kill Mr. Williams. My intent was to stop the threat." But the four pedestrians nearby testified that Williams did not pose a threat. Birk's statement of "no intent to kill" was critical for legal protection.

What Birk said next compartmentalizes the consequences of his actions, skirting accountability for taking Williams' life. Birk said, "We don't decide who lives or dies. It's a terrible thing."

I am uncomfortable hearing this statement. I hope you are too. "We don't decide who lives or dies." I assume the "we" Birk referred to are police officers. If so, Birk is hiding behind his badge. I suppose that police "don't decide" means that officers take action based on hard-wired training and unbiased policies, that police are just doing their job, that whatever a police officer does is necessary, no matter the result. Birk's testimony suggests that he decided to fire with no intent to kill. So if he didn't intend to kill Williams but Williams died from his shots, who is accountable for that mistake? By shooting four bullets into Williams without taking responsibility for killing, Birk is somehow blaming the system.

Let's look closer at this system. Eighty police officers told their stories of deadly force in a 2006 book *Into the Kill Zone: A Cop's Eye View of Deadly Force*. The "kill zone" is the area where a suspect might kill an officer. This "kill zone" surrounds every suspect where police are trained to fear for their lives. This zone, where police are vulnerable to attack, is the place where they are legally protected to use deadly force. Understand, the police detect an invisible kill zone around every one of us. Whether you know it or not, police are trained to use deadly force in this zone. Birk was trained to use deadly force, was legally protected in doing so, but he didn't intend to kill. That doesn't add up.

A common question asked of people applying to be police officers is, "Will you be able to shoot, and perhaps kill, another human being?" One officer in the book *Into the Kill Zone* responded, "I read a lot as a kid. I read a lot of everything, from cowboy books, to quite a few police books, to a lot of spy novels. I knew from all this reading and from watching occasional news pieces that there were some seriously bad, evil people out there and that there was a potential that I would come into contact with them. I knew that I would be able to handle it. I never questioned my ability to take somebody's life if it was a situation of where it was them or me, or them or my family, or them or some innocent person they were trying to victimize. So I always felt that I would be able to shoot somebody if it was necessary." My question is, what if it isn't necessary? What if an officer makes a mistake? And what if these mistakes happen in the kill zone?

If the officer believes you have a knife, the kill zone surrounds you in every direction for twenty-one feet. It doesn't matter if you actually have a knife. I doubt John T. Williams realized where his kill zone was. Birk entered the kill zone for Williams. Will you be aware when police enter your kill zone? Do you see that you are at the center of a place where police are legally justified to kill you because they are afraid? How much more lethal is your kill zone if the officer thinks he's in a war with people of color? Who will speak for the victims at the center of their kill zones—Amadou Diallo, Michael Brown, Philando Castile, Alton Sterling, Che Taylor, Charleena Lyles, John T. Williams?

The length of time between Birk's first "Hey!" and his decision to fire was seven seconds. Then Birk quickly squeezed the trigger five times. One bullet missed. The other four hollow-point bullets pierced Williams in his right side because he had not yet turned around to face Birk. Hollow-point bullets mushroom on impact to cause more tissue damage in the wound path. One bullet entered Williams' chin on the right and exited on the left. Another entered the back of his upper right arm, exiting under his right collar bone. A third entered the middle of his right forearm, the arm holding his knife, and exited the other side. The fourth, the most deadly, entered his right chest above the nipple, traveled through his lungs and heart, and exited his left armpit. Williams fell to the sidewalk. The Chief Medical Examiner concluded in his Coroner Report, "The manner of death is homicide."

In just under seven seconds, Birk escalated from making contact to assess a threat to fearing for his life. He decided Williams was a threat and needed to be shot. Birk deviated from policies and training to create the situation that increased his own risk. Why? We may never know. The Firearms Review Board ruled that the shooting was "unjustified."

So what should come from an unjustified homicide by a police officer? I believe that an officer should be held accountable for his actions. Under our Declaration of Independence, John T. Williams was endowed by his Creator with the inalienable rights of life, liberty and the pursuit of happiness. Birk took those constitutional rights away. Who will pay for that theft?

But Washington State law is not on the side of police shooting victims. Our law contains the strongest protection in America against police officers being convicted of homicide. The Revised Code of Washington, Title 9A, Chapter 16, Section 040, Subsection 3 states, "A public officer or peace officer shall not be held criminally liable for using deadly force without malice and with a good faith belief that such act is justifiable." In plain English, that means a police officer without evil intent in Washington State cannot be charged with killing a human being. This is where Birk's statement of "no intent to kill" shields his actions from prosecution.

It has been lawful for police in Washington to shoot and kill a fleeing suspect since 1909. But the Supreme Court ruled in 1985 that using deadly force to prevent the escape of an unarmed suspect violated their constitutional rights. In response, two Democratic senators from Seattle sponsored a bill that would merit lethal force if there was a perception of peril to the officer or anyone else. The Washington Association of Sheriffs and Police Chiefs inserted the good faith and malice clause. Leo Poort, legal adviser to the Seattle police chief told the Seattle Times, "We wanted it clear that if you were acting in good faith, that a prosecutor should not be able to charge a crime." The bill became law in 1986. So we are left with this rule. Awful but lawful.

While Washington State law may be terrible, according to a 2015 Amnesty International report, "all fifty states and Washington D.C. fail to comply with international law and standards on the use of lethal force by law enforcement officers."

Maybe the death of John T. Williams will change things. Five months after he was shot, the Justice Department opened an investigation of the Seattle Police Department. Eight and a half months later, the investigation confirmed that "SPD has engaged in a pattern or practice of excessive force that violates the Constitution and federal law. Our investigation further raised serious concerns that some SPD policies and practices, particularly those related to pedestrian encounters, could result in discriminatory policing." Seven months later, Seattle agreed to a settlement for a consent decree to address these concerns. But a consent decree is dispute resolution between two parties without admission of guilt.

John T. Williams' death led his brother to embody the peacemaker teachings of his elders. Rick kept his knife pointed to art, not anger, and carved a thirty-four-foot totem in John's memory. In front of the totem at Seattle Center, architect Johnpaul Jones, the architect of the National Museum of the American Indian in Washington D.C., has designed the Wa-Nish Circle of Peace to welcome all indigenous people.

The crosswalk at Boren and Howell has been decorated with a symbol of the peacemaker, and the utility box next to the place where John was killed is now covered with a story of the peacemaker, White Deer, as told by a tribal elder. This elder, Sara Jack, talked about why there is repetition in the story, the repetition of visiting an old tree to receive the power of White Deer. The elder said, "Why is it repeated several times? The ritual of going back again and again. Going home and going back to where there is knowledge. It is work. You have to work for knowledge. You have to go back and forth, back and forth. You have to study where you walk, wherever you walk, you have to study yourself; you have to feel things. You have to keep that within your heart and humble yourself. It is a lot of work to do that. That's the meaning of that, going back and forth."

As a community we need to study where we walk. I want to study where I walk—where John T. Williams walked. 📖

*The Passerby*, Painting, by Gregg Chadwick

# Snow White Woke

## Mare Heron Hake

She was young and she thought, flawless. A sexual innocent,
an untouched purity. No one had forced a roughness to her
skin, stretched her inside and out, made her comply, made
the walls of her vagina give, made her happy to lie naked
in the dirt with the full grown weight of another pushing
her backbone over the rocks. Her hair was the color of that
kind of midnight tryst, long and flowing to the slender waist,
ready to camouflage the perfect shoulders from prying eyes.
Shoulders not yet bent under the heavy hand of her mother,
not twisted to fit the matron's apron, but straight enough for
the songbird, a bluish bird of some bright type, to light upon.
And yes, a folksong followed her every step of every day, a
twiddling, a tweeting a whistle while she worked but then
again, her work was very easy.
Outrageously so, as if no one had the heart to wake her
from a dream, or could think of anything meaningful for her
to do except clean a little bit, or dust just a tad, or sing with
that too-red mouth, the pouty-never-been-kissed-princess.
But when that eveningsong came near, another repetition
of buzzing rang swiftly through the frost melting
in the uncut grass and came riding up the listener's legs
to the vacant
body where it seeped into her bones like a sudden draft,
a cold awareness
until most of the watchers turned their faces away,
eyes cast down like frightened little toadies
not kings or princes but dwarfish fools preferring
for that moment
to think her dead than to be so obviously beyond
their small-fisted reach,
a woman now woke in these manly woods
who doesn't need and won't give a bloody
              thing.

# By Water and Blood

## Sharon Hashimoto

I t's the high whine of the last syllable I can't stand: Mom-*meee*. As in feed *me*. Hold *me*. It's this chain of Mom-me demands that shatters my sleep. I rub my eyes and glance at the alarm clock. In three hours, I have to get up, ready everyone for work and school. *What now?* I ask myself, wishing the moment away.

My daughter stands in the doorway of my bedroom like she's afraid to enter, but wanting—always wanting—for me to fix some problem, some trouble—as if I can read her thoughts. I count her father's three snores, hoping she'll fade away, that she's part of some unhappy dream. But there's the creak of the hardwood floor as she shifts her weight from foot-to-foot, panic in her jerky actions.

During the day, I'm fitting household chores around my steno pool job at the Veteran's Administrative Hospital. During my coffee breaks, I'm calling Maytag about washing machine parts or checking the coupons I've clipped. Thirty minutes for lunch are thirty minutes of listening to my co-workers complain about our supervisor.

My government job is to schedule appointments and type reports in triplicate; the battered sheets of carbon paper barely conveying an imprint. Mornings at home, I cook Coco Wheats for Mary's breakfast, the wooden spoon scraping burnt pieces off of the bottom of the pot; sunny-side up eggs and bacon for my husband. I lean against the stove, bleary-eyed, remembering to take the pound of hamburger out of the freezer for dinner. Kraft American cheese slices go into sandwiches along with a bag of Fritos and an apple. I can't believe I've been doing this for three years.

Then I see Mary, barefoot in her pajamas, the hallway light silhouetting her in a reddish hue.

For the second time this week, I rise. My nightgown's hem swirls around my ankles; knowing feet search for their slippers.

I see the wads of Kleenex spotting with blood that Mary presses to her nose, head canted forward. There will be dime-sized drops on the hardwood floor that my daughter has trailed from her bed.

Her father wheezes, that sound he makes when he's coming up for breath—cranky to enter the waking world. "Quiet," I hiss, grabbing Mary's chin in my right hand and lifting it up. The other hand holds her sweaty forehead. "Don't wake Dad."

It's an awkward walk in the dark to the bathroom. The two light bulbs under the frosted glass are harsh when I flick on the light switch. The tub and toilet are a stark white. The sink stands on its stainless steel rods, the exposed water pipes silvery and cold. Mary coughs and spits into the sink, whining in fear at what she sees.

I swing open the medicine cabinet and reach for cotton balls to twist and shove into Mary's nostril. I see my face in the mirror: circles under my eyes. The hard pink plastic curlers askew on my head.

Mary sags, her belly pushed up against the sink, her two small hands gripping the edge. She's half-gurgling, half-choking as I pull away the soaked Kleenex. Bright blood drops fall against the white porcelain, rolling and colliding into a stream like the rain on our windows. A blurred streak finds its way down the drain.

I run the tap to dowse a washcloth, to rinse away the red. Blood is dripping down Mary's right nostril and I can't tell the striped pattern of her pajama sleeves from the streaks of her blood. "How many times," I say, "do I have to tell you? Don't pick your nose."

She gives a whimper. "I just rubbed it a little. And then . . ." Her voice hitches in her throat.

"It started bleeding," I finish for her. I'm stuck in a loop. Hadn't Mary said the exact same words two nights ago. "All this, all over again." My daughter is captive in my grip. If she weren't bleeding, I would probably shake her. Instead, I pinch her nose holes shut with the washcloth. I do it hard, knowing I need to apply pressure, knowing how my thumb and forefinger will tire, knowing that I can't let up.

Mary's voice is muffled by the washcloth, by her trying to breath through her mouth. I know she is trying to say that she's sorry but that angers me even more. Sorry isn't going to clean up her mess. Sorry isn't going to stop her from picking her nose again. Sorry isn't going to help her grades in school.

My daughter is such a timid child. Before she turned ten, I sat down with her at the kitchen table and checked her arithmetic homework. How she'd struggle with story problems. Always that pinched look, the raised eyebrows as if she could find the answer in my face. Mary doesn't try. Even when she does, it's a feeble attempt. Always, I'd end up telling her almost word for word what to write down. When she came home with a poor work slip, I drilled her on her spelling and vocabulary. Most of those she got right. Her report cards were mostly As and Bs then.

Mary gives a little burp, retches, and spits into the sink. I have to let go of the washcloth as she finishes. There are liver-colored clots, long and ropy, and a line of drool that I have to wipe away with the towel. It's disgusting. I know I'll have to soak her pajamas and sheets in cold water to get the stains out. I run the cold water and for a moment the sink is white again. Then one drop, two, a third strike the porcelain with the steady rhythm of a heartbeat.

Steady pressure for ten minutes while my feet grow chill. I lay cold compresses against the back of her neck. Mary shivers. I say nothing, thinking of my own mother—those days she hated on the farm—how in her work clothes, in her apron, she'd sit at the kitchen table peeling roots off of onions. I didn't know if she was crying because of the fumes, or because money was so tight. Japanese farmers worked hard; we had food on the table, but not much else. Somehow, I thought times would get better. But I'm trapped in the same scenario as my mother.

Mary's short straight hair is sticking up. There's a new pimple on her forehead. There's the rhythmic inhale, exhale as she breathes through her mouth. I can't tell if it's fifteen or five minutes. I want to go to bed. When I check, Mary's nose is still bleeding, a slow and irritating drip, drip, drip.

This is my daughter, I think. Blood should connect us, but all I see is the smeary nose—the small half moons of her eyes disappearing in the vacant blank space of her face. She is nothing I expected. When I was a little girl, singing lullabies to my Japanese doll in a kimono, all I thought of was clean skin beneath my chin. She would grow up to be pretty with long straight black hair, to be graceful and smart. Mary always looks disheveled, her skirt twisted with the side zipper riding to the front. A polka-dotted Swiss Sheer Dress looks beautiful on a hanger, but too tight around the arm holes and too big around the waist of my daughter. The full-time job I took on, not only to help my husband with the house payment and to buy a second car, but maybe to purchase a piano—music lessons for Mary. We never bought the piano. Mary was sick the day I saw a classified ad for an old upright for $200.

I can't think of anything else to do, to stop this nightmarish morning. It's an old Japanese wives' tale from my mother, but I'm willing to try anything. Without any explanation, I pull Mary's hair away from her neck and with the side of my hand, I strike the bare skin three times like an executioner. Mama used to tell us that this would disrupt the flow of blood. But instead, Mary starts crying. Nothing. Her skin is hot and flushed. The drip from her nose is faster.

"It's your own fault," I hiss.

Mary's words back up in her throat. "Mo-Mom-my . . ."

This isn't what I want to hear—no more pleas. Her groveling makes me angrier. I want to strike back. I want to see some kind of spark light up inside her. "You can stay there and bleed all night. I'm going to go back to sleep." I throw the washcloth into the sink and walk out of the bathroom.

There's an anguished wail: I'm afraid my husband will wake. Mary is my job and there's nothing he can do. At the edge of the diffused light, I can see that I'm in the hallway standing on the drops of my daughter's blood.

I don't want to, but I make myself go back. 📖

# In the Anthropocene

*(In Memory, Sam Hamill 1943-2018)*

## Alicia Hokanson

Winter doubles down
on Spring, slaps fists of rain
against the marchers

who take to cold streets
and chant, their signs
laminated against

the damp. Some carry
slogans written on umbrellas,
*Science not Silence.*

In the march of ecocide,
the small subtractions
(one poet's death)

loom larger
in the scheme of things,
where such a voice

could wake us
before we drown.

*In the great*
*not-knowing*
*there is only the learning,*
*the path,*
*the Way.*

You brought those ancient
poems across the centuries
to show us our time

and place—rain-filled
mountains and rivers
without end—

part of a continuum
we cannot rip,
though we have tried.

# Letter Home

## Kathryn Hunt

*The town has become accustomed to the war in the
way one can get used to old age, the thought of
death, to anything at all.*
—Sándor Márai

We said we'd be old like our uncles, have girls who
wouldn't leave us. Now this instead. Another country
under my boots, sand the color of piss ticking against
my helmet. Some days I feel I'm at the beginning of time,
the Imperial Star Destroyer hurling away without me.
I can't even remember the smell of my own room,
the shorts I left on the floor. Tell me: What color
are Mom's eyes?

Day after day rage enters me like a god or a machine,
even my dreams. Without it I couldn't go on. The
terrible things we say we'll do, we say without shame
like a football chant. When the guy next to me cried
out I thought of the train near home, the way it feels
to stand close as it goes by, like the sound of a horse
breathing—it came out of him—the air so hot,
the world tumbling backwards like a bright Millennium
Falcon. Strange how quiet, and the sun in the sky
where it always was. The guy moaned. I put my mouth
over his mouth the way they showed us. I pressed
my hand against the wound. This place: different than
what they said. I followed him all the way to stone.

# I Vote Present

## Heikki Huotari

My homeowner's policy endorses sixteen perils but explicitly excludes a multitude of others, such as floods, floods, floods and acts of God. I'm voting Present as there neither ought nor ought not be a law. The maples in the headlights briefly green, the music, what there is of it, is in the overtones, such as they are, and where the horizontal tangent is, the stationary point is also. I am present—no heroic measures for me please.

# Pike Place Market: Prelude

## Ann Batchelor Hursey

### 1976

The first time I visit Pike Place Market, I buy fresh raspberries for my hostess gift and choose two pints from a grid of green boxes heaped with red promise. A tourist from Ohio, and recent backpacker from California's Sierra Nevada, I celebrate Seattle and eat my first wild salmon, its meat tender and pink, baked with sliced lemons and *Walla Walla Sweets*.

> For dessert we pour
> fresh cream over red berries
> our tongues swallow sighs

After drinking our last bottle of red wine, we unroll our sleeping bags on my friend's living room floor, lay our heads on borrowed pillows, and fall deeply asleep. I want to say I dreamed of you, *She Who Watches*—but I did not know you then. I did not know your Great River. I did not know your Wishram Village, or the inundation of Celilo Falls. Nor did I know anything about Coyote, his tricks and his blessings. What I can say is like the

> Salmon, I return
> imprinted by the scent of
> rain, smoke and cedar

*Into the Unknown,* Photograph, by Theodore C. Van Alst, Jr.

# What Movie to Watch?

## Christopher J. Jarmick

A few days after my mom's 90th birthday
my sister Jackie called and asked
if I had read my emails this morning.
I did not.
"Mom died this morning."

I talked to Mom 4 days ago.
She sounded better than she had
for quite some time.
We talked about old movies, about
Cary Grant and we laughed.

When she turned the phone over to my dad
I said "I love you." She would usually
just say, "you too," But this time she said:
"I love you too. Here's your dad."

Sometimes the quiet and stillness
even with jazz from the NPR station
playing in the background is comforting;
now it is surreal as an overwhelming
number of memories mash into each other.
Old 8mm home movie images
flickering, kodak moments.

Later,
when I talked to Dad, he said his last words
last night to her were: "I love You."
When he left for church service this morning,
she was still sleeping. When he returned
and checked on her, he saw her eyes
open, her lips slightly apart. He sighed:
"Oh Gussie."

He is glad she went first.
"She's such a private person,
it's good she didn't have to deal
with someone else trying to take care of her.
She couldn't take care of herself, you know.
I'm grateful for this. We've been together
67 years . . . and I've never
really ever been alone."

Mom and Dad moved nearly four years ago
to an assisted living community
a few miles from my sister and brother-in-law.
Mom didn't go out, didn't socialize,
refused to go to the doctors
and even if forced was uncooperative.
But in recent weeks medications
were adjusted; things seemed to be improving.

Dad is glad family is close by.
"I'm not going to worry about
anything for at least a month.
There's a lot to do right now with Easter,
Good Friday, Stations of the Cross, a lot
I'm involved with but I'm not going to
do anything for a month."

"Good Dad," I say, "You have the right priorities."
"Yes, take care of myself," he agrees
and then a long sigh. "I'm not sure
what to do, I just want to talk to her some more.
We argued sometimes, got mad, but I
never thought of being without her.
I want to talk to her some more, ask her
what movie do you want to watch?"

# In a World of Danger

## Elizabeth Landrum

Some begin each day offering orchids,
mangoes, rice and papaya to gods
who might visit their spirit house
then drape the prow of a long-tailed boat
with colorful sashes and garlands of lotus.
Some chant prayers for the sharpened arrow,
for the cougar, a moonlit path home,
while others knit, count stitches,
repeat a poem before sleep.

Once I shared a table with other women
discussing what they carry each time
they walk through a city's dark parking lot.
A nurse holds her clamps and scalpel
close in her pocket. Another showed us
her hot pink "lipstick" pepper-spray case.
When asked what I take I said, *my wife—*
her eyes and ears sharpened by experience,
mine dulled by denial.

But what of the mothers,
the fathers, trying to breathe
before the school bell rings?
Some will brush their daughters' hair
counting an even number of strokes, or
kiss a son's forehead exactly three times,
then walk them up to the entrance repeating
*you'll be fine     you'll be fine     you'll be fine*

# Arc

## Lynn Knapp

She pushes the cart,
high heels clicking
across the pavement.
She pauses, lifts the box
up, up, still higher,
in one practiced arc
to the top of her head—
modern woman
striking ancient pose—
just as grandmothers
and mothers before her,
but not on a worn path
between the well and the house—
from Costco to her car.

# life sentence

## Andrew Lafleche

I don't feel, not for them
her or the child, not for
      the dogs, both huskies
I don't feel for anything

it isn't personal, she's a
nice enough girl, they are
      but I've been this way with
many before, and it always
ended the same: alone

like I am in this single
bedroom apartment: woman
      and toddler, two large dogs
no yard to shit in so they
need to be walked, a lot

then there's the beta fish
who needs to be fed and its
      tank cleaned. all of this foreign
to me, the martian here

at least I have the stoop
eight steps of solitude, perched
      on the concrete, walled on
one side, the metal rail to my left

I sit here smoking
cigarettes and drinking beer
      and when the sun sets I'll
switch to wine, a cabernet

I don't feel, for them, for
the cars rushing past on the
        freeway behind the trees. I don't
feel for the kid with the
flat top, air jordans and
        basketball as he dribbles
lacklusterly down the walk
I don't feel, not for
        them or the kid or the
man on his front porch
        who smokes late into the
night, the man I only
know is there from the
        pulsing cherry of his cigarette
and occasional cough. what
am I supposed to feel?

subtracting minutes and hours
until sleep has arrived
        to wake and do it all
again. this life sentence
is enough to kill a man

and it will, only not
on desired terms or at
        the right time. I don't feel,
less the cool menthol I
suck from this lit tube

and the wet forming
on the outside of this can.
        except for these, I
do not feel. and these even
I could do without

# Daddy Volcano

## Loreen Lilyn Lee

**N**ever, never take pork on the road across the Pali, a popular route cutting through the mountains and connecting Honolulu to the windward side of Oʻahu. Don't even try it or you'll be sorry. The stories are legion. Your car will break down; the engine suddenly dies and won't start up. It could be Madame Pele, goddess of the volcano, preventing any form of pig from passing through these mountains in her rivalry with Kamapuaʻa, the pig demigod. Or moʻo wahine, the lizard woman disguised as a beautiful human trying to lure you out of your car to your death over the cliffs. Or hungry ghosts wanting the pork. Hundreds of warriors plummeted to their deaths here in 1795 rather than face defeat and possible torture by King Ka-mehameha and his ten thousand warriors, who succeeded in unifying the islands for the first time under one sovereign ruler. He and his attacking army drove Oʻahu's warriors back to the Pali until there was nowhere to go except off these cliffs, nearly a thousand feet high.

If someone is stupid or foolish enough to carry pork over the Pali. . . . Auwē! Auwē!

However, the remedy is simple: just remove the pork and leave it on the side of the road. The car miraculously will work, and you can avoid a horrible fate.

Growing up in the islands, all us kids heard these stories and understood the existence of things we could not see, of things supernatural. We loved hearing these ghost stories that gave us chicken skin.

\* \* \* \*

Telling ghost stories
had power that transferred
to listeners. I listened trembling
with awe and fear.

Magical thinking came naturally
as a child. Merging worlds
made perfect sense.

\* \* \* \*

Daddy loved to entertain. A respected Chinatown business-man, he was in his element when we had houseguests, usually members of the huge Lee clan from Manila or other Asian cities. And we were happy knowing that, focusing on our guests and wanting to impress them, he was unlikely to show his temper. Fear mostly motivated our good behavior because we did not want his anger to fill the house. So the presence of visitors brought a welcome reprieve, for which we were grateful.

"*Holoholo*. Let's go!" Whenever we had visitors, we piled into the family's Buick sedan, a full car with three or four adults and us three younger kids—a brother, younger sister, and me. Daddy was going to show our guests the natural wonders of the island starting with Pū-o-waina or Punchbowl Crater, just ten minutes away. Daddy drove up the road circling the mountain past Papa-kōlea, a residential community of Native Hawaiians. Making the turns, we kids in the back seat slid back and forth on the wide, vinyl bench seat. With nothing to hold us in or to hold onto, we were all arms and legs jostling each other and trying not to bump our guests, who sat in the back with us. At the top, we scrambled out to visit the National Memorial Cemetery of the Pacific located inside the crater. Rows and rows of white, square stones lay flat in the lush green lawn to mark the remains of U.S. servicemen and servicewomen, many who had served in wars in Asia. Thousands of graves, a sobering sight, reminded us of the human cost of war. The adults automatically lowered their voices as we walked the grounds and we kids followed their example. One translation of Pū-o-waina is "hill of sacrifice." In ancient Hawai'i, this was the site for ceremonies of human sacrifice and the execution of those who broke traditional laws or kapu.

We were familiar with Honolulu's urban cemeteries, tradi-tional graveyards from earlier days around which the city grew.

Death also entered our world with television gunfights, cowboys and Indians killing each other with rifles, arrows, and tomahawks; my older sister Marleen's burial of her birds and kittens in our yard when they died; and our ghost stories.

Besides Punchbowl, there was another cemetery we visited. Once a year we honored our grandparents' graves in Mānoa Valley because we believed in the spirit world of our Chinese ancestors; if we took care of our ancestors, they would take care of us. Since April was designated for Ching Ming (Chinese Memorial Day), our extended family would join us early on an April Saturday or Sunday. Several cars caravanned up to the cemetery loaded with adults and children and everything necessary to set up an altar, including candles, incense, dishes, a whole roasted pig and other foods, firecrackers, paper offerings, umbrellas in case of rain, and gardening tools. The grounds were overgrown with grass and weeds, unlike the immaculate grounds at Punchbowl. We younger kids stayed out of the way and told jokes, while the adults and older kids chatted and cleaned around the large gravestones carved with Chinese calligraphy and names and dates in English; gravestones of all sizes and shapes dotted the crowded cemetery. Other Chinese families also arrived to attend to their ancestors' graves. When the cleaning was done, we burned candles and incense, set up the food to feed our ancestors, prayed, and burned firecrackers and paper offerings. After the ceremonies that honored my grandparents, everyone came back to our house for lunch.

Now at the rim of Punchbowl, we made an obligatory stop for our visitors to ooh and ahh at the view and take photographs. The city of Honolulu sparkled below us. Daddy pointed out the landmarks. At that time, in the 1950s, Aloha Tower stood out from the landscape with the lovely aquamarine ocean beyond.

He informed our guests, "That was built in 1926. It welcomes all ships coming into Honolulu's waterfront. It's always good fun to see the big cruise ships coming and going. Hawaiian music and hula dancers greet the passengers or send them home. It's like a big party. And the lei sellers, they do big business. Big business!"

Turning to the right, we could see Pearl Harbor, and to the left, Wai-kīkī with Diamond Head presiding over a landscape not yet blemished by high-rises. Pearls and diamonds! Pictures of jewels and treasure chests swam in my head as I looked out at the panorama.

Next we headed southeast through Wai-kīkī for a closer look at Diamond Head or Lēʻahi (brow of the tuna). Our visitors were impressed with its graceful profile. "It looks just like the postcards!" Daddy took photos of them against the background of this famous landmark, contrasting with the flatness of Ka-piʻo-lani Park. Its highest point faces the ocean, then the ridge line swoops gently back before angling down to the ground.

Going to Ka-piʻo-lani Park was always fun, but we had seen Diamond Head umpteen times already. No diamonds were to be found on this mountain, not even sparkly rocks. Mommy liked coming to the park for the Kodak Hula Show, and we visited the Honolulu Zoo nearby. But neither of these were on today's schedule. When I heard the elephants trumpeting, I wished we could go visit the animals, but pressed my lips together to prevent these impertinent words from escaping. Instead, Daddy bought everyone sodas.

Back in the car, we headed past Diamond Head toward Ka-lani-ana-ʻole Highway, Koko Head, and Hālona Blowhole. This was a longer drive, and I wondered if my younger sister Jean might get carsick. Mommy was concerned too, and switched places with one of our guests in the backseat to comfort her.

We found ourselves on the edge of the Pacific Ocean where wind and waves join forces to send geysers of water shooting up through black lava rocks. As we waited for the show to start, ocean waves came crashing over the rocks—a preview of the drama to come. I overheard someone explaining: "See, dakine ol' lava tubes underneat' da water. Dey make like one vertical pipe in da rocks. An' den, when plenty water in da pipes, big waves come and push da water out. Real strong, da waves. Da water gush out so high, can be even twenty feet! Sometimes more!"

I stood behind the barrier, but it was no guarantee for staying dry. I yelped with shock and glee with the sudden shower and tried to run out of range, my flip-flops splashing in the puddles. I played tag with the unpredictable sprays. They won and I got wet, but the sun quickly dried me off. We didn't know how often the hole would blow forth its water. It could be a quick series of fountains or lengthy pauses might occur in between. The suspense was exciting.

Every so often I glanced side-eyes at Daddy for any whiff of disapproval for my exuberant playing and running around. So far, so good. He smiled and chatted with our visitors, mostly in Cantonese, in the upper viewing section away from the sprays.

\* \* \* \*

Everything is possible to a child.
Anything is possible.
I didn't question
how Hawaiian legends and myths,
volcanoes as tourist attractions,
visits to cemeteries, and my strict father
fit together. Or if they should.
This hodgepodge of Chinese,
American, and Hawaiian cultures—
This was my normal.

\* \* \* \*

If we had time, we stopped to view Hanauma Bay, a visually stunning array of greens and blues in this collapsed part of Koko Crater that created a snorkeling paradise. But not today. We were tired. On the drive back into town, we heard little conversation in the front seat as we kids dozed in the back.

Maybe thirty minutes later, I felt the temperature change. The coolness of Nuʻu-anu Valley stirred me from my lethargy. We were going to the Pali, the final stop on our way home. We passed Queen Emma's Summer Palace, now a museum open to the public, and the royal mausoleum where Hawaiian royalty are buried. Ooh, kings and queens! But we never stopped at these places. Daddy controlled our itinerary and would not deviate from the natural landmarks. We traveled past and Daddy turned onto the Old Pali Road to the lookout. This high point in the Koʻolau Mountain Range offered a view of the windward side of Oʻahu with the cliffs framing and directing our vision to the towns of Kāne-ʻohe and Kai-lua in the distance.

Millions of years ago, these mountains began with Koʻolau Volcano spewing burning red lava. We locals looked to our mountains, now benign and familiar landmarks. A layer of soft velvet greenery covered the sides and cliffs flowing down from the peaks and ridges. We had little need for compasses; no matter where we stood, we beheld either mountains or ocean, and sometimes both. Even when the mountains were not visible, we had confidence, an ingrown instinct, about where we were. We knew that clouds often congregated where mountains rose, its cooler air and mist a contrast to the hot, sandy shores. Although extinct, these mountains felt alive, with wind and waves tangible expressions of the life force emanating from the land. No one talked about this mana, this power, when I was a small kid, yet it was always there.

We loved going to the Old Pali lookout. It was a game just getting out of the car and feeling the wildness of the wind. The lookout was a wind tunnel with strong gusts whipping through my hair and plastering my shirt and shorts to my body. It took my breath away, but I giggled as I made my way leaning into the wind to the edge of the lookout to take hold of the railing. "Look, there goes a hat!" We watched the rascal wind kidnap a brimmed hat from an adult's head and make skirts fly up; tourists unfamiliar with the Pali were caught unprepared for the strong gusts.

Over the side, the mountain fell away, a sheer certain-death drop, but my attention was fixed on the lush vegetation that covered these green mountains. In the distance, waterfalls cascaded down—white ribbons against green. I gazed down and saw banana trees growing wild along with ferns and a dense growth of other tropical flora. The richness of the earth with hints of fruits and flowers scented the air, and when I raised my head, the sun spangled the ocean, the buildings, and homes beyond.

I pointed out some of these sights to my little sister Jean. As the wind continued whistling around us, I told her the story of King Ka-mehameha forcing hundreds of warriors to their deaths below. "Can you hear the ghost voices in the wind?" She listened hard.

"By the way, don't wander off. I'm too skinny, but the ghosts like fat-cheeked girls like you." I smiled ghoulishly at her and pinched a chubby cheek. A carload of unruly tourists suddenly appeared, heads down against the wind and holding onto their hats. One of them gently bumped into her by accident. She jumped and ran screaming to me.

"Wa-a-a-a-a! No, don't let the ghost get me-ee!"

The wind carried her wailing to our parents a few yards away talking with our guests. Daddy came striding over with a dark face. He spoke in a low growl. "What's the matter with you!" It wasn't really a question, but I muttered, "I didn't do anything."

He took my sister's hand and looked at me. "You! Get back in the car! Behave or you'll get lickings!" He turned away and put on a face that said, "Everything's fine," while I headed to the car.

Of course, our guests enjoyed their visit. When they left, they thanked my parents again and again. I wished they could have stayed longer. Their presence ensured peace and calm in our home for a while. Their visit also reminded me of what I took for granted—the origins of our volcanic homeland. One volcano or another was ever near.

* * * *

Unknown to others
Daddy's unpredictable rages shaped
an emotional landscape
we could not escape.
Lava could fountain and rumble
the earth with no warning—
Daddy Volcano was no joke. 📖

*Peach Beach*, Santa Monica, California, 2002, Photograph, by Toni La Ree Bennett

# Vivien to the Universe

## Simone Liggins

*"It's not that I've been dishonest. It's just that I loathe reality."*
—Lady Gaga

This time last year, I no longer carried you.
No more shadowed eyes seeking
you out from under my flowing blouse.
It wasn't your home anymore.
In my reality, it didn't need to be.

The collective modern world barely has a conscience to start
with little balance to boot.
Here, the unknown life is more cherished
than one with a face, years—a personality to it.
It's tragic irony that the soon-to-be-born being
will one day be as scorned and detested
as a currently random one walking.
What was once fresh potential, pure life
will soon be just as wounded, rotten, destroyed
over and over and over and O—
more bodies for bombs,
more bodies for iPhones,
more bodies for overcrowded degraded soil—
All trivial facts compared to the highest turning
profit for the ultimate form of human consumerism.

So, my lovely little mudblood!
In a world that would throw you in a can on a curb
for possessing that ever-envied blend of waterfall curls,
in a world that seems to have little choice but to hate you
because you are a beautiful, beating testament

of boundless human bonding, I see no need
to make you suffer my time.
My love recycles yours, reduces, reuses—
here's to your re-destination
for a better millennium.


# Tanka Trio for Center City

### Rita Mookerjee

I scrape a tangle
of dark hair with a boar brush
between my breasts a
silver pendant swings heavy
and cool: the ouroboros.

philadelphia
leaves me to bad habits and
the pulsing ache of
a still limb that fell asleep;
an orgasm in reverse.

I prowl the bar at
XIX; the wide balcony
hums and I look for
more bad habits while my rings
swell tight between my knuckles.

# We Too

## Loreen Lilyn Lee

Twiggy was in vogue when a young Seattle woman went
to apply for a waitress position in an upscale restaurant.
They told her flat out, "We're not going to hire you
because you're too fat." She knew she wasn't fat, but
neither was she stick-thin.

Too many women have hidden stories they are ashamed to tell.
They think they're at fault or something must be wrong with
them. They store them away with their guilt and fear: boxes in
the basement, in the backs of closets, on high shelves beyond
reach, in locked drawers. In the dark. They try to forget, but the
pain or humiliation rankles, unraveling ambition or waving red
flags about their self-worth. "Don't be silly! You can't be a doctor
or lawyer or CEO!"

The English professor strode into a large lecture hall like
he owned it. He said, "If you are female, please cross your
legs." He waited a few minutes. A soft rustling indicated
that the young women, who then wore dresses and skirts,
were complying. He continued, "Now that the hell gates
are closed, I can start."

It's not new news. Across centuries and many cultures, these old
lies persist: *Being a woman is a crime. Women deserve abuse—emo-
tional, psychological, physical, sexual—because they need to be kept in
their place.* Power and cruelty are often twin weapons used to shore
up male entitlement and superiority. To quash fears of weakness.

A college teacher accused his Phi Beta Kappa
female student of plagiarism because
he insisted, "No woman could have written this."

Decades later, over a summertime lunch, one elder tells her story. Then others share theirs. Not isolated incidents, they explain why the Women's Movement was necessary. It rallied women to remind them they have value, they have choices. Naming this cancer in our society—inequality—ignited sparks of clarity, lit the flames of hope, sanity, courage, and grace to countless female lives. Women came out of the dark.

> A college journalism teacher told his female student, "I
> think you should move to the Midwest and find a nice
> young man in plastics to marry." After the shock came the
> tears, but she didn't stop. She dropped his class,
> completed her degree in journalism,
> and went on to work at *Time* magazine.

Gender discrimination. Sexual harassment. So it was. Laws like Title IX and women's raised consciousness and dauntless spirits helped. Women persist. So has the darkness. Today despite the rising numbers of women getting college degrees, taking leadership roles, and breaking glass ceilings, women are revealing stories of toxic masculinity that have turned more aggressive, violent, pervasive: penis power and privilege. Street harassment. Digital trolls. Sexual assault. Abuse. Rape. Murder.

Too many, too many women are crying out, finding solidarity in telling their stories. They keep coming. Me too, me too. 📖

*Old House*, Photograph, by Manit Chaotragoongit

# belongings: handmade home

## brenna lilly

belongings—fish on desk, book on shelf, ash on windowsill, and
the curve of our torsos in unison, twin mattress, 4am,

continuing until there is no time left, or until the time we have is
spoiled.

round belly on a sun-trimmed easter-egg hunt.
12 peaches in a white fridge.
opal yawnings of a blue-laced bird on our doorstep and
enough ink to tell you about it.
music humming from a muffled booth in the basement.
bare feet on cool wood,
tender.

we will be naked in water, running bath and small splash the
only sounds in our small house.
sing back to the birds—they watch us make life.

sing while i cry, while i scream. gentle openings and closings
mark a genesis.

you sing happy birthday and stitch up my wounds,
pet my head,
and we greet the coming afternoon with
our voices as howls,

primal in a handmade home.

# the self, elemental

## brenna lilly

aeriform and breathy, stretching outward like a
birch tree seeking light,
i lean toward the luminescence of something
greater than Just Me for a moment,
asking the light for its wisdom and for all benevolent
tidings.

oceanic, swaying closer *this* way and ebbing further *that*,
i coalesce, dually-bodied, like a sea turbulent,
a mind unfettered,
beseeching of the moon to cast me away in its
womanish pull.

built of soft clay and not yet put to the kiln,
brushing softly against freckled skin,
i rise above ground level, rooting myself like a pigeon on
newly lain concrete,
gently sticking and becoming, for a moment,
before flying away, a piece of soft earth.

standing over fire, heavy in its impact but weightless in
being plasma, being bathed in ash,
twigs and kindling burn at my feet. i am a salemite witch and
no one has bothered to ask Me
how to properly burn sage and where i buy
my silken skirts.

# Reflections on a Photograph Hanging in my Hallway

## Kaye Linden

**R**eflection One:

What are we celebrating in this black and white?

There I am, the skinny blonde girl of five or six, in the faded photo, its tiny cracks and folds a colorless tapestry. I stand dwarfed by others, next to an older, taller, mousier sister in a grown-up dowdy dress, too long, too dark, unfrilly, and plain. The skinny blonde girl that I am, stares ahead with a shadowed smile, chin-length fine straight hair. There's Grandmother, bent over, arthritic, scoliotic, fractured grin on her face for the photo op. She's stretching over the older girl and why did they put Grandma in the back row when, apart from the blonde, she's the most scrunched up, tiny figure in the portrait?

My mother stares from the photo with a half-smile, thin-lipped, hesitant, eyes glazed over with a tired look of "let's just try and smile for the photo anyway." She wears a lovely gray dress I know was red. Lace embellishes a high collar and hangs in a flouncy way down her chest with a clandestine frill hiding the heart of the fact that she wants to stay in Jaffa, in the land of milk and honey, not return to Australia, but stay in this foreign place with two little girls, who must stay on her insistence and attend diplomat schools in the oldest city in the world, Jephthah. The girls will want to go home to Australia. They will cry for their father, especially when the blonde girl has her doll snatched from her hands after school by a man with fleeting sandaled feet.

Next to Father and Mother stands Grandfather, maternal side only, my father's Scottish Glasgow parents long gone. Grandfather resembles my mother, his daughter, with the bulbous hooked nose and large, sad, pale blue eyes. I know his eyes were blue because I met him the day of the photo when I was just a skinny blonde girl from Sydney, a clueless grandchild, who tried to speak broken German to the man with sad eyes.

My grandfather stares ahead, beyond the photographer, dark circles under each eye, so deep I think I can place a coin or two in the pouches. He stares into that Second World War space, memories of eight brothers and sisters who refused to leave Germany, claiming rich Prussians stayed immune to hatred. Grandfather's eyes conjure up the brother who slipped away by train to Poland, but the soldiers searched him at the border, discovered wads of cash hidden in sewn up coat linings, money removed from his German bank accounts. He never crossed the border—shot against bleached bullet-holed blood-stained walls and thrown into a ditch. I know this from the German Certificate of Death found after the war. I filed it away, the lone death certificate of one uncle written in lovely German handwriting with impressive curly q's and tails on the y's and j's.

Old grandfather knows more than his blue eyes say and he straightens round shoulders, offering a frown of deep lines between two thin eyebrows; he doesn't smile or show teeth except perhaps in dreams. He has learned to bear it, because he got out.

He got out.

How he got out was through the wisdom of the rare ones who knew hiding money wasn't the journey, but the journey mandated letting go of the money, of the city block of dressmaking factories, letting go of teams of German workers who sewed the seams of fine silk jackets that hid the money.

He knew.

My grandfather knew.

My mother said he was one of the wise ones. This grandfather lived because he stayed quiet, shared superficial pleasantries, "Wie sind Sie," and "Good day, Herr Bracht," stayed quiet, shunned neighbors. Grandfather herded his wife and children onto a train in the middle of the night, with nothing but the clothes they wore, simple clothes, dark in color, the children's shoes filed further down and harshly scuffed so not to attract attention. They left behind an estate, even then, worth millions, an estate they would never see again, millions that the children's children's children would never see again because it didn't matter.

Five people rode the train out of Germany, my mother with one little doll that she could not leave behind, a moth-eaten doll made from cloth and bandages, a doll that looked even sadder in the photograph with its stitched down-turned mouth and one eye black from a child's surgical overcorrection. The doll's eyes stare out beyond the photo frame, beyond the photographer, hanging from the blonde girl's hand, a mother's gift to her little girl, an over-hugged, raggedy, damaged doll. The train puffed the family across Europe and into the land of the Bible, in a time when Israel existed only in ancient texts. They came to the Levant, the land where the British ruled, 1935, approached by boat, in the cover of night, in desperation, by those who believed in Zion.

# R eflection Two:

Some years ago, I walked through hallways of shoes at the Holocaust Museum in Tel Aviv: red shoes, cracked dried leather, dehydrated skeletal remnants of baby shoes, little boy shoes, little girl shoes, one pair with one bow on, pairs with one shoe missing, old man shoes, old lady shoes, tired, beaten, hacked, moldy, rescued from mud. My stomach flipped upside down as witness to history, to the broken promises of these children's shoes.

Afterwards, I said to the taxi driver that my mother escaped Germany during the Second World War to "Palestine" and he ranted at me in English and Hebrew that "Israel has always been Israel as it was in the Bible and in ancient days and always was and always will be Israel" and why am I calling it Palestine, where did my parents come from anyway, a blonde woman with white skin and green eyes, an Australian American, an ignorant one who should have known, but did not know the difference and my chin-length, straight blond hair curled up and stood on end, with the "horror, the horror" of offense. I explained in broken Hebrew that my mother had married a man whose heritage claimed Scotland and neither Germany nor Europe, whose parents knew poverty in

Scotland and immigrated to Australia, that my mother had married this Australian soldier, traveled ten thousand miles by ship through India to a foreign country (and why the hell would she do that after escaping Nazis?). As I ranted, I realized how crazy I sounded, trying to explain to a stranger such a phenomenon, and I shut up midway through my explanation when my husband kneed my knee and I realized how crazy how crazy how crazy the story sounded and how crazy how crazy how crazy that story really is.

# Reflection Three:

There stands my father, the Australian soldier my mother married, now on the wall in the black and white photo, tall and proud, dressed in a tweed vest, long-sleeved, white starched shirt and plaid tie (in a hundred Middle Eastern degrees), in man pants with one ironed pleat down each leg, his bald head reflecting light (perhaps from sweat), a ring of ginger hair softening the hard pate, a handsome man, sharp defined nose and face, a twinkle in his black and white photo eyes that I know were green because I missed seeing his eyes the times he left us. I valued him as a best friend and trusted in a little girl way that he might do the right thing, but the right thing left his wife and two little girls in the Levant, a foreign country, a language in tongues not understood, a people not understood, a country of shadows, groaning camels, sweet orange blossoms, hands-on breasts and butts and in those days, in the 50s, things were not as they are now.

# Reflection Four:

What are they celebrating in that photo?
How dare they celebrate in a foreign land.
They are saying goodbye. Bon Voyage. My father is going back to Australia for a year, but I know now he didn't return, and I shed tears, begging to go home, but my mother said: "Don't be silly."
What was the matter with that little blonde girl who cried little girl tears when big girls "don't cry?"

# H ow dare they say Bon Voyage.

The little girls stand as foreigners in a foreign land, this blonde child remembering oodles of colored streamers thrown from the ship where father waved goodbye to no one in particular while laughing and talking with another passenger beside him, too distant for the little girl to see, blurry and far away, so far away, but she glimpsed that glass in his hand waving and gesturing in conversation amid the pinks, blues, and reds of gaiety, despite thunderous warnings blasting from the ship's funnel. 📖

*Unaccustomed to Frost*, Photograph, by Jury S. Judge

# Dancing on the Edge

## Anna Odessa Linzer

Pull the tansy, I was told. And like all interlopers dancing on the edge of the tickertape of time and memory, I ignored the Islanders' imperative. And watched. Waiting for the bold yellow, the aromatic scent. Thinking I would hastily pull them just before they seeded, I enjoyed their brash presence. They too come from other shores, uninvited. At dusk, I walked the edge of the knoll to admire their wicked alien ways, as if meeting a secret lover. And there in the fading northern light: a riot of workers garbed in prison stripes of black and yellow, a chain gang of smooth skinned larvae. The offspring of cinnabar moth, that delicate black moth with red dots and calligraphic brush strokes on wings that fluttered through our doors and unpacking days in May. Field guide in hand, I read aloud to their low crunching, made as if in agreement with me, as they hear what they had always known: the tansy ragwort and cinnabar moth are married in a dance. The cinnabar sworn to fidelity, the tansy her only partner. I go on and read: *more effective than pulling is the use of the caterpillar of the cinnabar moth*. How can one need the other so completely, with such faithfulness, as each kiss strips away the season's hot promise? And now, days later, I see bare stalks, flowers only a memory in the fatted blimps of the caterpillar clutching the last lower leaves. And the earth is suddenly a memory of color: red and black and yellow and green. How strange this dance, this alien world become familiar, settling in, each dancing their own last dance. And yet, just down the ridge I see: three perfect stalks, fully flowered. Away from the tight busy neighborhood above the rock ridge, they lean coolly into each other, as they gaze into the bright mirror of the day, and then turn, whispering as soft as summer breeze, to slowly thumb through the pages of the calendar, marking time.

# Running While Old

## Alice Lowe

**Age divisions** keep older runners in the game. We may be out there with swift twenty-somethings, Olympic athletes, and human gazelles, but the competition that matters is in a five-year gender-delineated block. I was thrilled when I placed second in a field of thirteen seventy to seventy-four-year-old women in the San Francisco Rock 'n' Roll Half Marathon, a far more meaningful achievement than my ranking of 2,841 out of a total of 3,758 women.

**Brain, back, bones, and beats** are my reasons for running. Now more than ever. Scientific evidence of the benefits of aerobic, weight-bearing exercise—running and walking—to health and heart, mobility and moods, lucidity and longevity, is conclusive. I do it because I can and will continue as long as I can.

**Chocolate milk** at the finish line is a liquid life preserver. One of running's proven superfoods, it helps muscles recover and replaces carbs, glycogen, and burned calories. Last year I ran the Hot Chocolate 15K and was rewarded on completion with a cup of hot chocolate and a bowl of warm chocolate sauce surrounded by chips and cookies and other sweet and salty treats to dip into it. Recovery never tasted so good.

**DNF** is the nadir of initialism, a badge of infamy. The dreaded "Did Not Finish"—you'd rather come in last—might have a justifiable cause, but playing the age card won't make it less of a defeat. I came close to dropping out twice during half marathons, once due to an electrolyte imbalance that made me woozy and lightheaded, a year later with a foot injury combined with leg cramps. Pride and the coveted race medals kept me going. There's also DNS (Did Not Start), which seems a lesser evil. I was sidelined for two races but pleaded age and infirmity on one and was given a deferral.

**Electrolytes**—sodium, potassium, chloride, calcium, magnesium, and phosphate—regulate the body's fluid balance, but we expel them when we sweat. I used to shun sports drinks—why imbibe artificially colored and sweetened crap when you can drink life-sustaining water? When out-of-sync electrolytes caused my near-DNF, I became a believer. Endorphins are the brain chemicals responsible for the blissful "runner's high." Sometimes leaping endorphins can step in for lagging electrolytes.

**"For your age"** is an increasingly common though no less irritating qualifier, even when it's unspoken, even or especially when you apply it to yourself out of false humility or as an excuse. Younger women I run with don't say it, but it's implicit in their praise of what would otherwise be unremarkable achievements. When a fast and frequent marathoner tells me how awesome it is that I'm training for my tenth half, she means well. I accept the accolades, but add the rejoinder, "for my age."

**The Golden Gate Bridge** is the mental pinnacle of the San Francisco Rock 'n' Roll Half Marathon. Running across it I felt myself levitating, my legs propelling my motion about a foot above the pavement.

**Half Marathon** signifies part of a whole, a smaller portion, like a half sandwich or a half pint. It sounds like an apology when you find yourself saying you're doing "just" a half. Yet 13.1 miles is no fractional achievement. It wasn't "just" a half when I challenged myself the first time shortly after I turned seventy. I wasn't running then, but I was a fast walker and held my own. When I passed walkers and slow runners, young and old, I teemed with energy and satisfaction. Sometimes I smirked. When my first race medal was hung around my neck as I crossed the finish ahead of my three-hour goal, I was champion of the world—the whole world, not just half.

**Intervals** are the late-blooming runner's buddies. At first I was content to be a power walker, thought it wise not to risk my stiff and squeaky joints to the hazards of running. Then I read that people with osteoporosis—mine is classified as severe—can maximize the benefits of walking by running just one minute out of every mile. That was easy enough, and I found that using different muscles for short spurts felt great and improved my walking. If a one minute surge is good, what about two, three . . . you see where it leads. With cautious training and lessons learned through trial and error, I've built up to comfortable intervals, stronger and faster outings.

**Jogging** is what runners don't do. "Run as if someone just called you a jogger" is a frequently-seen sign along a race route. We're serious about it—it's not just an excuse to buy cute outfits or drink more beer. But no one's sure of the parameters. Some say runners are faster, but how much faster—does an eight-minute mile qualify you as a runner or do the speedsters think you're still jogging? Is it frequency? If once or twice a week makes you a dabbler, a Sunday jogger, and five or six makes you a serious runner, what about three or four times a week? Does entering competitive races make you a runner? Does it need to be a marathon, or does a 10K count? Maybe you are whatever you think you are, and I'm a runner, by god.

**Kilometers** are 1000 meters, 0.62 of a mile. Races are designated 5K (3.1 miles) and 10K (6.2 miles), but shift to miles at the half marathon mark (13.1). Maybe our imperial system brains can't compute metric equivalents this far, maybe it's just what we're used to. A marathon—26.2 miles, 42.2 kilometers—is spectacular no matter how you express it. The numbers sound arbitrary, because it's a place—the Marathon battle site from which a Greek soldier named Philippides ran 26.2 miles to Athens in 490 BCE.

**LSD** is recommended once a week—I do it every Saturday. The hallucinogen doesn't increase running speed, to my knowledge, but "long slow distance" does. "LSD" makes sense at any age, but maybe more so for older runners with less juice to spare. Your body gets used to more miles without having to worry about pace or risk incurring injury. Save yourself for the real thing.

**Medals** are motives to run, moments in the sun. You stand tall and proud, no matter how sore and exhausted you are, when a chipper young volunteer drapes it around your neck at the finish line. It's a short-lived thrill, but a thrill nonetheless. Then you go home and take it off, hang it on the wall or put it in a display case, maybe into a drawer or a shoebox in the closet. The high stays with you after the first one, but it wears off faster and faster each time. Like a narcotic, you want more. Last year I ran the Triple Crown, three successive half marathons over several months. In addition to a medal for each race, there's an extra disk for completing the trio, a big heavy one. At Carlsbad, the first one, I skimmed along the shore like a sea bird and scored my personal record (see "PR"). The La Jolla Half features a slog up the long, steep Torrey Pines grade, but the reward at the top is a gorgeous panorama of the Pacific. I finished in spite of burgeoning plantar fasciitis in my foot. I trained for AFC (America's Finest City), last in the series, and my foot got worse. I sought treatment and kept at it—I was determined to run that race and complete the Triple Crown. I hobbled the last couple of miles, but I did it. Was it worth it? I look at my four medals and chartreuse Triple Crown hat, the aches and pains long gone. Damn right it was.

**Nine miles** is my optimal run. Long enough to be significant, short enough to leave me with energy for the rest of the day. My nine-mile training route circles parts of Mission Bay, and I can tailor it to more or fewer miles as needed. Nine miles is 15K, the distance of San Diego's Hot Chocolate run, which adds to its appeal, but the race is scheduled within a week of the San Diego Half Marathon. Younger, more agile runners may do both, but I can't, so it's one or the other. Nine miles is a respectable race—no one would call me a wimp for choosing it—but this year I opt for the half, unwilling to surrender to senescence.

**Old, older, oldest.** Katherine Beiers, the eighty-four-year-old former mayor of Santa Cruz, California, was the oldest participant and the only woman over eighty in this year's Boston Marathon. She started running in her fifties and now has run thirty-some marathons. Harriette Thompson of Charlotte, North Carolina, completed the 2015 San Diego Rock 'n' Roll Marathon at the age of ninety-two, the oldest woman to complete a full marathon. It was her sixteenth. World War II Marine Jonathan Mendes, ninety-six, is believed to be the oldest unofficial finisher in the New York City Marathon's history. He crossed the 2016 finish line after more than eleven hours, when official timing had stopped. "You have to have goals in life," he said as he rested up with a shot of Scotch.

**PR**—woohoo! Setting new personal records is the ultimate high, because you're challenging yourself rather than competing with other runners. Mine was last January in Carlsbad, the first leg of the Triple Crown. Now that I'm back on track after foot problems, the record confronts me. I'm determined to beat it, but it won't be easy—the natural flow of life is to slow down, not speed up. I won't admit it's my goal—that would jinx it, tempt the fates. A former coach suggests having three goals for any race: the modest one you tell everyone about (and that you're pretty sure to reach), the one you aim for but keep to yourself—doable but a stretch—and the PR, always in your sights.

**Quads** and calves, glutes and hamstrings, knees and ankles, heels and arches, toes and toenails, neck and shoulders, hip flexors and iliotibial bands, muscles, tendons, and nerves you didn't know existed. They're all connected and all susceptible to soreness and stiffness, aches and pains, previously unimagined and unheard-of injuries. They happen to young and old alike—well, no, not alike. Older bodies are more fragile, brittle, worn down. More liable to twists and tweaks. So you stretch and roll, roll and stretch, do squats and lunges, lunges and squats, anything to keep the wolves at bay as much and as long as possible.

**RICE** equals rest, ice, compression, and elevation, a handy mnemonic when shit happens, as it's bound to do sooner or later.

**Senior Masters**—I am one! *A Runner's World* article identifies these as runners between the ages of sixty-five and seventy-four. It's an age "where simply lining up for the start of a race is something most peers would never attempt." Next year I'll be a Super Master (seventy-five+). A reason to keep plugging.

**Training**, like flossing, is forever once you've acknowledged that you want to stay mobile / keep your teeth. I follow a ten-week training schedule to prepare for half marathons, which means that if I do one every three months—my goal—I have just two weeks after a completed race to slack off before I have to start up again, increase the LSD runs, get out six days a week (on the seventh she rests). When I falter I remind myself: I'm doing this because I want to.

**Uphill.** Course designers are sadists. Rare is the race without some significant elevation—short and steep, long and gradual, or all of the above. If it's early in the race, you get it behind you. If it's closer to the finish, you hope the momentum will carry you through, one foot in front of the other. But what goes up must come down. Good news for the runners who blaze down hills, taking precious seconds off their time. Not me. Steep downhills terrify me. I pick my way down, leaning back, my brakes on. It's a gravity thing—I fear falling forward, hurting my back, tumbling down like Jill and Jack.

**Vibes: vigor, vitality, vanity, virtue.** The first two represent how we want people to think of us, radiating health, strength, and youthful energy, but the latter two have their place as well. When I joined a running club, younger women in the group would tell me I was a role model, an inspiration. At first I bristled at being called out for my age, but I learned to take it in stride and eat up the kudos, their calories padding my pride. Non-running friends closer to my own age express envy at my stamina and resolve. Their murmurs of awe cause a warm wave of smug self-righteousness to wash over me.

**The Wall**, hitting it. "I can't run another step . . . I'll never make the finish . . . I don't care anymore. . . ." Energy flags, breath is labored, incentive nil, every footfall an effort. The experts say it's most likely to happen two-thirds of the way through a race, when you're running out of fuel. I carry salt and carbs as well as water, so barring leg cramps—my nemesis—I mentally reboot at around that point. I trust that the race does have an end and that I will reach it in spite of what my body may be telling me. I visualize the finish line and start the countdown: "three more miles, two-and-a-half, yeah, you've got this. . . ."

**XT** is my training calendar's command every Thursday. I resisted cross-training for a long time, but when recovering from various running injuries I have to do something. I don't ride a bicycle, don't swim, don't play tennis or racquetball. Recumbent bikes, ellipticals, and treadmills will never be my exercise of choice, but I've incorporated the gym into my schedule to give my feet a rest while I use new muscles and get my heart pumping. The clincher—I feel stronger on my runs since I've been doing it.

**You**, as in "Better you than me." My husband says this, like a CD on repeat, whenever I do something he's happy not to do, every Friday night as I'm setting out my gear for my long slow Saturday run.

**ZZZZZZ.** 📖

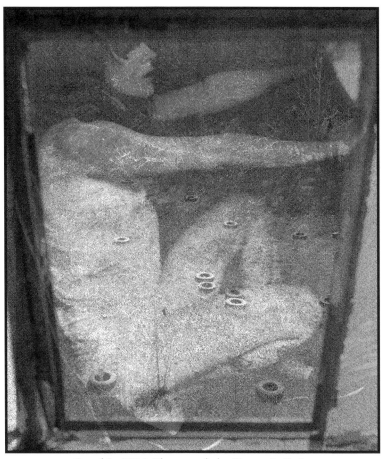

*Boxed In*, 2016, Photograph, by George L. Stein

# Reckless, 1977

## Tim McNulty

Two a.m., well past
last call at the Moon,
and the last pilgrims
are shambling out the door,

but a weaving drunk is
still raving over our table,
hasn't finished his story yet,
or his beer.

Fuck you, bartender,
he sings, sloshing and slurring
some idiotic detail, and

my country girlfriend
is strangely fascinated,
attracted to the humming current
of danger or expectation.

Come on, we say, we've
seen this, it isn't
gonna be pretty. And
it wasn't.

Not when the barman knocked
the glass from the drunk's hand
shattering it on the floor,

and not when the drunk
took a poorly aimed swing
with his left, and paid
dearly for it. She's

not laughing now
as we haul her out the door
into the cool night air
of 45th.

It should have hit me,
drunk as I was, maybe
a little too reckless back then
even for me.

# Up Here on Naches Heights

### Terry Martin

I wake to a rooster's crow
Mexican music in the orchard
ladders already reaching up, up
into trees thick with apples.

Stubbled fields and sky for miles.
Lupine and balsamroot
splash purple and yellow
on a sagebrush canvas.

Sometimes these hills reassure,
rolling on and on.
Ahtanum Ridge to the south,
Mt. Clemen, to the north.

Mount Adams always there,
like a birthmark. A loyal sentry
guarding the horizon.

Tumbleweeds and goatheads ask
if dying might be something I'll be able to do
without being scared out of my mind.

This landscape is teaching me things.
How to gather it up, take it all in.
How to kneel where I am, and pray.

*Rattlesnake Ridge*, 2017, Painting, by Judith Skillman

# Agnes Borglum's Three Cures

## Michelle Matthees

### I.
### *Whiskey*

It's ridiculous, isn't it
trying to stay here with my bad
focus, one hand skulled

around the precipice's ledge?
Apparently I can hang like this
for years. One hand free to take

the cup's sour mash, its
punch through glass
into a twenty-below dawn.

My wrist is slow and white
beneath the light of a juniper
beyond the cuff of my robe.

I draw up my legs.
I'd not thought of any of this.
Winter in the desert,

my hell of resting. I relax
a hand and fall
into the mind's antiseptic.

### II.
### *Capsicum*

The nurse of dawn comes
to my ice-eyes beneath

my hood's imp point.
Here is her red-pepper torch

my soft lady liberty.
Here my vast plant, radial
crown, summer peacock
in the eye's core chilling

beneath the stillborn,
open window. I hear
an early engine and
the progressive man on the red

tractor discs through my mind.
A typewriter of birds
crashes behind, white
gestures. Behold

my capsicum sunrise
with a stare as bold as
a broken horse's morning.
Red climbs up

the pipette, fist over fist.
Strike the vein of pain
in a rock formation
stacked, dew time

in my original desert.
The divine red candle
flickers green.
Relief. Deep relief.

But I remain below zero.

### III.
*Tobacco*

I'll not be sour if I get
my twist of tobacco.

A fool's gold sun rises,
and I'm apt to follow it.

Come closer. I want
to speak more clearly.

Last night Ida Slatten pounded me
with a bed pan. Now

my hands are blooming
in the after effects of defense.

I'm the magi adrift
in a ceramic night

and I light the coal of my pipe.
It's fine if you fall

short, if you can't follow me. It's
enough that you've come

bringing like a gift
yourself to yourself.

# My Mother(s) Remains

## Jessica Mehta

*Do you want to go to the Bahamas?* I opened
my mother's ashes and was taken
by the color. Somehow, I thought she'd be slate
but she was like Florida,

coarse and tawny. What remains
is heavier than you'd think, full
of bones and grit. The weight
tugs you down. As I spooned
her into the little glass
jar, I remembered being six,

my aunt packed tight
in a carboard urn while the lot
of us boarded a shaky propeller
plane. The pilot never said
to hold it low, let the wind
lap what's left—she swarmed
us like wild things, left a thick
coating and we licked her chars
from philtrums. Brackish and dry, she shot
to our innards, became a burrowing,

permanent part of us all. I thought,

I don't want my mother
to stay. Haunt my organs,
blow like smoke through dreams. How long
can someone stick
to the familiar? Cling scared

to all we hate? Like the gold
beggar children in Mexico, I brushed
her from my skirt and held my breath
against her dust. Maybe,
if I sprinkle her in the turquoise
of the tropics, salt the rim
a little more, she'll finally
(after so, so many years) release
those bitten nails and let me go.

*Decades Ago*, Visual Found Poem, by J.I. Kleinberg

# The Realm Between

## John Mifsud

As usual, arrivin early pays off cuz it's Saturday night and Bookie's is SRO! The Detroit swelter is almost bearable. It's stiflin but that ain't stoppin this tall, light-skinned brother from callin the D.C. Shuffle. A few of us join the small ensemble on the floor responding in uniform steps to The Hues Corporation singin *Rock the Boat* in three-part harmony. Everybody's beamin! It's contagious.

Pleated bell bottoms and fringed leather vests accentuate the beat. Graceful double turns are followed by full kicks on cue. We're shakin our groove thing and competing to see who can swing their platform heels the highest. Honey, it's jumpin and the Children are all in it!

We already sweatin but everyone knows it ain't half as hot as it's gonna get.

My gut tells me this evening will be another unforgettable night at Club 870. What I don't know is I'll still be tellin this story forty-five years later.

It's so damn humid and there's no AC. An oscillating fan whirs red and blue streamers in the back of the bar. Footlights spill on our front-row vantage. Swirls of smoke smellin of cloves ascend from our glasstop reflecting overflowing ashtrays, Cuba Libras and spent wedges of lime. After nailin six of the best seats in the house, we ain't budgin. So we wait. What choice do we have?

Leonard has his arm wrapped around me and I cannot tell you how happy I am. He is so damn dashing in his black and orange dashiki. I love him like no other. I sensed the joy would last a lifetime. Who knew it actually would?

Miss Dede and Kitty start complaining, as usual.

"Damn!" Kitty barks. "I wish this heat would let up."

"I'm okay with heat," I reply. "It's the humidity that's wearin me out."

Miss Dede grumbles, "Can we get this goddamn show started already."

Tonight, Dede's wearing overalls and a white tee with two simple silver hoops. Kitty's in her usual black pants and turtleneck.

Danny hennaed his beautiful, long hair and his turquoise and black bone choker is a striking compliment. He has eyes for every man that walks by.

I'm wearing my teal vest and bell bottom ensemble with a ruffly, magenta silk shirt. I guess I'm goin for some kinda queer buccaneer. Javier is in yellow overalls with wedgies. He's so high on pot, his eyes look like two watermelon seeds floatin in a pan of water.

Leonard asks, "Are you comfortable?"

"No complaints here," I chirp. "I feel like the luckiest queen in the room."

He gives me a peck on the cheek. "Me too."

Miss Dede groans, "Would you two please stop spooning? It's tiring."

I snap right back. "When it comes to tired, you're the expert."

"Bitch!"

"Ya basta!" Javier barks, "Don't start or I'll get all Puerto Riqueña on you. No será bonito. Let's have some fun. Sherrine's why we're here so knock it off!"

Kitty grabs her empty glass. "I need another drink. Can I get anybody anything?"

Danny winks. "Yes. That cute bartender's phone number please. The one with the beard."

Kitty returns with another vodka martini, shaken, not stirred. The deejay fades the disco so the show's about to begin. The whole place quiets down. After the usual canned fanfare, the booth brings up some parade music. No one knows what to expect but we straighten up, facing the proscenium, anxious for the magic to start.

It had.

We just didn't know it.

It's so damn dark, no one at our table noticed. Sudden applause from behind catches us off guard. We turn around to the camp surprise at the goddamn front door! First, two muscly men in go-go boots and red, white, and blue bikinis march in on beat. Behind them, a dyke in navy uniform and one tall red-headed queen in full army regalia. They are both highly decorated and waving flags. Everyone stands at attention as they pass.

Sherrine suddenly jumps into the dazzling follow spot from behind the foyer wall and proceeds to strut to the stage. Amazed, we join the growing ovation following her to the boards. Left. Left. Left, right, left.

As she passes, we all salute.

She's wearing some big hair. I mean very big hair, okay? She musta had three falls seamlessly stacked, one on top of the other and teased into a colossal brunette bouffant that flipped pertly at her shoulders, thank you very much. And if that ain't enough, the prima donna is wearing her own goddamn GI jacket with **D-E-N-I-S** appliquéd across her left breast pocket. (Snap.) Just try and beat that! (Double snap!) She's the grand marshal at her own gay pride parade!

Sherrine's a vet. Oh, yes she is! Served in 'Nam and thankfully got back home to lip sync about it. Please do not ask me how she managed to be gay and on active duty during a goddamn war. I don't even want to know, but somehow Sherrine prevailed. There are times when we all know what it means to be on the front line.

She certainly is tonight!

Her khaki jacket reaches right above tight black panties. Honey, she has all her stuff tucked away under fishnet hose, okay? She's lookin like a real woman. She always does. And those stilettos. Girlfriend! She's six feet anyway. I ain't lyin. Those pumps and all that hair made the bitch seven feet tall!

Her talent is likewise gigantic. Tonight she opens with Freyda Payne's *Bring the Boys Home*. Her dancing and gestures are superbly choreographed as always. She lip syncs the lines impeccably, quivering her ruby reds like she's actually singing every note in her own voice. I scrutinize her technique. She simultaneously whispers and accentuates her consonants so it sounds like the words are coming right outta her mouth and not the blaring speakers. If you're within earshot, you actually hear her enunciate the lyrics almost out loud.

*(Why don't you) Turn the ships around*
*(Everybody oughta) Lay your weapons down*
*Bring the boys home (bring'em back alive)*
*Bring the boys home (bring'em back alive)*

Every weekend, we make our fifty-five minute pilgrimage from our beloved Ann Arbor to the Motor City. It's 1973, and we are some young, fiery activists fulla moxie just when the U of M campus is a hotbed of political activity.

*"END APARTHEID!"*
*"OUT OF VIET NAM!"*
*"WOMEN ARE NOT CHICKS!"*
*"GAY RIGHTS NOW!!"*

Girlfriends, we are strong, united and uber radical; a troop of intellectual skag-drag queens gender-bending to raise consciousness and promote civil rights. Demonstrations are our forte, our lifeblood. Our presence is powerful, our voices loud and clear. We are passionately connected and make national gay history as often as a good queen changes pantyhose. Okay?

Our petit bourgeois college town is the first to elect a lesbian to City Council. This is truth talkin here. If you didn't know, Kathy K is the first out gay person in all of these United States to win public office. That's right! The very first! She runs as an independent and our alternative ticket prevails! A big dyke beats out the Democrats and the Republicans with our radical platform! Hard work pays off for our victorious third party.

We believe it'll last forever.

Ann Arbor becomes the first City Council in the country to declare Gay Pride Week. We organize the first official Gay Pride March and parade we do! Oh yes, Honey, it's true! Local television stations shot rare footage that historic day.

A few months later, the American Psychiatric Association convenes in downtown Detroit and we organize our own national conference: *GAY IS MENTAL HEALTH!* (Snap!) You got that right! (Double snap!) We work that assembly of shrinks and their institutionalized homo-hatred.

We are not playin, okay? We are some serious business.

The very next year, the APA finally removes us from their list of pathologies! You do the math. They sure as hell do! You may think of us as an anomaly but being queer is certainly no pathology. We put an end to all that hetero-fascist propaganda. Nipped it. I'm tellin you, we are a powerful force.

The Detroit shows are our relief. Resistance is vehement so we need a break. The Saturday night spectaculars are more than just a good show, more than mere escapism; they're actually our refuge; our spiritual practice.

And we are head over spiked heels for the queens, Honey. They use gender as performance and absolutely personify our politic. A few dollars worth of make up, a wig, a dress, and matching pumps and these queens illustrate just how simple it is to cross over. Generations of conditioning cannot stop them. Not hardly. Even if they wind up being a man's idea of how a woman should look and act, for us, their short jaunt is exhilarating and inspiring.

Conforming gender dynamics do not interest us. Not today. Not ever. We're human beings. We're not meant to fit into boxes. We want out. We perceive gender as a feeble social construct and a bad one at that. Abandoning the limits of traditional sex assignments, we explore the rich realm between, the natural, often mystical integration of the masculine and feminine. You want your sexuality to conform? Fine! That's your psychology. That's your business. Just keep us out of it.

A classy drag queen further proves our point. They establish our culture. We come to honor our queens as the stuff community is made of. So every Saturday night, we drive to Detroit without fail. It's healthy. It's church.

After Sherrine brought the boys home, Beneatha Sheets does a flawless Carmen Miranda singing, *The Lady with the Tutti Fruity Hat.*

*Awakening*, 2018, Graphite, by Drake Truber

*Some people say, I dress too gay,*
*But ev'ry day, I feel so gay,*
*And when I'm gay, I dress that way,*
*Is something wrong with that?*
*No!*


Then Miss Lolly Pop comes out and does Bette Midler's *Boogie Woogie Bugle Boy* on roller skates! What a hoot! Tiffany Middlesex follows doing an exquisite Streisand with a blonde beehive regaled in sunshine taffeta and more petticoats than Scarlett O'Hara had at Tara.

This is some show, baby! Unparalleled. One amazement after another.

We love all the performers but Sherrine is our ultimate diva, okay? She's mixed race. She looks Black but out of makeup, she's got freckles. I asked her to dance once and she told me she's also part Native. Regardless, the room fevers up when she hits the lights. I'm breakin a sweat just talkin about her! She gives you reason to fan yourself, Honey. The humidity is one thing; Sherrine's another. She turns it up just right. Some kinda hoodoo's happenin and we're about to be spellbound.

For the finale, our dear Ms. Denis walks onto the Bookie's stage wearing a plush pink coat with a sable collar. This is totally atypical for Sherrine. We are so surprised to see our supreme drag star dressed like some suburban housewife.

"Epale!" Javi yells, "Look at that cute pink pillbox."

Dede backs him up, "With a thin gauze veil covering her face."

"Where the hell did she get those pink gloves?" Danny asks. "Not to mention those matching patent leather heels?" Danny leans over and whispers, "You knock her over. I'll grab the pumps."

I don't know what to say. "She looks like she's going to church on Easter Sunday!"

A matching, rectangular pink paten leather handbag swings on her left hand pinky.

Kitty declares, "That's a big ol' purse, Honey!"

Leonard tells me, "Sister's struttin around like she's lookin for trouble!"

We are tremblin with excitement just thinkin bout what she's gonna conjure in this pink get up. Sherrine's always gotta gimmick so we know she's up to somethin!

Tonight, it's like Miss Thing is signifyin the preacher and his wife after a Sunday sermon. She's casually strollin the stage, strikin poses and makin quick turns, lookin back over her shoulders with gloved fists on her hips. Her lip syncing is high art. Being in her presence is total reverie. It's holy. She is the very best drag queen ever which is why I'll never stop tellin this story.

Sherrine's doin' *You Better Leave My Man Alone* by The Raeletts. It's humorous but we know Sherrine. She's got some kinda crazy ass plan in store to be sure.

> *Now I don't wanna start no trouble girl,*
> *Lord knows I don't wanna start no fight,*
> *So take this advice and stay away from my man*
> *And everything will be alright.*

Dede growls, "This song is sooooooo politically incorrect!"

"Silencio," Javi orders. "Mira, it's going be a real showstopper. Esperate."

I turn to Dede. "Darlin, this is so over the top, you just cannot take her too seriously."

> *You better leave my man alone,*
> *'Cause I'll poison ya,*
> *'Cause I'll scratch your eyes out.*
> *'Cause I'll cut ya . . .*

Then, in a split second, she pulls out a long butcher knife with a big ol' shiny blade she's been hidin in her huge pink purse. We are not at all prepared. Caught up short, we start to come undone but not Miss Sherrine. No. Uh uh! She's prancin all over the stage. The knife is gleamin light and she's wieldin it like she gonna put it to good use.

Javi starts howlin. "Esta loca! Okay? Chicas, you do not want to mess with Sherrine."

Danny answers, "Noooooooooo Honey!"

"This bruja is not someone you take on."

I can't believe it. "I don't care how many bricks you got in your purse, if she ain't your ally, you might as well pack up your tiaras and move the hell outta town."

"Okay?" Leonard snaps.

Kitty coos, "Try Kalamazoo!" and snaps again too.

We are absolutely outta control; laughin so damn hard, we're cryin and we can't stop even when it starts to hurt. We're wheezin, doubled over, holdin our bellies with tears streamin down. Then, if her perfect lip syncing, the pink ensemble, the sheer hilarity of the interpretation is not enough, our would-be church lady ends with one arm akimbo, and, daintily holds the big black handle of the thick, stainless steel pointing down. She deliberately stares down the audience from left to right and lets it go. Wouldn't you know, that blade sticks straight up in the wooden floor, vibratin back and forth with a twang like the final frames of some goddamn Looney Tune Cartoon.

We go craaaazy, Honey! I mean Yosemite Sam kinda crazy! Everyone simultaneously jumps up to cheer, the second standing ovation of the evening, but this one is on fire! I'm talkin about a four-alarm, Baby. The laughter is so overpowering, our exhilaration and joy so embodied, hysteria descends on the entire bar and holds everyone hostage.

It's obvious. We feel it. And we own it.

In another hot flash, Bookie's is chaos! Girlfriend, we just can't stand it. Sherrine ignites something wild and buried inside of us and we want more. We must have more! She aligns our emotional interior with the outer world and manifests the two. Sherrine's transvestite magic becomes our bridge to the other side. Just as she crosses from male to female, we cross over to a new, timeless landscape we've longed for but can barely describe.

She pulls the knife out of the floor and prances back to her dressing room.

We're screamin, "Encore! Encore!" A bartender puts a cardboard box out on stage for Sherrine's tips cuz she ain't got time to be nice. We're tossin in tens and twenties. We gave her our rent money Honey, cuz we know she's comin back!

"Encore! Encore! We want more!"

We do not stop until the music comes back up and the diva starts the tune from the top. Ms. Thing has to do the routine all over again. She has no choice. Sherrine is the boss of us while she's performing, but after that knife trick, Darlins, we take over! Now, the audience is in charge and we're givin the orders.

How many hours must she have rehearsed to perfect such precision? Once the blade quivers back and forth in the floor a second time, it's as if someone throws our composure in the blender behind the bar and hits frappe. We wig out! I mean all the way. Our applause is deafening.

We're shriekin! "Get back out here, girlfriend!"

"One more time, Honey."

"Do it again. Please!"

"I said one more time, goddamn it! One more goddamn time!"

Sooner than expected, she's back out and does a third rendition. Each brings us closer to feeling the full daring she emanates so gracefully; a real palpable power infused with camp and pink leather pumps. Her head is cocked to one side, givin you some real tough attitude. She's funny and sexy and scary all at the same time but now it's starting to make sense. The smoke is thinning. We're internalizing something as yet unspoken, something completely apparent but just coming to consciousness. Never underestimate the power of a man in a dress.

Although we're all just having some big fun, Sherrine is actually threatening violence, albeit benignly. Here she is, a tall man wearin a pound of makeup, a big wig, and a woman's wool coat. Her invitation is to know the strength in our own femininity. She's doing just that and demonstrating fierce command.

With skillful timing, that butcher blade stabs the floor, three for three and Sherrine strikes a pose that etches in our minds forever. Naturally, we insist on a fourth encore, stompin and carryin on.

Kitty says, "No queen has ever had more than two encores at Bookie's."

"Sherrine's makin history," Leonard offers.

I'm clear, "She knows it too."

And so do we.

For what seems like forever, we're demanding, "Do it again, goddamn it! Do it again!"

The music starts up and our drag star finally returns without her big pink purse. We're lookin at one another all bewildered.

"What the hell is she gonna do?" Javi asks.

I'm thinkin out loud, "How she gonna pull this off without the butcher knife?'

She improvises down the steps and into the aisles. Near the igniting lyric, she signals this brother near the bar to get offa his seat. He obliges. What choice does he have?

It's a large perch, Honey, stuffed leather, brass studs and a wrought iron frame with a little loop at the top. Don't you know, Ms. Thang swoops up this big ol' chair with her index finger and slings it over her back like it's a goddamn pocketbook. She climbs back up on stage and just when she's comin to climax, the lezzie on the light board cuts to black and flicks on the strobe.

Now, in flickering slow motion, Sherrine flings the chair over her head with one finger and smashes it on the stage floor. Two wooden legs go flyin. Fairies stage right jump outta their chairs in fright. Somebody could definitely get hurt. The armrests are asplinter. That fat leather four-legger is all busted up. They kill the strobe and the house lights hit. Everyone's dumbfounded with goose bumps tingling up our arms and down our spines.

Bookie's dangerous diva holds out her right hand to check her nails. Nary a chip on the culprit that fucked up the furniture. She cups her claws, blows on them, brushes them on her sable, adjusts the hair and curtsies, skippin off stage in pink patent leather spikes. (And around the world and back snap for that!)

Now, we're all fired up, flamin and verbose!

"You have got to be goddamn kidding me!"

"This ain't no joke, Honey."

"You got that right."

"Naaaaaaw, this is for real."

Or is it unreal? Now she's really gone too far. An adrenaline and testosterone cocktail floods our veins not to mention the booze. Now she's not just harmlessly threatening violence for laughs, she is actually treacherous. She's crossed over from male to female but instead of abdicating her power to align with traditional notions of what it means to be a woman, she's got physical prowess. She crosses over then crosses right back, all in one song.

No one gets hurt but she's unintentionally summoning our cumulative rage after a lifetime of being called names, spat on, slammed up against lockers, humiliated, heads dunked in toilets, tossed into dumpsters, publicly beaten, raped, and, yes, murdered or left to bleed to death. We know what it means to be outnumbered. It's in our bones. All of our lives, we have faced heartless, brutal men who know no mercy. It may very well have been a stranger or just as likely our own blood.

Simultaneously, we're also coming to know the strength of our community, our combined conviction, and the wrath of our resolve. When Sherrine destroys that chair, we are suspended in history; involuntarily vested. She's living proof of our capacity, our potential, individually and collectively. It's empowering and feels supernatural. Although we are adamantly dedicated to nonviolence, we're all riled up. Sherrine's strength demonstrates what we can do when we're pushed too far.

So we keep pushin. Can't help it. Our energy just won't quit. We keep stompin our feet and bangin on tables. We're chantin in earsplitting unison, "Sher-rine! Sher-rine! Sher-rine!"

We stop when the lights grow dim, signaling her reappearance. She comes out and leaves the main curtain open. A backstage lamp lights her up from behind. She's holdin somethin but it's dark and we can't tell what the hell it is.

And there she stands. A towering silhouette rising above the wreckage of her fourth encore, eerie and defiant. Otherworldly. Our freckled, Black and White, Two-Spirit enchantress. A giant among men.

The music starts again as the lights fade up real slow.

Honey, she's got a fire hose in one hand and the big red tank in the other!

She proceeds to work the aisles and showers the house down with $CO_2$! She's not pointing the funnel at anyone, she's shootin right above our heads fillin the bar with a cloud of soda bicarbonate and pearl ash. Sherrine's still lip syncin flawlessly but Darlin she's ready to call it a night and subdues our delirium definitively. We're burnin up, a ragin wildfire and she puts our asses out! We're doused. Once the song ends, the diva throws the hose and tank on stage. They land with a clunk and a thud and Sherrine walks off. (Another triple snap for that!)

"Amen! Amen!"

"She's done."

"Hallelujah! Thank you Jesus!"

"Girlfriends, this show is over!"

"Got that?"

The staff is so flabbergasted they forget to announce, "Last call."

We're exhausted, okay? Stunned. Everyone in the audience is coughin, chokin, and powder-coated.

Maybe next time, you'll believe me when I tell you she truly blew us all away.


The fog of fire retardant does not dissipate, just lifts slowly, an ethereal haze rising to obscure Fresnels hanging from the ceiling. Their rays are unearthly, emanating through a canopy of incandescence. It looks like some kinda UFO mother ship is hoverin right over our heads before a warp speed takeoff. We've definitely been visited.

Our cohort leaves Bookie's bewitched, devotees staggerin from the voodoo.


We drive back to Ann Arbor in no hurry and in silence. No radio. No nothin. The windows are rolled down. The cool rush feels so goddamn good. Leonard and I are cuddled in the back but we cannot sleep. Couldn't if we tried. Every now and then, synapses spark simultaneously and we revisit the evening's magic, speakin all at once.

Danny's driving. "I still can't believe it."

"That was the very best show ever," Kitty whispers shotgun.

Leonard replies, "Who you tellin?"

"She turned it out, chicas."

"I'd say she ripped it up."

Dede agrees, "She sure did. She ripped it to shreds."

It's a mum carpool home. We need quiet. We're absolutely speechless . . . mesmerized but full of energy . . . the good kind.

I'm tellin you, those queens have an indelible affect on us. And I'll say it again; it's not just entertainment. Bookie's is our sacred ground. The floorshows, our fevered dancing, and an array of intoxicants usher us into altered states. The disco rhythms drum through the night, pounding with the beat of our hearts. The mirrored balls spinning overhead bless us, charming the entire room with a sparkling glow, a bonfire burning til dawn. The female impersonators are our spirit guides, our shamans courageous enough to cross over, reenacting tribal, ritual transvestism from evening into night.

We pull off the freeway and find an all night diner in downtown Rawsonville. Coffee all around. Greek omelets, chili dogs and baklava are breakfast.

We get back on the road and silently drive west. The clear sunrise promises good weather. It's almost 5:00 a.m. and the windows are still wide open. The fresh air is invigorating. In the rearview mirror, an alluring dawn graces the horizon while another awakens within. 📖

*Tail of a Tale*, 2017, Cartoon, by Don Swartzentruber

# Nic-town.

## Jack Miller

*—For James Rathe*

We're standing in a small cafe by Castro
I order extra large
You shaved your head recently,
grassy tufts of thread
lock onto the empty space
Your red flannel, your
Spirit cigarette,
lit by the stucco wall facing the sidewalk


The lights all crumble under your gaze
purple neons, streetlight reds
The road fills up with
sad orange light. The park migrates to the
staircase
We trade liquor for teeth
lost in this mess of green
Let it go.


I tell you stories of another time
not so far in the eternity
long past now
Nic-town.
Stuck here, trains all gone from the subway
The people here are uncertain.
You're uncertain.

# Yard Work

## Kevin Miller

You love the scuffle hoe,
extend, pull, and scrape
the surface a thin skim
as if removing the moles
on your spotted skin or
peeling a layer of years
from the face of it all,
leather and weather,
crows feet and furrow,
tags and other bits.
Or this spring you use
the handle as support.
You see the way weeds
cover the bed you made,
the lie in it others want
you to see, straight edges
and borders, the order they
love. You want a smoke,
the ease of exhaling
while you ponder. Each
season you rework skin
to callous, the other side
of liver spots, you joke
about connecting dots,
the constellation of scars
for stars, a map to trace
labor days, buck twenty-
five an hour, ten cent beers
and fears this was your life.

# Selecting a Reader

## Rocio Muñoz

I would have him be invisible.
When searching for him in a photograph,
You would not find him.
He would be lost in the chorus, silently sitting in the front,
hiding where he belongs, in his world of words.
Avoiding our decaying one that is slowly losing its musicality.
He will walk into the bookstore,
Allowing his finger to guide him through the endless
   maze of bookshelves.
Thumping all those different spines
That proudly compose their own unique sound for him.
Until he finds it. That tune he did not know he was missing.

*Transformed*, Drypoint Etch & Aquatint Print, by John Timothy Robinson

# Our Tribe

## C.A. Murray

"**A**re you Webster's buddy?" asked a young man from the driver's side window of a grey SUV.

"Yeah," Jim said as the wind picked up in the parking lot of the diner fifteen miles north of Cantwell. "Is he here yet?"

"We were going to ask the same thing," the driver said.

"Are you coming?" asked an older man in as few syllables as possible as he leaned across the driver to get a good look at Jim.

"He better come. We need the help, especially since Webster didn't show up at my house and he ain't here either," the driver said. Jim popped the trunk of his car, grabbed his bag and jumped into the SUV. They pulled onto the highway and went north.

"You ever go hunting?" the passenger asked. He was a larger man with a dark beard and wonky ears.

"When I was a kid," Jim replied.

"Good. My name is Ronny," the passenger said, "and this is Paul." Paul looked back and forced a smile.

"I'm Jim. Do you have any idea where Webster is?"

"Who knows, Jim," Ronny said. "There's not much that boy doesn't get up to."

Jim should have known this would happen, knowing Webster. He did not know exactly what made him get into the stranger's SUV. It could be because he knew Webster relied on his share of the meat or that he finally wanted an Alaskan adventure. He knew he wouldn't miss his usual weekend routine of shooting pool at the veterans bar, making comments on uploaded classical pieces online, doing errands at the office supply store, and maybe masturbating in the late morning.

Jim was twenty-seven and had managed the same restaurant for the past five years; during the first two years he was still getting his degree in English. Between high school and graduating college a whole lifetime had passed him by. At least it felt like it.

He had a girl call him in the middle of the night once, telling him that she had a miscarriage, and he still cannot with confidence remember her name. The four times he called in sick to work in the last three years were all related somehow to the strip club, and his first college attempt ended when his girlfriend kicked him out of their apartment for cheating with the same girl twice.

\* \* \* \*

Paul, Ronny, and Jim stumbled through the patches of trees and bogs that felt like gelatin. They abandoned the trail in the first fifteen minutes from the gravel pit that they parked at, and they soon walked along the tree line of a mountain. They glassed the nearby passes searching for caribou. Once they were past the earshot of the ATV's on the trail, Paul got out his rifle and held it with the butt hugging the top of his rib cage. The sun tried to force its way out of the morning fog, and they walked with their heads hung low—like a funeral procession—as they avoided the rain. Jim felt like he had joined the company of pallbearers but instead of carrying a body, they carried the tools to create one.

The caribou was shot on the second day. It froze in shock and half-ran, half-fell down the mountain towards them like a drunk horse in a rodeo. It took another bullet to the head to kill it from Paul's .30-06 that he pointed between its murky eyes. As they were gutting it, the insides spilled out onto the dirt almost elegantly as if it was a cordial pouring into a goblet. The snapping of the knees and hip were the only act that seemed barbarous to Jim, but it was done with such grace as flies swarmed and blood dripped down their arms. They disassembled the animal like a piece of furniture and sequestered the meat into the quartering bags, everything else tossed into the lichen and blueberry brambles.

\* \* \* \*

Ronny decided that Paul should drive to Cantwell for burgers since it was his idea to stay the extra night in the gravel pit. Jim and Ronny sat around the blazing fire pit leaning back and swiping bugs away, not the least bit deterred by the smoke. Ronny groaned with hunger and Jim tried to shut him up by trying to get him to cook up some of the caribou.

"It's not tradition to taste the kill the first night?" Jim asked.

"Not that I know of but sounds like witchcraft," Ronny said tossing his cigar into the fire.

"There should be," Jim said.

"How do you know Webster?" Ronny asked. "I've been meaning to ask."

"I met him outside of a hotel," Jim responded.

"There is a story behind that and I want to hear it."

"I had been bar hopping in the middle of December. I met a women who invited me back to her room. She took my hand and led me to a hotel but when we got to the door inside she told me to wait until she checked to see if her sister was up in her room. I waited for the young woman to return to let me inside from the cold. She never came back and as I waited for her, I bummed a cigarette from some guy who was also waiting for something. This turned out to be Webster."

"What was ol' Webby waiting for?" Ronny asked.

"He told me that he had paid a prostitute already for her services and was waiting for her to come back downstairs to retrieve him. It turned out that he had been waiting over an hour. I took it as a sign to give up, then Webby and I took a cab to the strip club."

The SUV pulled up and lurched to a stop. Paul jumped out and tossed them each paper bags with their burgers folded in aluminum foil.

"Jim over there almost convinced me to pop a back strap on the fire since you took so long," Ronny said.

"You two are animals. I made no stops."

"Aye, never did I lose faith," Ronny said, washing down the burger with cheap beer.

"Up in my village, it's custom to give the first cut to the elders," Paul said, who was half Alaskan Native and half white.

"It's no good unseasoned anyways, and needs to be cooked right," Ronny said leaning into the fire. They had all finished their food and were quickly downing a bottle of Monarch Vodka so they could sleep through the cold night. They had only a large enough tarp to fit all three underneath and some shoelaces to tie it up. The sky darkened and the northern lights came out, faded and moving slowly. The bottle was tossed around between the three. Paul told an ambitious story of creation about his parents when they were about twenty, the age he was now. It was in response to Ronny asking why he did not bring a jacket. They were up in Barrow and the condom that his father had brought had become frozen on the way up to a cabin they were staying at.

"I was conceived in the cold and created because of it," he said to end it with the widest of grins.

Ronny told a story too about the trip last year to the same area with Webster. "We must have walked as much as this trip, at least it felt like it, all uphill, and we had gotten up earlier in the day. It was hot as any day, and everything but us were catching some shade but that did not stop us as we went up on the spine of the nearest crest.

"The one we got was the bigger out of a group of four or five. They all scattered after the shot had been fired. One of the caribou ran straight toward us and when it passed us, Webster went running after it. He almost caught up to the thing but could not gain enough ground. He must have been chasing those things around for about an hour. I don't know what gets into that boy sometimes. I don't know why Paul keeps inviting him on hunting trips." Ronny pulled out the heart from the quarter bags. He slapped it on the coal for a few turns, then Jim took a few bites from it as Ronny cheered. Jim asked Paul if eating the heart had broken the tradition but he wasn't sure. It only bothered Jim.

\* \* \* \*

When Jim was fourteen, his dad took him hunting for the first time. Jim remembered knowing that most boys would have killed to be out hunting in Alaska with their dad. He was embarrassed about it all because he had tried to get his mom to let him stay home. This was before she left his dad for a fancy woodworker in Missoula, Montana. His dad spent hours on the internet researching the different approaches and techniques to tracking caribou. When it came down to the hunt, they stumbled onto a herd after climbing over a small crest to a gully within the first hour. There were about twenty in the herd all scattered. Jim and his dad were crouched behind a small spruce tree watching in frozen awe at the caribou, slowly walking towards them. One of the caribou got downed, and seconds after there was a shot from the other side of the valley. The herd scattered and his dad screamed and cursed, trying to get a shot that never came as the rest of the herd ran in different directions.

"We were there first," he kept saying as they hiked back to the truck.

It must have been an hour after walking back that Jim noticed far behind them was a caribou. "Look dad," Jim said, "we can still get one."

"I seen that one for a while now following us. That dumb shit. It's a baby with no meat on it," his dad said.

"Why is it following us?"

"It got separated from its momma, or maybe she was the one shot. It doesn't know what else to do."

The little caribou followed them for hours. Jim's dad would look back and swear under his breath. It got close enough to them they could hear its tendons on its feet clicking.

"Should we feed it? What should we do?" Jim asked.

"Nothing," he said annoyed.

It got closer and walked right behind his dad and he turned around and scared it away by shooting at the sky. Thirty minutes later it came right back up clicking along. His dad turned around in one motion and shot it square in the nose. Jim did not talk to his dad for months after. That was the last time he went hunting before taking Webster's place on Paul's hunt. Jim told a rendition of the story to Webster at the locals bar in downtown Anchorage and that's when he convinced him to come on the trip.

\* \* \* \*

*Over the River,* Photograph, by Theodore C. Van Alst, Jr.

There was a voicemail from Webster on Jim's cell made from the Jailhouse and he went to bail him out after leaving work early. He waited in the lobby after being patted down by a security guard. The bail was set at $300. The guards escorted Webster out of a short hallway. He walked slowly, looking as scruffy as ever behind two women security guards who looked back twice making sure he was still behind them. His shirt was torn down his shoulder, and he looked confused.

Once outside, Webster said, "I'll pay you back for the bail, sometime soon."

"Yeah, take your time. I expect you will tell me what happened to you."

"Can you take me back home? I'd appreciate it. I don't have a way back and I don't want to hitchhike; I don't think anyone will pick me up looking like this."

\* \* \* \*

They drove up north toward the lodge that Webster worked at not far from where the caribou had been bagged. The leaves were beginning to turn on the side of the highway toward the military base.

"Turn off the depressing music," Webster requested.

"It will fade soon once we get out of range," Jim said, turning it up a little. It was one of Chopin's Nocturnes that he recognized but it was faster than he was used to.

"Did you go with Paul?" Webster asked.

"Yeah," Jim replied

"Who else ended up making it?"

"It was Paul and a guy named Ronny"

"I know Ron. Christ, how was it?" Webster asked. "Sorry I missed it."

"We got one."

"Dam, and I missed it for some stupid shit," Webster said. "Death can be bold if you want it to. For five years now I have been going up with Paul and helping him with the caribou. Every time I come back from it I feel better, maybe it's the whole sacrifice thing." His voice faded into itself and he stared out the passenger window towards the lower spine of the Chugach Mountains.

"Is it good meat then?" Jim asked.

"It's better than Safeway," Webster said.

"You can have my share that Paul said he would give me. I don't cook much at the house anyway, because of working at a restaurant and all. Too bad you missed the hunt this year."

"I know. The first time I went with Paul," Webster said, "I took the antlers home and bolted them to the front of the house I was staying at. I liked the way that they looked and they were so heavy when I picked them up. Can you imagine having them on your fucking head? They bleed too. It's not like hair, even though they fall off."

"What do the antlers have to do with it?" Jim asked.

"I began to understand that we grow antlers of our own but they do not fall off in winter," Webster said.

"Shit. What did they do to you in there?"

"Nothing. I slept a bit. It was not peaceful," Webster said, "but at least the jailhouse is filled with people who don't want to be where they are either. I've never had something in common with that many people in one place. I tell you, if I still was a drug dealer it would have even been better. It's like a business convention in there, except only for drugs."

Jim mentioned that there would be snowfall in the coming weeks. Webster shrugged, and asked him if he had a cigarette. "You know I don't smoke," he replied. Webster leaned his head back against the window.

It started to rain.

"My downfall was my television," Webster said.

"A TV set?"

"On my sixteenth birthday my parents bought me a television. One of the very few possessions that I took with me when I left home. It was one of the older ones with a VHS player at the bottom. I lent it to a woman who works at the lodge too. I am guessing I don't have a job when I get back, but she was not on good terms with the lodge when the cops were called.

"Anyways, so this woman and I were drinking in her room and we had an argument. I was in the wrong like always. I smashed the TV. The noise incited a response from the troopers and they asked her if the TV belonged to her and if she felt in harm's way. She replied yes to both."

"Shit, we'll get you a lawyer, for all that they're worth," Jim said.

"We will see. I just need to get to work. They are going to have to fire one of us because there is a restraining order active. I would not be surprised if it was the both of our asses."

"Why did you smash the TV?"

"I was pissed off at her," Webster said.

"Have fun explaining that in court."

"It will be my pleasure. I never thought in a million years I would be expected to explain to a judge whether or not the TV I destroyed was mine or not."

"The day has come," Jim said in an ominous voice.

"The crazy thing," Webster said, "is that she had dared me to do it after she tried to smash it herself. If she wasn't so drunk she might have been the one to do it."

"Did you feel in harm's way?" Webster asked.

"You mean before or after the troopers showed up?"

Webster told a story about the woman he had been with at the time of his arrest for the rest of the car ride. White birch trees rustled in the wind and crows flew from up the mountain.

"We lived on the same street on the east side of Anchorage. We must have been in the seventh grade when we started learning about all the Native Americans on the west coast of the lower forty-eight. The two of us made up a tribe. Across from the main road by our house was a forest and it was there that we constructed a hut over an already deep hole in the eroded soil. We had dug the hole out and created a roof with tree branches. There was a name for our tribe and everything.

"One day, we got to our village and everything had been destroyed. The branches were all tossed to the side and our shelves we carved into the roots were filled with dirt. She had broken the code we had created and told another boy about our tribe and had gone as far as showing him the location. We soon found the kid not far from his house. I offered to let him join. I never planned on letting him in, and he agreed without knowing the steps he had to take in order to join. They were rules for joining that I made up for him. She went along with it all because of the amusement, I think. We made him drag a wet log for a while and then told him to do some other tasks. The kid did it all. He must have liked her because he agreed to the last and brutal test.

"I told him he had to fight one of us. I was certain that he was going to choose her because I was bigger. I was planning on telling him that it was a trick question and that fighting women was forbidden in the tribe. He chose to fight me and knocked me out pretty quick and she just stood there watching it all. For the longest time, I had the creeping suspicion that she was the one that had destroyed our village."

"You have a history of violence with this woman; maybe you could tell that story to the judge," Jim said laughing.

"Maybe you will be there as a character witness. Start thinking of how great of a guy I am."

"Get some real sleep Webby," Jim said, letting him sleep the rest of the way to the property that he rented in the back lot in a tent.

* * * *

After he dropped off Webster, Jim pulled into the only bar in the little town close to the lodge. The building was a cabin next to a gas station with a large empty dirt lot with only two cars.

Inside the bar was brighter than he imagined and wanted it to be. It was like they had replaced every light bulb that morning. He sat at the end of the bar towards the dirty kitchen that was visible through a small window on a swinging door. The bartender, a very fat woman, walked over and did not ask him what he wanted until she was standing right across the other side of the bar.

Jim drank his beer and thought about the hunting trip with Webster's friends, and then about the one he went on with his dad. Webster told him that he would have done the same thing and that the baby Caribou would not have survived on its own.

Someone always knew better than he did. He wondered if that was why his dad shot it all those years ago. Had he misinterpreted his dad's kindness for a savage brutality?

Each time the bartender gave him his next beer they would exchange a few words about how drinking a few during the day was not the end of the world. The other person at the bar was a gentlemen who watched the baseball game. A young girl entered the bar talking on her phone. She ordered a vodka and soda, and while it melted paced around the back of the bar by an empty pool table.

"I don't know what I am going to do," she said, "'cause I don't have a job or a place to stay now." She agreed with a few things that the other person on the phone said and then disagreed with a couple of them after that. She said thank you three times and put the phone back in her bulky backpack. The girl was young with short blonde hair and thick black-rimmed glasses. She had little skinny legs coming out of her tight cargo shorts. A few more people filtered into the bar and sat down. One at a table, a few at the bar between Jim and the girl that did not know what to do.

Jim sauntered over and sat next to the girl. He called the bartender over and ordered them both another drink.

"What's your name?" Jim asked.

"Danielle," she said quickly, knowing he knew he was going to ask.

"Danielle. Jim," he said, tipping his beer toward her. Jim tried to make some conversation with the girl but she was reluctant to talk much and he was about to chalk it up to what it was.

"Are you going through Anchorage?" she asked Jim.

"I live in Anchorage and I'm headed in that direction. Do you need a ride or something? Where you going?"

"My friend just got me a job interview at the ski resort out in Girdwood, so unless you are planning on going through Anchorage and heading south down the arm, then you can't really help," she said, stirring her drink with two skinny straws like they were chopsticks.

Jim shrugged his shoulders and got another round. Danielle mentioned being recently employed at a lodge near town. Jim took a guess that she was the woman who had a restraining order against Webster. He said that he had been meaning to make his way down to the lodge because the owner was trying to hire him on for the winter, which was not a complete lie because Jim knew the general manager who tried to hire him a few years back.

"You can ride with me," Jim offered.

"You're not one of those psychos who wants to steal my panties or something?" she asked.

"No, but I am flattered," Jim said.

"Aren't you charming?"

"I can be," Jim said.

* * * *

At the ski resort where Danielle had a job interview, he got them a room. She went straight to the shower after seeing her friend that got her the interview. Jim sat at the bar that was a part of the restaurant on the third floor and waited for her to come down. It was empty other than the bartender, a worker or two getting off shift for a quick beer, and Jim. The lights were dim inside the lobby that was met with a big set of stairs with a big red rug running the length of it. When she met him, they had a drink and then made their way to the room. He bought a bottle of wine from the bar and had the young bus boy take it up to their room. Danielle played music from her phone, the moon shined, and they drank straight from the bottle.

She was not what he pictured her to be from what Webster had said. He noticed her dimple on one side of her face when she smiled, but it was too late for Jim. His plan to get the truth from Danielle was already in play with his smart phone set to record every word that she said. He did not want to be a character witness in Webster's case because he was not good at lying and he knew very little about him. He knew that he only graduated high school because he was sent to the alternative school for juvenile delinquents where they gave out diplomas just to get the students out of their hair. He also couldn't count on his fingers all of the bars in Anchorage that Webster had been 86'd from.

"Do you want to watch a movie?" Jim asked.

"Yeah, that sounds nice. It's getting late though."

"We can watch most of a film."

"What kind of movie?" she asked.

"I saw it on the catalogue. It's a mystery," Jim said.

"Let's see if we can find it, she said. She turned on the TV and sat down on the bed against the low headboard. "What is the name of it?"

"I'm not sure. It was about the mystery of a broken TV."

"A what?" she asked.

"Yes," much like this one I assume," he said, walking over to the television. He unscrewed the back, picked it up and opened the sliding door to the balcony that faced the inlet. Jim held it over the railing and shut the door with his foot.

"What the hell are you doing?" Danielle asked as she pried the sliding door open.

"Do you want to see me drop it?"

"No. Why would I possibly want that?" she asked. "It'll definitely fuck up my chances for a job here."

"Wouldn't it be poetic," Jim asked, "losing two jobs over a television? Will you lie about this one too?"

"Who are you?" she asked.

"I told you who I was. You don't know me but I know who you are."

"He threatened to kill me, okay? I lied about his TV but I did what I had to do."

"Who threatened to kill you?" Jim asked, while the TV chord clanged in the wind against the railing.

"Webby did, but he was out if his mind."

Jim brought the TV back over the railing and put it on the stand. Danielle faltered, watching his fixed stare on the window. He was not looking out, but at his reflection, and for the first time not recognizing himself.

"Are you going to tell anyone what I told you? Did you know Webby then?"

"Yeah, I know him. I picked him up from jail and had to drive him back home. Should he expect a job when he gets back?"

"No. How was he? I didn't want—you were not there," she said.

"Jail was not good for him, but I guess you know him better than I do."

The glow of the moon was gone. Jim had the proof that he wanted, that she lied to the police. He had thought of Webster as someone who always got the short end of the stick and, now, for the first time, he could do something about it. Danielle led him backwards to the bed, holding both of his hands. He held onto her, waiting for the light to filter into the room. 📖

# In Flood Season

## Jed Myers

I dreamed a rock island.
     I lived there alone.
Sky, like the stone,
    gray, a great haze.
Sea a smooth tarnish,
     all the winds gone.
Nothing to burn.
     I wouldn't live long.
I thought of the streets,
     trees and cars,
houses and crowds,
    what had drowned.
I knew of no other
    island but mine,
this mountaintop.
    So I sang,
to no one, to all
    the cosmos. I sang
like a child. I howled
    like a dog, or a wolf.
I cried like a gull.
    Like an eagle I screeched.
I growled like a bear,
    or I tried.
I tried to roar
    like the fire we'd made,
to whisper like the smoke
    roof of the world.
I kissed the void
    and it chirped like a bird.

I stood and sang
                    on my rock till I woke.
Out of my throat,
                      a last voice cracked
the cracking of the last
                            cliffs of ice.

*Cloudbank*, 2015, Painting, by Judith Skillman

# Bookstore Poem #56
# In the library

Kevin J. O'Conner

1
The reflection
in the glass
of the light fixtures
hanging from the ceiling
do not
include me

The lines
of the window frames
curve gently inward
along with the light
the panes let through

The waste product
of electricity
obscures the rest

2
The reflections
in the wedge-shaped mirror
that decorates the corner
smooshes the room
into a shield

In that inverted world
I am too small
to be seen
amidst the clutter

but my escape route
is clear

# The External Me

## Sue Gale Pace

I am not a hero nor am I someone who has the energy and drive to overcome any obstacle. I am neither beautiful nor athletic. I'm a decent cook and a terrible pianist. I don't cheat on my husband or my taxes. I love my children.

I write fiction and non-fiction and poetry. I've been published in *Newsweek*. My novel can still be found on certain library shelves. I was writer-in-residence for Seattle University's Creative Writing program. I have taught workshops at national conventions and Young Author conferences.

That is the external me.

Then there is the internal me. She is a woman who sits at the computer trying to remember if she wrote the poem on the screen or if she found it in a literary journal and copied it because she liked it and wanted to study the internal rhythms and external alliteration; a metaphor, perhaps, of her own life.

I say the words of the poem aloud then analyze the choice of nouns and verbs. It seems like the kind of thing I would write. It seems to fit the world I inhabit. It seems this poem could be one I've written and even if it isn't, I'm usually scrupulous about giving credit to others where credit is due and there is no indication that this is someone else's poem.

I listen to the whir of the printer then take the single sheet from the tray and walk into the kitchen where my husband is buttering toast. I hand the paper to him.

"I'm putting together a file of old poems and I can't remember if I wrote this," I say. "Have I ever shown it to you?"

He brushes crumbs from his hands, reaches out a pale arm and scans the page. He frowns thoughtfully and hands it back.

"So," I ask, "did I write it?"

"I don't know who else could have."

He is careful of my feelings. He tries to be gentle and humorous and neutral. Neutral is important because I don't want to feel foolish or stupid. I reread the poem. I mentally delete a word that pops up twice in the second stanza. I move a phrase to a line further down. There is no feeling of familiarity but I can logically deduce these are the images I would choose. These are the rhythms I favor.

I return to my computer and tap the changes into the file that contains the poem and when I press "save" I close my eyes and give myself a pep talk. I am okay. My loss of memory is slight in the total context of life. I have made adjustments and I have compensated. So has my husband. So have my children. But tears sting my eyes. I liked the person I once was—before I lost my inner self to the haze of seizure medications—and I am sad to not have her with me.

A few years ago I sat in my parents' family room while my father told my mother about his golf game. My father tells a good tale and the story moved smoothly from golf with friends to golf with coworkers to one man in particular.

"We were on the way to the clubhouse and he had a seizure right there in the parking lot. It was because of his heart medicine and there he was, jerking around like a goddam puppet with all those people staring at him." Dad shifted uncomfortably in his recliner. "When he finally stopped you could tell from the smell that he'd not only pissed himself but he'd shit himself, too. I felt so sorry for the guy. I don't think any of us can know just what that moment meant to him."

"I can," I said.

"No, Susan. I don't think any of us can understand what he went through."

I tried to keep the edge out of my voice. "I'm epileptic, Dad."

My mother was on the couch, crocheting an afghan. Her voice was almost a whisper. "I read that calling someone epileptic is offensive, like calling them a homo or a retard."

I refused to be sidetracked and my own voice instantly filled the room with decades of anger. "I've told you both this before. I wasn't just a dreamy kid who didn't pay attention. I have temporal lobe epilepsy. The neurologist says I've probably had it my whole life. A few years ago it morphed into something worse. I've been on medication for grand mal seizures for ten years. I can understand."

There was confusion on my father's face, a long pause, then an abrupt nod. I was forty-three years old and my father finally got it. I, too, have lost control of my bowels and jerked around like a goddam puppet. I, too, have been the object of someone's pity.

I tuck that incident deep into my center. It joins the lost poem. It joins the images and sounds and confusion that, try as I might, I cannot seem to translate into coherent sentences. When I am being whimsical, I picture those lost bits and pieces holding hands and waiting, like frightened and dutiful servants, for the real me to come home.

As a child, I had many, many falls down stairwells, off cliffs and bicycles, and tree branches and beds. Twice, I fell into rushing rivers. Once into a deep, green pond. Often, I crashed my bike. I fell on roller skates. It was attributed to day-dreaming and clumsiness and inattention and naughtiness. As an adult, I was considered funny by my friends, eccentric by my enemies, and imaginative by my husband. Forty years of marriage have proved to me that being seen as imaginative is a gift.

This "imaginative behavior" became even more pronounced during my third pregnancy. The twitching and hallucinations intensified though the gestation, labor, delivery, and increased again through two years' worth of nursing my daughter.

In the middle of all that, I was referred to a neurologist. He was small and quick and inherently skeptical. He read the referral and frowned over gold rimmed glasses. "Why are you here?"

"I keep having these visions, sort of dreamlike, only during the day, and people no one else can see are talking to me."

"Talking to you?

"Yes. They yell at me or, sometimes, they ask me questions."

"And no one else can see these, um, people?"

"No. Just me."

"And do you answer these questions?"

"Of course not! They aren't real!"

At which point he scheduled an EEG and a series of head x-rays. A week later he called me. "Well, you don't have a brain tumor but you do have some hinky EEG patterns in the temporal lobe area pointing to a partial complex seizure disorder." He sounded excited. "You have no idea how many patients with Schizoaffective Disorder come in with the same presenting symptoms. I'll send my report to your personal physician but I think it's best if you don't take any heavy-duty medications until your pregnancy is resolved."

By that I assumed he meant everything was to be put on hold until after the delivery. Then put on hold again, for two years, since I had decided to nurse this daughter like I had the other two. It was years before my body was wholly my own again. I walked wherever I needed to go. I lost or misplaced a great deal of time, information and (sadly) money. I twitched and jittered. But I had healthy babies who became, eventually, healthy adults.

I worried about misplacing my children so I began a series of medication trials. It took a while since I was allergic to one and others made me sleep twenty hours a day. Finally, the right one came around. I tolerated it until, like many who suffer seizures, I grew lax and had the mother of all grand mals. It scared me into beginning yet another round of medication tryouts, with a variety of truly dangerous side effects, but I gritted my teeth and kept at it and, bottom line, I have been completely seizure free for over fifteen years.

I am not the person I was before that first grand mal but, in spite of the side effects of my medication, I have become a reasonable facsimile of my former self. I miss her, though. The brighter me. The quirky me who didn't have occasional short term memory problems or, at the very least, the one who remembered writing a poem about kites and the tug of dreams against a steady wind of the bland and familiar.

After my father's golf story, he rose from the recliner, kissed me on the forehead, patted my back in that one-armed fashion of those who are uncomfortable with the expression of emotions, and headed to the den. Driving home that night, I pulled into a Safeway parking lot and tried to sort out the evening. I thought my father was aware of what was happening to me. My mother had stayed with my children as I went through one after

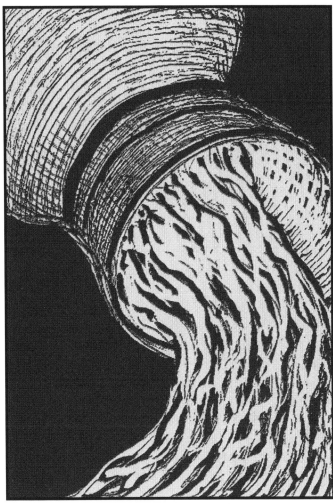

*Living Waters*, 2017, Pen, Ink, and Marker, by Mary Zore

another allergic reactions to medications. During family gatherings (Thanksgiving, Easter, summer picnics) I had even shared a couple of poignant and, I hoped, lightly humorous stories about seizures at inconvenient times and places. My father was there, in his recliner, when those stories were told.

Given all that, how could he have insisted that I wouldn't be able to understand his coworker's experience?

I ask that even as I rush to my father's defense. He isn't stupid or uneducated. He did what many people do when faced with a painful reality. He denied its existence and, to be honest, my mother joined him there.

In fact, we all rode that horse for a while.

After that conversation with my father—a night I privately refer to as "the unveiling"—my parents reacted to the diagnosis of epilepsy as if it was a temporary condition like the measles or chicken pox—something unpleasant but quickly gotten over. Then they graduated to the idea that it was simply an inconvenient flaw—like left-handedness or color blindness. Something that was an occasional annoyance but certainly, with a little effort, a flaw that could be gotten around.

There are many reasons why it took so long, decades, to diagnose my temporal lobe seizures. I even went to counseling and talked about the rare but confusing hallucinations as if they were dreams. I should have been honest with my counselor but I am someone who always asks, "is this my fault?" first.

And, honestly, I was quite willing to live with confusion. It was comfortable and, sometimes, entertaining. In fact, my conceit was that these early flights of imagination proved how special I was. I had a family. I was published. People envied me.

And then things changed.

My middle daughter came home to find me on the floor with bruised legs and arms and a cut and bleeding mouth. I was in my office, tapping away at my typewriter (in the days before word processing or computing), and I remember feeling my internal world slip sideways. Apparently, I fell backwards and proceeded to whack myself again and again against both chair and desk until, finally, the seizure subsided.

No other full-length books have been published. I also quit writing plays. I kept with short stories, though. And poems, personal essays, and shorter non-fiction pieces. I do not tell people why I am concentrating on the shorter stuff. I don't want flip statements about being in good company because a lot of very talented people had seizures. I don't want lectures on Dostoyevsky, Tolstoy or even Susan Boyle. I want to concentrate on the over one hundred pieces published in both literary and commercial venues. I want to feel good about my craft, not bad about it.

Over the years, I have not been particularly secretive with my diagnosis but neither have I taken out an ad in the newspaper announcing why there were years when I walked everywhere. I never put down the diagnosis on a job application.

Sometimes I don't recognize people and I perfected the sentence, "Please tell me your name again, I must confess I am Proper Noun challenged." The reason I am not terribly forthcoming with my history of seizures is threefold. First, I do not want the looks of pity, however brief. Secondly, I do not want the assurances of friends and family that I am exaggerating. Everyone has lapses, they assure me. I'm making something out of nothing. I should listen to their own stories of forgetfulness and silly mistakes. Why just the other day they forgot to pick up their daughter at soccer, where they parked their car, even the name of their sister-in-law.

Thirdly, there are the competitive types who want to assure me how truly awful-horrible-terrifying their own life, seizures, marriage, arthritis, parents, kids, exes, job, cancer, neighbors are. In the world, heaven knows, there will always be someone worse off. At the very least, the message goes, I'm a lucky duck and I should be counting my blessings.

I do count my blessings. My children. My husband. My friends. My family. The fact that I live in this beautiful little corner of the world. I have food and clean clothes and I live in a small but quite serviceable condo. I have health insurance.

I know I am a lucky duck. I count the good years. I count the good doctors. I count the effective medications. I appreciate having the ability to drive and swim and dance with abandon. I count the laughter and not the tears.

Over the years, I have read books, blogs, and magazine articles that are profoundly anti-medication. Be your true, artistic self, they urge. Don't let your mind and creativity become befuddled with the toxins used to control your seizures.

The thing these anti-medication folks don't understand is that after that first grand mal seizure I felt that some essential part of me was forever lost and I could not find my way to it or to home, either. I felt like a hollow woman, like a partially built house without furniture or electricity or plumbing. No laughter in that house. No love. No light. Just a roof and an ice cold floor. Just walls and echoes. The hollowness lasted for weeks.

My current medication gives me the illusion of belonging in my body. It gives the woman I used to call myself a place to enter, to sup on bread and good soup and to sleep without the panic that comes of perpetually falling down an elevator shaft.

A few weeks ago, I handed my now-grown daughter the poem that I hoped was mine, and told her I was thinking of writing a personal essay about being someone with epilepsy. "It would be a small essay," I said, "because I know, objectively speaking, I have it easy."

She tilted her head. "What do you mean by that?"

I told her about my best friend in high school whose son went to college, got a good job doing something with computers, and died during a grand mal episode. He was inconsistent in keeping up his medication regime. A lot of people couldn't understand why it was so hard for him to simply take the prescribed number of pills.

I could understand, I told my daughter. I tried to let her know how I feared the "hollow woman" but also how I hated not being who I used to be.

My daughter said she remembered clearly that grand mal. She confessed how frightening it was to come home to a mother who was bloodied and disoriented. She was fourteen and it was the first time she had thought about having a parent die. Her voice quavered a bit and she swallowed, hard, before finally saying, "You only talk about what you have lost and not what you have gained."

"What have I gained?" I asked.

She talked about growing up with parents who showed up for sports and plays and dance recitals. She talked about having a normal life. She talked about feeling safe, as a child, and not worrying whether one or the other parent would go away, perhaps permanently. She talked about having children of her own and wanting to feel okay when we took them to the playground or the store or hiking. She talked about not always waiting for the other shoe to drop.

"Back then, I didn't want to think about you having one of those seizures when you crossed the street or at my graduation or while you were in the bathtub. I didn't want to come home, ever again, to you all bloody and in a mess."

I nodded.

"Now," she continued, "I don't want my own children to see you that way, ever."

"Same here," I said.

What I didn't tell her was how hard it is to give up the wish of turning back the clock to the time when the external me and the internal me presented a united front. Logically, I accept that a united me is only a figment of my imagination. Emotionally, I am conflicted. I want to feel complete and confident but there are the missing words and the missing names and the missing months and money.

"The medication is here to stay," I tell my daughter. "Did I show you the new poem I am working on?"

"Yes," she smiles and hands me back the sheet of paper. "I read it twenty years ago. It's lovely." 📖

# Elwha River Night Walk

## Christopher Pierson

Walk along a backcountry river trail
near bear droppings and gutted elk carcass.
Count the trees to identify patterns
in their 300 year-old calligraphy,
note the direction of the river.

Your only guide on a moonless night,
a dark-green glow from the depths
surrounds you  as you wobble on the edge of the trail—
let it swallow you,
and read the hieroglyphs
of those old-growth branches.

*Mother,* Photograph, by Theodore C. Van Alst, Jr.

# The True Vocation

## Mary Randall

### Preface

That was the year Mama worked in the credit Department of Milan's Jewelers. We lived in a little house that had once been a summer cabin in the hills of north Oakland. The only child of a single, working parent, I walked the eight blocks home from school alone, stopping every day at the foot of the steep flight of steps that led to our door to bring in the mail. One day the mailbox contained a large manila envelope addressed to me, Belle Randall. It looked like a letter for grown ups, and I knew it was against the law to open anyone else's mail, but there remained the incredible fact of my name on the front. I tore open the envelope. Inside was a manuscript with a note from the editors of *The New Yorker*, telling me that they liked my story and would reconsider it, if I would make some changes to the ending.

It was dark by the time my mother got home. With her return, the lights came on. While our casserole was warming in the oven, I gave her the envelope, pointing out my name, in case I had done something wrong. She laughed and explained: she had written the story and submitted it to the magazine. Why was it addressed to me? I don't remember her exact words, but there were few boundaries between us. She told me that she liked the name—the name she had given me—so much that she had borrowed it, for the purposes of getting published. She hoped I didn't mind. Writers often did that. It was a *nom de plume*.

Last week, digging through cardboard boxes stored in our basement, I found the yellowed manuscript of my mother's story. I have saved it all these years, with no particular purpose in mind. I don't know if my mother ever made the changes *The New Yorker* requested, but I do know she never published it, nor any other story. The demands of being a single parent, and, perhaps, ambivalence about her own ambition, silenced her.

—Belle Randall

\* \* \* \*

There was a large sampler in a carved black walnut frame, hanging in the upstairs hall of our home when I was a little girl. It said, "Honor thy father and thy mother." It hung just off the main hallway, in the little side passage that traveled the length of the wing where all of us children had our rooms. None of us could get to our rooms without passing it. When I did wrong, that sampler used to give me a chill. After I passed it, I could feel a draft on my back. It made the hall cold.

That was Gertrude's work. The house was full of it. There were garlands of petit point roses on the bell pulls, petit point covers on all the dining room chairs, and more moral messages, all worked in petit point, all signed modestly in the lower right hand corner G. v. W. because our last name was von Werk.

I never really knew Gertrude. There were ten years and a sister between us. I was only seven when she left home and she never came back. I have an image of her, playing tag with me in the garden. Laughing, darting quick as a hummingbird in and out of the shrubbery, while I plodded after her. She let me catch her under the lilac bush. The sunlight tangled in her fawn-colored hair. There were little beads of sweat on her full upper lip. But that was forty years ago. One day she packed her bag and put on a little straw bonnet, a plain white blouse, and a long black skirt, and went to join the Carmelites.

Once, a long time later, I saw the convent where she lives. Driving down from Carmel toward Big Sur you pass the mission, and then before the car dips down into the valley, there is a moment when you see the convent spread out below you, across the valley to the south. It looked like a lovely place to live, looking down on it from the hill, so near the sea, the grounds all green and open to the sun. But as we drove across the flat of the valley, I saw the iron fence. The buildings seemed to withdraw as we got nearer. It was a lonely place when you got up close. I suppose God sees it as I saw it first, from above.

No one told me she was leaving. My sister, Theresa, buttoned me into one of my Sunday dresses and a white organdy pinafore and told me to button my own shoes, she had to see about Clara. Mama came rustling in after a while, all dressed up in her new white summer suit. She buttoned my shoes and clamped my bonnet on me as if I were a kid. I didn't know where we were going, all dressed up.

We had been to church already.

Theresa and Clara were sitting waiting on the sofa in the upstairs hall. They looked like a pair of Alices in Wonderland. Clara whispered that Gertrude was going away to the convent. I looked over the banister, down into the hall downstairs. The door was wide open. Gertrude was standing down there, in her plain black and white outfit. She was looking out into the front garden. I suppose it really wasn't sudden at all but I was seven and no one told me 'til then. Mother had her new hat on. Father was standing beside the carriage, holding the horses. He had on his top hat and his long coat. He looked like an old and scornful crane. I knew, the way he put us in the buggy, he didn't like what was going on. He sat me on Mama's lap and said, "For once you can wrinkle your skirt." We were quiet riding Main Street to the station. It must have been Sunday, the streets were so empty. Mother reached over and patted Gertrude's hand and said, "Our little saint."

Father called back once, "Take a good look, Gertrude, this is the last you'll ever see of Annaburg," as if he hoped she might change her mind about leaving.

The train was crying out in the distance when we got to the station. Gertrude laughed and chattered (she made little gurgling sounds and said "I can't believe it's here!"). Her hands moved as she talked as if she were tatting. She leaned over Mama and me, patting our cheeks, and dabbing kisses on us. And then the train was there, black and hot-looking under the sun, puffing great black balloons of smoke and making so much noise I couldn't hear what

Father was saying to Mother and Gertrude. He carried her little bag into the train. We watched them through the window talking together, and then Father got off. His eyes above his beard looked tired. His cheeks were flushed. The train began to move. Mama got her handkerchief out, as if she expected to cry.

I saw Gertrude staring out at us. She wasn't laughing anymore. She looked surprised and a little dismayed, as one does when something is suddenly real that has only been imagined before. She looked at us almost reproachfully. She forgot to wave, and the train carried her away. She hadn't even taken her coat with her.

In the carriage going home, Clara began to weep in earnest. She said now she would never see Gertrude again. Her face got all red and her hat was crooked. Mother said, in that sweet voice she reserved for religion, "Clara, that is our little part in this sacrifice." She helped Clara blow her nose.

"We'll go see her, Clara," I said.

"Oh, no. Will we, Mama?" Clara was eight years old. She knew more about this thing that had happened. "No," Mama said, Clara was right, we wouldn't. Carmelites were a cloistered order and they only spoke at certain times and to certain people. Clara began to whoop again. Mother went right on talking. Gertrude's hair would be cut off, her name would be changed to Sister Mary Something. She would be everyone's sister, not ours. That didn't sound nice at all to me. But I saw Mother thought it a fine thing. Her eyes were wide and dark, behind the veil of her hat, the way they always got when she talked about religious matters. She was using that sweet, almost lisping, voice. "Your sister has done a noble, self-sacrificing thing. It isn't as if she were a girl who couldn't have married. She had several offers. But she gave up all that most of us hold dear to devote her life to prayer and meditation. She will be the bride of Christ." I patted Clara's hand, "Maybe Gertrude won't stay, Clara. Maybe she won't like it and they'll send her home."

Mama gasped, "Not stay! She has to. I told her that. Now that she's told everyone and gone—people would laugh." The awfulness of this possibility silenced even Clara.

Mama sat, straight as the line she drew between right and wrong, her Manila straw bonnet properly level atop her rather yellow curls. The veil came down over her face and tied with a black velvet ribbon around her throat. It cast little shadows like a web across her cheeks. She broke the silence to remind me, "Don't crush my skirt, Dear, stay away. Stay in your own corner, Dear."

Well, Clara wanted to know, what would Gertrude do all day, if she couldn't talk. "Prayer and meditation!" Mama brightened up, "and embroidery. She will embroider altar linens and garments for priests. You see, all the time she spent on petit point was not wasted. She was learning a skill that will be useful to her now."

Papa turned on her from his perch on the driver's seat, "My God, Anna, you talked one child into Carmelites. You want them all to join?"

"August," Mama said, "there are worse things that can happen to a girl than a religious life."

"True," he said, "and to many men. You'd have done both me and the girls a favor had you married the Lord, yourself." I looked at Father on his perch. Tears were running down his cheeks and hiding in his beard. He looked like a wet bird.

We turned off Main and drove along Water Street, between the rows of drowsy houses resting under the sun. At one corner, two little boys in overalls knelt in the dust of the road, drawing a circle for a game of marbles.

Father didn't turn the horses onto Elm Street the way he should have. He kept right on driving down Water, past the Normal School. Mama looked annoyed. "August, what are you doing now?"

"I'm going to Frank Weaver's house."

Mama's face smoothed out. "Good, we'll tell them that Gertrude is gone."

Mr. Weaver published *The Annaberg Record*. He was Papa's best friend. Privately, Mother didn't think much of the Weavers, even though they were Catholics. But she was always very polite to Mrs. Weaver, because Mrs. Weaver wrote the Ladies' page in *The Record*. In spite of Mama, Father and Mr. Weaver went right on being best friends. Evenings, summer and winter, after cook

THE
**NEW YORKER**
NO. 25 WEST 43RD STREET

EDITORIAL OFFICES
BRYANT 9-8200

December 27, 1951

Dear Mrs. Randall:

      The editors hadn't forgotten about,
or lost, the two manuscripts of THE TRUE VOCATION, but
we have indeed kept it longer than we usually do or
should, and to our sincere apologies I have to add the
confession that the story is not yet in shape and that
the fault is mine. If you will let us hold it a little
longer, say till the end of January, I think I can promise
you a decision on it, one way or the other. And if you
would prefer instead that we mail the two manuscripts
back to you, we will, of course, immediately do so.

                    Sincerely yours,

                    William Maxwell
                    William Maxwell

Mrs. Mary Randall
2309 Bowditch Street
Berkeley 4, Calif.

had washed the dishes and put them away, found the two of them, sitting in our kitchen, in their shirtsleeves, drinking beer, and talking, sometimes late into the night. In the winter they took off their shoes and rested their stockinged feet on the open oven door.

When we drove up to the Weavers' place, Mrs. Weaver was rocking in the hammock on the front porch, like a feather bed, airing in the wind. She was a big, flabby, loose-talking woman. Mr. Weaver was down by the side of the house, pumping water into a big bucket to pour on his flowers. He put down the bucket and came across the lawn toward our buggy, his face shining with welcome.

"Well, this is an honor, August, and Anna with you." He turned to call Mrs. Weaver, but she was already struggling up from the depths of the hammock.

Father ignored the greeting. "Frank, we just saw Gertrude off."

"Well, come on in. We'll have a little something."

"Yes, do, Mrs. von Werk," Mrs. Weaver panted, coming up behind her husband. "I'll tell Patty" and, as good as her word, she began calling to her in a sing-song voice as she walked toward the house. Wherever Patty might be, I thought, she was sure to hear. "Listen how she calls," Clara whispered. A large colored woman came to the front door. "Yes, ma'am."

"Patty, the von Werks are here," Mrs. Weaver said, as if Patty had been waiting for us.

The grownups arranged themselves in the rockers on the wide veranda, under the shade of the vines. Clara and I sat side by side on the top step, afraid to play because we had on our good dresses and our long white stockings. We looked at each other and folded our hands, waiting to see what Patty would bring us.

We heard her inside the house, and then the drum of dishes and glasses as she rolled a little cart along the hall out to the veranda.

Mama spread her white skirt and sighed loudly, "Mrs. Weaver, dear, our Gertrude is gone." Mrs. Weaver shook her head and said, as if she had nothing to say that quite fit the occasion, "It's come at last."

Father leaned back in his rocker. He looked at Mama and spoke in a voice that sounded as if it were coming from inside a cave, "And that's not the worst of it, not by far." Everyone looked at him. None of us were prepared for what he said next. I've often wondered if he had come to the Weavers' with this purpose in mind, but I don't think so. Once he got there, I think he was just inspired. I see us, as I saw us then, caught, by some accident of memory in that moment, all staring at Papa, wondering what he meant. He sighed and covered his eyes, reverently, with one hand. "Anna, too, wants to join an order."

Mrs. Weaver put up her hand and tapped her mouth, three times, ceremoniously, "Your wife is married."

Father waved that aside with his hat, "That makes no difference. The church has not forgotten those who marry. For those with a true vocation, there is still the Third Order, the order of the world." He licked his lips. "Of course, she must sacrifice, she must abstain—no social life, no finery. Anna will live as Gertrude does, pray when Gertrude prays, but to do it in the world. She has decided. We're very proud of her."

Mother stood there staring at the back of Father's head.

"Why, Mrs. von Werk! You have a 'vocation'? You feel called?" Mrs. Weaver blinked.

Mother said, "Well," as if she were tasting words.

Mr. Weaver interrupted her stiffly, "August is joking."

"I am not," Papa said flatly. He looked sideways at Mama leaning back in her chair with her eyes closed. "Anna was saying, just driving down here, "Worse things could happen to a person. Uncurl my hair," says she, "Cut it off. That gold chain on my bosom, that watch" says she, "How can I rise heavenward with an anchor like that. Cast it off."

"I'm a selfish man," Papa explained. "I talked it all over with Father Lannigan. He says these women misunderstand hairshirts. He says a corset is a crown of thorns. She can do penance right here at home wearing tight little shoes and her curl papers. Why, to hear him tell it, them that retires to the convent are just leaving the field for want of strength."

He swallowed his drink in a gulp and unfolded his long sad body from the rocker.

"Come children. Come Anna. I'm a selfish man. I want my supper." Mama had not found her voice. She followed him meekly down the steps and across the lawn.

Father shook the reins. "We must go. Good day. Print it, Frank, print it."

Mother fell back in the seat beside me. The buggy lurched away, leaving the Weavers standing there, in the dust, staring after us.

In the carriage, Clara said out loud, "Papa made a scene," and no one denied it.

Mama sat all doubled up on herself, the rest of the way home. Her hat was on crooked. She didn't tell me to stay off her skirts, but I did. I stayed in my corner of the carriage as it swayed along past the church, past the Normal School, toward the uncertain haze of late afternoon at the end of the avenue of trees. As we turned into our own drive, I saw that she was crying.

Papa got down from the driver's seat and helped her from the carriage. Mama spoke uncertainly, as if repeating a phrase learned by heart, the meaning of which she did not remember. "I'll make you sorry for this, August," she said.

Father stood beside the carriage, looking up at her twisted face. "I'm sure you will, my dear," he said, but he was smiling.

The next day, the Ladies' page of *The Record* told all about Gertrude leaving and Mama deciding. It said that Mrs. von Werk was withdrawing from her many social activities to devote her time to religious contemplation. Theresa and Clara and I cut the article out and pasted it in our scrapbook.

The following morning, the Ladies' Altar Society began arriving in surprised little flurries, one by one. They all said Mama was awfully noble. Father Lannigan came in the afternoon, solemn as a Bishop, and talked to her for a long time in the parlor with the door closed. Father spent the day drawing diagrams on the ground with a stick and talking to a carpenter about adding a wing to the house, in which Mama might have her own room, and a little chapel, where she could meditate and pray.

When the new wing was finished, Mama moved into it. And after Father died, she spent quite a bit of time praying, in the chapel he had built for her when she was not yet old. 📖

*Faith and Urban Life*, Photograph, by Manit Chaotragoongit

# Biblical Summer, 2017

## Sherry Rind

I long for the days of simple faith
when King Kong and Godzilla duked it out,
stubbing their toes on skyscrapers
and breaking off radio towers like twigs.
Oh, the joy of screaming until we puked.
And then it was over.

They're real enough.
Instead of evolution's organic soup,
Godzilla bathed in nuclear muck.
I'd be angry, too,
with those radiation keloids.

Say he wasn't shot off Empire State,
Kong would've gone like Ishi
or the last passenger pigeon
housed in a museum
until death from a white man's disease.

We know, even before they loom into sight
there's always some hotshot
who blows his load and becomes a just dessert
and always a man who says *wait*
and a beautiful woman everybody loves
for being kinder than god or man
and the extras who get trampled—

those would be us.
But we know ways of escape
in helicopters or sewer system or the London underground.
We are as ants to those monsters,

yet we sweep them away every time
and love them so much that we bring them back
so we can win again.

*Guilded Life*, by Judy Xie

# The Wisdom of Finishing

## Jack Remick

Finishing.

The wisdom of finishing tells you that to finish is to understand how to begin. When I taught at conferences, I opened with this joke—Writers have just three problems—How to start. How to keep going. How to finish. When you lick those three, you are in.

The beginning predicts an end. The end is predicated on a beginning. For the writer, the worst case is the stop. A poem, I tell poets, should end, it shouldn't just stop. The idea of an ending implies a structure. The idea of structure implies a shape. A poem that stops has no shape. It has no ending. The wisdom of finishing has its own problems.

How do you know when it's finished?

How do you know when to let it go?

If you just stop, you have done nothing. It is a bridge to nowhere, a road that peters out in the middle of the desert. A path to the top of nowhere.

Finishing, to me, implies not just a thought, but also a how—how do you begin in such a way that the ending is implied in the beginning? The wisdom of time gives us triplets. What walks on four legs in the morning, two legs at noon, three legs at dusk? The riddle implies a three-part structure. A life, according to Sophocles, is divided into a beginning, a middle, and end. We are born, we shop, we die.

The tripartite structure pervades the Western mind. In the wisdom of beginnings we see the wisdom of finishing. But the sense of time in the West is broken. And that, the question of time, inserts itself into the question of the beginning.

Had I written in the time of the Maya, I might have seen time in units of katuns. I might see a cluster of katuns as a baktun. I might see a cluster of baktuns as a sun. I might see the fifth sun as the end of time. In the Mayan mind, was the beginning inherent in the ending? To the Maya, time cycles into a series of beginnings. But the continuum is a hard nut for the Western mind.

Say that a life is on a continuum that can last for one day, one hour, 100 years. Faced with that, how does the writer of memoir begin even to think of finishing?

I know this—to finish brings me a sense of joy. If I begin a piece, I start with emotion, feeling, or a sense of place. Then, I imagine an ending. Without the ending, I have no sense of direction, no sense of purpose, only a sense of going nowhere. To see an ending, is to suggest 100 beginnings, 100 forks, 1000 choices. *If—then*, becomes the guide. If I do this, then my characters must do that. The if—then is a chain of guideposts, of mile markers along the way. If I have an ending in mind, then I can move from place to place on a line of divagations—subplots off the main line but always aimed at the ending, which might not be the ending you see at the beginning. Implicit in this is change, and the idea of obstacle. No story moves in a straight line except the dreadfully boring one. The difference between a Bach fugue and a Max Reger fugue is the difference between a chance encounter with a beast in the jungle and an encounter with a beast in a cage in a zoo. The confinement of Reger limits the possibility of the fugue whereas Bach by introducing anomalies produces a circus of accidents.

In nature, they say, there are no straight lines—except the line in quartz crystals, the lines in a grove of trees, the fall of water from a cataract. In writing it is the straight line that is the death knell for the writer. To finish is to overcome the accident, to conquer the obstacle, to value the anomaly.

In the beginning is the unknown. The unknown we learn of as we go, and the logic of going implies that the end will be there. If I climb a mountain, I expect to arrive at a summit. From the summit I see where I have been. I learned that Blake Edwards, who brought us the Pink Panther movies, always started with an ending. He then said, how did I get here? What comes before?

So the wisdom of finishing suggests that the beginning can be found. In this idea, I developed the notion of the walk back through time. It works this way. You have a beginning. A moment in time. You ask yourself what happened five minutes, one hour, one week, one month, one year, four years before the opening. So the logic of the ending is that every beginning is already an ending. The complexity of structure exaggerates our consciousness and implies the work of the mind we cannot know. You cannot interrogate your unconscious mind using the apparatus of your consciousness. Consciousness is a narrow window while the unconscious is a vast and complicated sea that speaks only in metaphor, never in logical syntax, always speaks in symbols, never in concrete objects with a single meaning. So, the structure comes, not from the conscious but from the unconscious as it tries to make sense of the journey.

Every story is a journey begging to be concluded. In this as, Aristotle says, art is an imitation of life. Life, however, is a defiant and rebellious child we spend years trying to tame only to find that in taming, we open other domains. Blaise Pascal wrote—*combien de royaumes nous ignorent!*

Finishing is of course a dream. If the beginning is an already made ending, then there is no such thing as a finish, but only another opening. Still, I sense when a piece is finished. I look at it, I see the way it develops, I see the plot points and, in the subplots, I watch characters develop with their objects and I see the characters wrapping up their subplots aiming at the finale—and when that happens, I, along with Conrad Aiken, say *Tetelestai*. It is finished. It is enough. Never the life, but the journey, and there can be hundreds of journeys in a life. To end, is a problem. To begin is a problem. But never to end is a horror.

The wisdom of finishing then is to know how and why and what. How do you know this? When is the beginning *the beginning*? When is the ending *the ending*? Do you know why an action happens and why the character reacts? In this we see both Pavlov and ourselves as god. Pavlov because we make the character react, god because we build the world the character inhabits. And then what?

Always the existential questions—what are we? What are we doing? Where are we going? What will we do when we get there? In the beginning, the ending shows. But always that question—what are we? Why are we here and how do we get here?

In the evolution of the mind, and mind is what brain does, the ride-along questions are always—who are we? Is this real? Is this a dream? I think of Pedro Calderón de la Barca and his *La vida es sueño*. Sigismundo awakes up—or does he? Is he dreaming that he has just waked up? Is he dreaming that he is waking up in a dream that he is dreaming about waking up in? This is the labyrinth of mind where Pirandello searches for meaning and an answer to the questions—who are we? What are we? Why are we?

To finish is to come to an end and to say this is all. *Tetelestai.* It is enough. To finish is to accept nothingness, the answer to all these fundamental questions—Who am I? Nobody. What am I? Nothing. Why am I? Because you are a beginning.

In the end, at the finish, the writer has to ask—is it done? Is it enough?

Is this ending the last ending? Is there a forever? The answer to that is, of course, no.

No is the finish. Niente. Nada. Nihil. Nothing. 📖

# a day at the avian cafe

## Frank Rossini

junco wren & sparrow flit
& flicker from bobbing
rosemary boughs to tubes
of seed & nuts
hung outside
our kitchen window

the big gray squirrel
is here perched
on the roof he contemplates
flying to the suet cage
embracing it with all
his little fingers his bushy
tail falling straight
to the cement
bath below where towhees
splash & shiver the cold
water from their feathers

three crows in black
robes stroll through wet
grass discussing
corvid business  a swarm
of bushtits dart by as I wash
the morning's dishes

in the evening my wife returns
from work  I tell her
how all day the nuthatch never comes
to rest but grabs a single seed

or a bit of nut & rushes
off to eat in the plum's
blossoming branches  we watch
the finches occupy every perch
of the three feeders
for their evening meal then leave
to light the oaks & settle
the night with a muted
rustle of feathers

*Remember Me*, Orange, California, 2017,
Photograph, by Kathleen Gunton

# Coyote Country

## Kathleen Smith

The whole plateau swims in fog: a liquid
landscape where songs of ghost dancers
swirl around. You got the call, so now
you're driving toward the hospital bed
where she drifts in and out of worlds and stories.

The radio is silent. Loose connections due to old age.
Then suddenly, between big river and the lake, it blurts
out its name: 99.9 Coyote Country. He did not need
formal announcement. You know you are on trickster
ground. There are no road signs in coyote's land.

Anything can happen here.
Anything can happen now.
The fog curls close
like a bright blanket sitting heavy on your shoulders.
Like the blanket of near death so soft and strangely familiar.

# The Arrogance of the Princely Mind

## Jack Remick

We live in an Age of Self. The Self devoid of its deities is lost and at war with the common good. Stripped of its connections, the self enters into a time of pure selfish existence. Without bounds on its greed, without regard for the other, the princely mind takes itself to be divine. All others exist so the princely mind can achieve its goal of total possession of everything in existence.

In the last few decades of the twenty-first century, we saw the self-elevated to princely status where only the "I" mattered. All existence was filtered through the lens of the "I." This tendency flattened out the culture of the others.

In the culture of the others, that is the culture of the past, it was incumbent upon each of us to think of the other while gathering for ourselves. In the past, we were encouraged and taught to think about the pain of the other, to see the anguish of loss, to understand what stamina of mind and being it took to stand on a corner, palm out, asking for alms.

Elevated to princely status through inheritance of wealth and assumptive greed, the princely mind does not see the ruin of civilization in the outstretched palm, but sees only the worthlessness of that other. The princely mind imagines itself at the pinnacle of the world. And in this insanity, there is destruction.

In extremis, the princely mind has no redeemer, has no hope, has no recourse because in death as in life the only essence of existence was the self, and so the princely mind, in extremis, laments itself, poor me, I must live forever. The mirror of time reflects on his or her own anguish as if divorced from the entire spectrum of humanity. Yet, we all came out of Africa.

In this time, we need to look not at philosophy, not at religion, but at biology to understand who and what we are. We must look to science for knowledge of who we are and how we came to be who we are and for the tools to understand how it is possible for the princely mind to distance itself from its own science of being.

What is the princely mind in this second decade of the twenty-first century? What is it if not the self exalting itself at the expense of all others, at the cost of endless pain and the damage of greed. The princely mind's arrogance sets itself apart from the ebb and flow of evolution to find in its self-love not the peace of no desire but the anguish of endless and insatiable and infinite greed.

The princely mind in its arrogance never asks how much is enough, but asks instead how much more can I acquire?

The princely mind, then, is the apotheosis of greed and exemplifies the death of democracy in a flood of gold and silver and possessions and jewels. The princely mind is a desert of its own making, not the result of millennia of natural and sexual selection. It is an aberration, a distortion, a fraud.

In the Paleolithic era, women chose males for breeding based on three traits—speed, size, aggression.

In this, the end of the Anthropocene, women choose males for breeding based on wealth, power, and position.

In the evolution of the princely mind, women are a reward, but the princely mind, ignorant of its own origins, believes that it, the arrogant mind, is the one choosing. In this, the princely mind is a complete desert of ignorance, a field of emptiness surrounded by monuments to itself—all at the expense of all others.

Eric Kandel writes, in *The Age of Insight*, that artists must learn to pay attention to the neurosciences. Writers, it seems, must also learn to pay attention to biology and desire.

Sigmund Freud knew that he did not know enough about biology to understand the human mind and its workings in its totality. He understood that all brains are the same, all driven by the same evolutionary energy, but he did not know why. He did not know the mechanisms. In his humility, Freud achieved a certain arrogance for which we can forgive him because he knew the truth lay in the body as it had evolved and he knew that he did not know the truth but anticipated it when he said that we are nothing but chemistry.

When Eric Kandel decided on a profession, as he writes in *In Search of Memory, The Emergence of a New Science of Mind*, he chose psychiatry so that he could find where in the human brain the ego, the id, and the superego resided. In his research, he discovered that that unholy triad did not exist in a locus but was a construct of mind. He saw that Freud was right—we are naught but chemistry—and Kandel led the notion to show us how the mind sees, how the mind constructs reality, how the man exists in his moments of forgetfulness, and he showed us how art filters into a mind and how edges do not exist except as gradations of light and dark.

In this, science of mind, the princely mind is lost in a Paleolithic swamp of selfishness, never seeing or understanding who or what it is. It lives only in the first of the selective triads—wealth. Wealth to the princely mind buys position. Wealth buys power. But forgiveness? No sin, no crime, no transgression cannot be bought with wealth and so the princely mind is not accountable to anyone or anything. But the glorified self it worships is a sham.

Thomas Gray writes in "Elegy in a Country Churchyard":

The boast of heraldry, the pomp of pow'r,
    And all that beauty, all that wealth e'er gave,
Awaits alike th' inevitable hour.
    The paths of glory lead but to the grave.

The princely mind lives in a constant denial of death, lives in a universe of ignorance, and dies in a splurge of nothingness because the arrogant prince does not see himself as a human being evolved from others, but sees himself as a great and powerful being, sui generis, the self-made man who owes nothing to the rest of humanity. In this the arrogance reaches its pinnacle of shame. In this the arrogant prince lives in a darkness of mind where there is no light except the light that fires his own eyes.

The princely mind is an impoverished island devoid of compassion, empathy, sympathy, and unity. To be human is to understand how we came to be and how we share not just the same brain but the same constructs of mind. We are, each of us, the center of our universe and we all die alone, but the good among us go beyond the ego to feel the lives around us, to feel with each breath the anguish of being human.

I recently read *Sapiens: A Brief History of Humankind*, by Yuval Noah Harari. It is a book that acts as a Summa. In it Harari summarizes the history of human beings and asks the fundamental question—What are we?

Are we simply a union of X and Y chromosomes led into the now so that we too can project the chromosomes into some unknowable and unseen future?

It is a good question. If we do not ask it, then we all become arrogant in our treatment of life. We kill, we destroy, we annihilate because we can, and in this create our own earthly desert devoid of everything but us.

The princely mind, then, is a projection of a future replete with insanity, pain, terror, destruction, and the filth of unfettered ego.

In the words of a poet, we are more than flesh and bone.

Harari asks the question—what is a human? I ask the question—is the arrogant prince even human? Do wealth, position, and power define the future? Without victims there are no strongmen. Strongmen depend on the weak for their wealth, their power, their position. Without the others, there is no pinnacle upon which the arrogant prince can stand. Is there anything left in the princely mind of the pain of ancestors? Is there anything left in the princely mind of the concept of the Commons?

In this time, we have seen, as Garrett Hardin writes in his article "The Tragedy of the Commons," how the range of the commons has been extended, from that small patch of pasture that defined the original commons, to the seas and to space in which the earth exists.

In short, the arrogant Princes in their arrogant mania, have despoiled the planet and now they are in the process of despoiling the space around the planet. The princely mind has to be an extension of the biblical dictum—go forth and multiply.

This dictum is the life breath of an ever-expanding Capitalism. Capitalism says we need more consumers to feed the coffers of the princes. So we must abhor abortion, we must control women's bodies, we must abhor birth control because each baby is a mouth, a consumer, possessed of an infinite hunger for things, and that hunger feeds the arrogant princely mind its wealth. But it is our own greed, and our own proliferation of self that is the agent of destruction. If we say No, the princely mind will shrivel back into its meager slime and cease to exist.

The princely mind tells us that death is our due. In this there is no end but extinction. As the commons is depleted there is nothing but death. In the princely mind is the end of humanity. 📖

# Bar Talk, The Squealing Pig, Provincetown

## Matthew J. Spireng

One was from Ohio and two others
called Provincetown their home for years,
and one said it was like towns everywhere
except it was different, and one said

the Ohio town was like towns everywhere but
there wasn't much to do, and one said *And they
don't like gays,* and they all laughed at the truth
of that, and then two discovered they both

knew Billy K., and that seemed awesome
that one not from Ohio knew the same gay guy
the other had gone to school with in Ohio, in
a small town, where gays were frowned upon

unlike in Provincetown, where they could
sit at a bar and talk like this, and none of the
couples around would think much of it, except
to be amazed, as they were, that both knew Billy K.

# Bending Moment

## Joannie Stangeland

Here I wear another year
like a ring inside a tree.
Middle of the island
where the creek runs wide,
a poplar leans a little more.
Winded and rain-freed,
it lowers like a supplicant,
an ordinary man,
returning from his mending
journey to the outer fences
and back below cloud wisps,
a break, the cataclysm of stars
reeling, his boots dew-swept
on the track across the gusts
and up the three wood stairs,
walks into the kitchen,
unaccustomed to the sudden
warmth and simmer, sets his hat
on the table, strips off
his woolen gloves, and steps
inside his lover's arms,
lets his body into that
peach and iron, hands and hair
where it parts, the ear
against his cheek and then breath
as though it is the center
of gravity's long, sure pull
the way the tree falls
toward the earth it has known.

*Sedona Sun Transforming Oak Creek to Molten Silver,*
Photograph, by Jury S. Judge

# Intimacy

## Martin Rutley

Camera one's overhead feed blinked steadily in the dreary half-gloom of Mia's aunt Amelia's faux granite kitchen. Of course, she'd been at the tramadol all evening, and even argued it had steadied her dystonia as she'd interrogated the parietal lobe. Once or twice, she'd dropped a little cigarette ash in there, maybe even a false nail or two, but otherwise things had gone more or less peachy. The craniotomy had taken the best part of an hour, which, considering the finite effects of self-administered anesthesia, had seemed an eternity—the poor woman couldn't tell a bone saw from a rusty pitchfork. Somehow, she'd managed to free the cranium and reassemble three irregularly-shaped pieces in a salt water fish-tank we'd reemployed as storage. She'd dumped the bone saw with the silver-tipped Tetras in the hot tub and insisted on a half hour meditation break. We'd split 900 micrograms of lab-grade fentanyl and argued over the ingredients of peppercorn ranch dressing. She'd sat out sulking on the balcony with a gin and tonic while I loosened the straps on the La-Z-Boy recliner and finished a crossword I'd begun the night before. Around two o'clock, we found our primary target and switched to camera two's macro lens.

Mia's Egyptian blue fingernail filled the video feed. "It feels like a god damn walnut."

"Advanced bio-synthetic polymer," I said. "Those Cal Tech bastards have been in league with ET for decades."

She drew away her hand and took the cigarette from her mouth. "So how'd they get it in there?"

"Same way they got to Ted Nugent," I said. "Molecular harmonic resonance."

"It's hideous," she said, and snatched a scalpel from off the table. "Let's get this thing out."

Mia, a bipolar sushi waitress I occasionally lied to, had begun as backup to my painter friend, Harris. The schmuck had left, pale and delirious, two nights ago to board a last minute flight to Chicago. You know the way Dr. Whoever drives up the bill and exaggerates long distance—your Father, hit and run, blood clot in the amygdala, get here tonight if at all possible. Naturally, I'd trashed my apartment, thrown my father's vinyl collection from the thirteenth floor, and come straight here. Before she'd fully woken, I'd pumped her full of scopolamine and told her she'd been bumped to first.

"Go easy in there, honey," I said.

"I'll guess I'll start back here," she said.

"Back where?"

The tip of the scalpel entered the frame of the video feed and nudged at the rear of the device. "Back here."

"Going with your gut, huh?" I asked.

"I think so," she said.

"Don't second guess it, honey," I said. "Hand that blunt over and we'll start right there."

She kicked off her heels, crossed herself, and brushed cheery red bangs from bloodshot eyes. "Love you."

Like the giggling sushi chefs she smoked out back with, she moved the blade quickly, in thin, horizontal slices. I marveled at her handiwork and caught the pieces as they fell from the scalpel into my cupped hands. As she worked, we shared a bottle of her aunt's tequila and finalized our plan to house the apartment in lead—we hadn't laughed like this in months.

"We haven't laughed like this since Tijuana," I told her.

Around twenty minutes in, she straightened, finished the last of the tequila, and tossed the scalpel over her shoulder. "There's something else in there, Harley."

I'd had x-rays, density immersion tests, laser-induced breakdown spectroscopy, diffraction pattern analysis, isotropic range tests, scanning electron microscopy—and still that potato-headed imbecile with the elfin ears at Facility 7 had missed something.

"Whatever it is," I yelled, almost choking on my tongue, "Get it out."

"It's down and dirty time, baby," she said, and pressed a hand against my mouth.

I took each finger separately, meticulously sucking from tip to knuckle. "You've had them everywhere else, honey."

She slipped in easily, parting the left and right hemispheres with surprising grace. In spite of her uncharacteristic tenderness, the vision in my left eye briefly cut out and I blurted some rot about astral travel with Crispin Glover in what Mia said was a near perfect impression of her eleventh grade science teacher.

She bent in close, placed her free hand around my neck, and kissed my forehead. "Breathe, baby," she whispered. "This is intimacy."

"Keep going, honey."

She edged a little further, reaching what I suspected was the basal ganglia. "Almost there."

"Go as deep as you need to."

"Let me know if it hurts, babe."

"You're the—"

"Bingo," she yelled, and pulled out her hand, holding it high above her head. "Let's get the fuck out of here."

"Show me, honey." I pleaded. "Show me."

She dropped a small metallic sphere into my cupped hands. "Let's celebrate—let's go fucking Rumba."

"Geez Louise, that's a DC-771."

She pulled out her cell and dropped into a chair. "We'll four-way with Denise and Roberto from Boulevard XS."

"Bastards," I yelled. "They've had cellular control of my temporal lobe."

"I'll wear the peep-toe boots and fix my hair like Veronica Lake," she said, her phone clamped against her ear.

"It's a miracle I haven't slit your throat and mailed your organs to the mother ship."

"Baby, where's Aunt Amelia?" she asked. "She promised me her marcasite drop earrings."

"Get the staple gun, honey," I yelled, and flipped the contents of my cupped hands into the air. "We're going dancing." 📖

# Goodnight

## Carol Sunde

Across boundary waters,
      a loon calls,
and, as I unroll
      my sleeping bag,
I let go of annoyances:
      that sputtering campfire,
a broken pack strap,
      your grumbles about
our endless hike.

A loon call is the last sound
      I hear—haunting
lovely loneliness—before
      I sleep.

Someday when we finish
      our final *love you-*
*love you, too,*
      I'd like to die
hearing a loon call.

*Have a Tao Day*, 2008, Photograph, by Rayn Roberts

# Innocence Lives In An Eyrie

## Vaibhav Saini

### Chapter One

?

**B**abudeep flipped through his notes minutes before *Primetime News Live with Babudeep Roy* on Expose IndiaTV. He occasionally looked up and into the mirror while his makeup man applied gel to straighten his curly hair.

"Sir! Sir!" His secretary barged into the dressing room.

Babudeep pressed his lips and kept on reading the notes, his back towards the secretary.

"There's a teenager outside the studio with a gun to his head," said the secretary, sweaty and flabbergasted.

Babudeep flicked his hand. The makeup man stopped and stepped away. Babudeep swiveled his chair to face the secretary.

"Sir, he is threatening to shoot himself unless you interview him." The secretary wiped his face with a handkerchief. "What should I do?"

Babudeep arched an eyebrow. He wanted to yell, "You fool, call the cops," but he refrained because a teenager with a gun held potential for primetime.

"Sir, the boy says he is a big fan of yours."

"So what?" Babudeep rolled his eyes. These days, everyone was his fan.

"He says he has a story that will make you believe there is no God."

That was it, the hook—a godless, reckless, hormonal teenager with a gun—Babudeep recognized opportunity when he saw it. Mental issues were the rage these days, and he had been thinking about covering the topic for a few weeks. Also, he enjoyed conducting impromptu interviews, for they generated momentous headlines and injected novel ideas into the mainstream. He tossed his notes in the trash can. He instructed the secretary to cancel the political commentators booked for tonight's show, and to confiscate the boy's gun before letting him in.

Upon entering the studio, Babudeep noticed that the secretary had allowed the boy to bring in a gym bag. When he questioned him the secretary said, "But, Sir, you told me to take away his gun. You didn't say anything about his bag."

Babudeep snapped, "You fool, I didn't know that he had a bag. Did you at least search it?"

The secretary opened and closed his mouth, but no words came out.

"Don't you think you should have? He had a gun. He could be hiding another in the bag."

The secretary moved his weight from foot-to-foot.

Babudeep shook his head dismissively. "Are you waiting for a priest to announce an auspicious time? Go, take away his bag. Now!"

The secretary raced to the boy and sprinted back to Babudeep. "Sir, he is saying his life is in it, and he will give it to you but only when you interview him."

Babudeep sighed because breaking news demanded a price. The boy's behavior thus far guaranteed an explosive interview. Babudeep enjoyed generating buzz while communicating quality content to his viewers. That said, the last thing he needed was to telecast live a shooting on the show; not that he minded it, in fact if it happened he would become a legend among news anchors, but he definitely minded being the target of the bullet. He was a newsperson, not a martyr. He asked the secretary to call the cops, just in case.

Chapter Two

*Primetime News Live with Babudeep Roy*

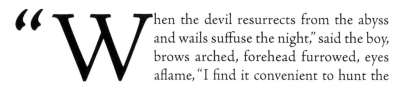 "When the devil resurrects from the abyss and wails suffuse the night," said the boy, brows arched, forehead furrowed, eyes aflame, "I find it convenient to hunt the

beasts." He relaxed his face, a countenance he preferred before unleashing pandemonium. He unslung the gym bag hanging across his chest and laid it on the off-white counter.

Babudeep, sitting across from the boy, leaned over, wondering who talked like that, except a full-on drama queen. The boy pushed the bag towards Babudeep and enticed Babudeep to open it with a twitch of his trimmed, shaped eyebrows. As Babudeep unzipped and upended it, he screamed and jumped out of his chair. A cacophony of screeching voices exploded in the studio: "AAAAAAA." "RRRRUUUNNNNN." "Hai-Ram." "Oh My God." "What The Hell."

Babudeep vomited. Two cops rushed to him and two flanked the boy, who smirked. One cop punched the boy in the spine and pushed him against the counter, and the other pulled his arms behind his back and manacled him. He laughed maniacally as a cop forced his face sideways into the counter. He muttered, "And, so, it begins—"

Chapter Three
Decisions

Amid the din, Babudeep processed the biggest story of his journalistic career spread in front of him. Seven severed legs, red-hued with clotted blood, glistened lividly against the dull ivory counter, and sickened with a morbid stench. Hit by a diabolical vacillation—to halt the primetime live feed and protect his viewers, which included families with children, from the trauma or to snatch the opportunity and expose the kind of story every journalist dreams of, the kind that gets coveted prizes, book deals, and, importantly, the much needed TRPs[1]—Babudeep made a pragmatic decision. After all, he had become a journalist to discover the truth. If the truth seemed ugly, the blame fell elsewhere, for life beguiled with hope and spat wickedness. Those too squeamish to accept reality could turn off their TVs. He whistled and broke the madness among his crew. "Guys," he yelled, "take your places. We are live. India is watching us." He sat in his chair, cops coloring the background

1. TRPs: Target Rating Points

khaki. He ran his palm over his hair, gulped, looked straight at the camera, and said, "I apologize for what you have just witnessed. But at ExposeIndiaTV, we are committed to telling the truth." He took a breath. "At this time, I will advise the viewers to please remain calm as we try to understand what has happened here." He nodded at the cops and said, "I thank the much-maligned Indian Police for their swift response." The camera zoomed in on each cop: The two behind Babudeep smiled and waved. The one pinning the boy's face to the counter drilled out snot with a finger in his free hand, and the other rolled the ends of his moustache.

Babudeep pointed at the appendages and the camera operator zoomed in on them. "To get to the bottom of this crime," said Babudeep, directing his hand at the boy and the camera followed, "we need to talk with our handcuffed guest here." He raised his voice, "Is he a criminal, a psychopath, or a victim?" The camera found Babudeep again. "Don't go anywhere. We'll be back after a short break."

Babudeep sped to the exit, shadowed by two cops and trailed by: "Sir, tell us what to do?" "Where are you going?" "Is the show over?" He looked back at his crew, following him like sheep, craning their necks towards him. He closed and opened his fist once at them, signaling a five-minute break. He paced to the lavatory. The cops placed themselves on either side of the restroom entrance. He pushed open the door, jumped to the urinal, and violently emptied his bladder, wondering if he should bail on the interview. He clicked his tongue and cast aside the futile thought. Though shaken, he reveled in the adrenaline rush. He predicted further momentum to building his cult, as if he needed it, ha? He had been number one as documented by numerous polls, and had an unbroken streak of Best News Anchor Award for four years straight. He smirked, remembering how he had snagged the prestigious award multiple times by tricking and exposing the linchpins of nefarious scams. By any means necessary, he had collected irrefutable evidence of their illegal actions. Then, he had offered deals at the intersection of corruption and blackmail:

"I will not expose your penchant for insider trading if you get me the award; I will not expose the hundreds of children killed by your vaccine trials if you get me the award; I will not expose your orgies with imported Thai Ladyboys if you get me the award; I will not expose the ecosystem disaster caused by the toxic chemicals spilled by your plant in the Ganges if you get me the award." In response, the elite crooks had loosened purses and pulled strings for mutual benefit.

After receiving an award, Babudeep had leaked the particular scandal to journalists at a magazine with a live blog but never at another rival TV channel. He had strategically informed the entitled malefactors five minutes before their crimes had become public online, lest the racketeers, pedophiles, corporate bullies, and polluters had had time to block the news. He had gained their trust and convinced them to give exclusive interviews by promising a sympathetic tone. In reality they had served their penultimate purpose—propelling his award campaign and providing him exclusive interviews, thereby addicting Indians to his show—and then they served their ultimate purpose—purging society of monsters, his goal in life. Because he had been able to control the timing of breaking news, he had trumped his competitors by booking the foremost experts to discuss their opinions on his show. Thus, he had setup a network of favors among print and online journalists as well as people in power, and earned his viewers' respect while making a difference in the world. He had reached the top by being as crafty as the corrupt he targeted. "*Zahar ka ilaj zahar se he hota hai.*" He chuckled. "Poison cures poison, ha?"

He zipped his pants and washed his hands. He checked himself out in the mirror. He thought of splashing water on his face, but forwent feeling fresh for his fans. His image remained his USP[2] and, under the circumstances, he would have struggled without patience if the makeup man had had to redo his face or hair.

"Oye!" He jumped.

The cops crashed in, pistols raised and cocked.

"False alarm," he said, pulling his intermittently vibrating iPhone out the pocket of his pants, and waving it at them.

---

2. USP: Unique Selling Proposition

He read a series of texts from the producer:

*Great show*

*You need to go back live*
*Sustain the momentum*
*22 million viewers and increasing*
*Raining money ;-)*

Babudeep sighed. Money, money, money—that was the producer's sole aim. Babudeep also appreciated the importance of rupees, but he desired more professionally. He had proven time and time again that reporting on difficult stories—those that could get you assassinated—was possible while acing the TRP game. Yet, the producer analyzed each new story through the prism of "Will it generate TRP? Will it make money?" Perhaps the producer was simply performing his job. But Babudeep was determined to use his platform to seek justice for the underdog because that was what he had sought for himself throughout his life. The producer knew his motivations, yet ignored their import.

Babudeep returned to the studio, swarming with uniformed personnel. He saw a forensics team collecting the limbs and six policemen leading the boy in chains out of the studio. "What the F!" he said.

One of the lawmen stepped forward and said, "Babudeep-ji, I am Inspector Kumar. This is a crime scene. We are shutting you down until the investigation is over."

"Are you kidding me?" Babudeep pressed his temples. "We are in the middle of a live telecast. You can't do this."

"Babudeep-ji, I like your show. But no one is above the law," said the inspector.

Babudeep's iPhone vibrated. He answered and heard a familiar baritone, "This is the producer's assistant. The producer would like a word with the inspector." Babudeep wondered how the producer knew to call at this exact moment. He passed his cell phone to the inspector who said: "Yes." "Yes, Sir." "Yes, yes."

"Yes, I understand." "My pleasure." "No, Sir, no problem." "Yes, Sir." "Thank you."

Babudeep smirked.

The inspector handed the phone back to Babudeep, unchained the boy, warned him against making a hasty move, and allowed him to sit again for the interview; and admonished the forensics team for their snail-speed. The team packed the limbs swiftly and left. The inspector positioned his juniors and himself around the room but outside the camera frame that included Babudeep and the boy.

Babudeep took his seat warily and guzzled a glass of water. He appreciated that the cleaning crew had wiped his vomit off the floor. He snapped his fingers. The cameraman counted to three. Babudeep noticed that the boy, dressed in a dirty, wrinkled, cream cotton shirt, tapped the counter nonchalantly. Babudeep addressed his viewers in a grave voice, "Tonight, we are investigating homicides." The video editor replayed the earlier recording of the boy pushing the gym bag towards Babudeep and the grisly human parts falling out of it. "Forensics personnel have confiscated the limbs and the bag. We thank Inspector Kumar and his team for their swift action and for their continued protection." The camera turned to the cops around the studio, and then back to Babudeep. "I will start by asking the question that has been burning on our minds. Who is this young boy?" The cameraman zoomed in on the boy who pulled his lips to one side and squished air. "Hello?" said Babudeep sternly. "Who are you and how did you come into the possession of that bag?"

"I am Raagini." The boy laced his fingers together. "It is my bag, now. Rather, that was my bag, but you took it."

Babudeep jolted backward in the chair. With bulging eyes, he asked, "You . . . Are you . . . You mean to say . . ."

Raagini unentwined his fingers and put his hands on the counter. "I hacked them to pieces."

Babudeep gaped. Nothing added up. He said, "You are claiming to have killed seven human beings, but to gain entry into the studio you pointed the gun at yourself whereas a killer would have pointed it at a hostage."

"If I had taken a hostage, the focus of the news coverage would have been the rescue operation. I wanted to get in here and tell my story."

"It makes sense," thought Babudeep, "and yet it doesn't." He frowned and wondered, "How can a mere boy brutally murder seven people? But a godless, mentally unstable, hormonal teenager with a gun can commit homicide. It happens in America all the time. But not in India. Well, we are living in a global world, isn't it? Yes, it makes sense. No it doesn't. Yes, it does. No, it doesn't." He exhaled imperceptibly and coursed his fingers through his hair, aware of the live camera. "Who is he? Or, rather, what is he? Does he have multiple personalities? Is he making it up? Or, is someone setting him up? Maybe a Don killed these people, then kidnapped his family, and is forcing him to take the blame—no, that is too far-fetched. I need to get him talking. I don't know. Should I end the show and hand him over to Inspector Kumar? Am I putting my life, my reputation at risk? Oh My God, this is nuts." He swilled another glass of water. He took a deep breath and reminded himself, "This is a great story. I—The One and Only Babudeep Roy—am uncovering the story of the year." He wrote *stay calm* on his notepad, placed on the counter in front of him, but when he opened his mouth he was anything but calm. "Whhhhhhai?" he stretched the word until it acquired a collo-quial pronunciation. "Uhh." He inhaled loudly and said silently to himself, "I am Babudeep Roy. I am in a suit." He straightened his back. "I am the suit." With confidence befitting Babudeep Roy, Babudeep asked, "Why?"

"They had it coming." Raagini shrugged.

"You have to do better than that." Babudeep raised his voice, "People are dead. You are confessing as the murderer. But why, how, where, and when did you commit the crimes?"

Raagini looked at Babudeep. As shadows etched horror in the constrained muscles of his face, Raagini stuttered, "My ... My ... My mother ...." He started breathing heavily.

"Yes? What is it?" Babudeep knew he stood on the edge of a scoop.

As tears poured down his face, Raagini managed, "I had to . . . I . . . He forced . . . I . . . My mother . . . My sister . . ."

Babudeep glared. "Are you saying someone forced you to kill your mother and sister?" "No," spat Raagini with crimson eyes. "I never said that. I love them." He went quiet. He hung his head. "I loved them." He jerked his head up and looked menacingly at Babudeep. "I sawed them because they deserved it."

"You cut up your mother and sister like vegetables because you loved them?" screamed Babudeep. "You crazy sociopath, I don't want to interview—"

The cops moved to put Raagini back in chains.

"I never said that. You are not listening," yelled Raagini, his entire frame trembling. "I could never hurt my family. They are no more. I don't have anyone." He gulped.

Babudeep realized that although Raagini seemed addled, a level of truthfulness permeated his tearful voice. "But, the best lies incorporate some degree of truth," thought Babudeep. He felt curious to untangle the story. He locked eyes with the inspector and nodded. The inspector signaled the cops to retreat.

Raagini formed his hands into fists. "I did what I had to. Trust me, it was long due."

Babudeep snapped his fingers for a break and advertisements brought respite to think it through. He downed another glass of water. Once calm, for the occasion demanded utmost professionalism, he snapped his fingers and was back in people's homes where he carried forth the unfolding drama. He said to Raagini, "Why should I," hit his fist on the counter, and added, "why should the viewers listen to you?" He paused. "India is watching you, Raagini. Choose your words carefully."

"Because my story will make you believe there is no God."

Babudeep snapped for another break. He knew neither he nor his viewers would sleep tonight. He drank another glass of water. He took a deep breath. He stared at Raagini who returned a lost look that unnerved him. What was it about the boy that shook him to his core? Perhaps the boy's mercurial temperament? That was part of it, but not the whole reason. Then, it hit him. He recalled the uncountable times when, just like the boy, he had questioned the existence of God. He surrendered to the memories that huddled like ghosts in a cemetery. 📖

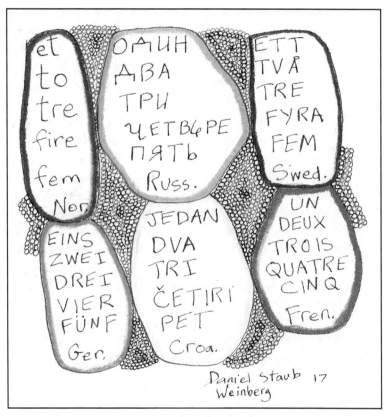

*6 Languages*, 2017, Pen, Ink, and Colored Pencils on Paper,
by Daniel Staub Weinberg

# Tolerance

## Mark Trechock

Not that I fear strangers, even though
newscasters always seem particularly thrilled
by unprovoked late-night attacks on those
whose real-life plot line calls for being killed
within or outside some town's seedy bar,
likely fumbling in purse or pocket for keys—
when you need them you never know where they are—
or because a beery attempt at jest displeased
a bully awash in alcohol and offense.

Thus, traveling alone and spent from work,
I seek a tavern within walking distance,
choosing a table lurking in the dark
(near the rear exit is the perfect seat),
order a scotch, preferably a Laphraoig,
with its aroma of fennel and canned Heet.
I fix my gaze on the glass, intentions vague,
yet of no interest. I order a second, a third.

No one will notice when I slip out the back,
my steps resolute, rapid, my eyes blurred,
but survival instinct keeping me on track.

# Rakija

## Ana Vidosavljevic

In the middle of October, when the sun still spread around its warm rays, my father and a few neighbors would gather in the backyard of our house to make rakija.

Rakija was a "fire water," as some Chinese tourist who had come to Serbia and tried this traditional Serbian alcoholic drink called it. I tried it many times under the influence of the grown-ups who claimed that it killed all bacteria, germs, viruses, calmed a toothache, and reduced a fever. But, honestly, I didn't like it. It was so strong that once you sipped it, and you had it in your mouth, you could feel its stinging drops spread all around the walls of your mouth cavity like tiny needles. And when you swallowed it, the warmth would spread so fast through your upper body that in a few seconds you felt the heat that skyrocketed your temperature to a thousand degrees. And you would start sweating as if you had been in a sauna. Your legs would feel weak and shaky, and it was better for you if you didn't attempt to walk for a while, otherwise, you would probably end up stumbling down and kissing the ground.

Anyway, my family and all other Serbs believed that rakija was a cure for everything. No medicine could surpass the healing effects of rakija. Also, no other alcoholic drink could cause weirder hallucinations. Our neighbor Stevo was fighting with anacondas after he left the *kafana* (a local Serbian bistro or pub), and he was so engaged in this fight with huge snakes that he ended up stopping the traffic on the town's main street since that was his battlefield. My cousin Vera got so drunk once that she believed there were fairies asking her to climb up a tree and join them. Vera climbed the tree and after five minutes she ended up on the ground again, falling directly on her butt. She couldn't sit on it for almost three weeks after this happened.

That warm October day, after playing on the street with other kids from my neighborhood, I came back home feeling weak. It was an autumn day bathed in golden and red, with leaves falling down from trees. Mornings were crispy but pleasant. The enjoyable warmth made people in my hometown wear summer clothes, shorts and T-shirts, but that day the hairs on my body stood up and I got shivers down my spine. The cold chills turned into shaking and I ran into my yard feeling sick.

When I opened the gate the sweet fruity smell of ripe plums permeated the air. It was delightful and provoked me to think about sweet purple plums. But no matter how compelling the sweetness of plums were, I was not feeling hungry. I went in the backyard and I found my dad and our two neighbors there.

They were gathered around our *kazan* (a still) and chatting. The three of them were holding small shot glasses and, of course, tasting rakija in the making. Needless to say, tasting rakija, again and again, while trying to make the best version of it, was obligatory. Not to mention that by the end of a day all tasters were usually so drunk that they couldn't tell the difference between my sister and me. And my sister and I were very different. They would wish Marina good night saying, "Good night, Lena." And I would be petted on my head with the words, "Marina, you are growing up so fast. You will be taller than Lena." I was four years older than my sister Marina and much taller.

That afternoon, I bid them good afternoon and told my dad that my head was burning and that I felt strange. Everything was spinning around and I was getting dizzy. He stood up from his stool, left his precious shot glass on a small, round wooden table, and approached me. He pressed his warm sticky palm, spreading the fragrance of rakija, on my forehead and kept it there for a few seconds. Then he said, "You have a fever. Go to Nana. She will prepare the best medicine for you. You will feel better after a couple of hours. When I was you age, I never went to a doctor. Nana was my doctor. Thanks to her I easily recovered from chicken pox, shingles, fever, and flu."

Nana was my grandma. Her real name was Lena, the same as mine, but in Serbia, we usually called our grandma "Nana," if we liked her. If we didn't like her, we would address her "grandmother" and avoid her as much as we could. My sister and I had always called my grandma Nana. I guessed it showed our love and adoration for her.

I entered the house feeling lightheaded and woozy. I felt like a terrible weakness was seizing my body. I began to suffer some dizzy spells. Everything around me was moving. I found Nana in the kitchen. She was making pancakes. Sweet vanilla and spicy cinnamon smells lingered in the air. Nana offered me a pancake with delicious apricot jam filling. My favorite. When I refused, she looked at me in surprise and said, "You are not feeling well. You look like a ghost and you don't have an appetite." I nodded.

"Come here," she said in a demanding tone of voice. She left her artistry of making pancakes and headed toward the bedroom. I followed her. Then, she told me to take off all my clothes and disappeared through the door that led outside to the backyard. After a minute, she came back carrying a bottle of rakija. I was confused but so weak I didn't have the strength to ask questions and demand explanations. I believed she was an expert and had a gift of healing. She told me to lie down because she wanted to massage me with rakija. I obediently did what she said. I was feeling cold and my arms and legs were shaking. Strange chills were ruling over my body and I felt as if I had been lying naked on an iceberg.

Nana poured a bit of rakija in her palms and then she started massaging my shoulders, back, arms, stomach, lower back, legs and feet. My body was heating up and I was comfortably numb. After Nana had finished massaging me, she grabbed one towel from the drawer, soaked it in rakija and put it around my neck. She told me to go to bed and try to sleep. I compliantly did what she demanded. She also told me not to remove the rakija-soaked towel from around my neck. I lay down and she covered me up with the cotton sheet and promised me that I would feel better when I woke up. She kissed my forehead and went back to the kitchen to finish her pancake art.

The room was filled with the strong smell of rakija, and even though I had never liked it, I felt that it was making me feel better.

I was sleepy, my eyelids were heavy, and they began to droop. I was half asleep for some time and eventually fell asleep.

I'm not sure how long I slept, but when I woke up it was pitch-dark outside and I could see the carpet of stars through the half-open window. I smelt of alcohol. Rakija left its after smell all around the bedroom, and even though I wasn't drinking it, I had inhaled it and it had made me a bit tipsy. But miracle! I was feeling better. No cold chills were running down my spine and my hands and legs were not shaking anymore. My forehead was not burning either. I finally removed the towel from my neck that Nana had soaked in rakija earlier. It was almost dry. I uncovered myself to cool off since it was pretty warm in the room. I put my T-shirt and jeans on and went to the kitchen.

Nana was sitting in a rocking chair and watching her favorite Latin soap opera where every minute someone cried and yelled. And the actors used a lot of gestures and talked too loud. A big pile of pancakes was on the table waiting for me and I was so hungry. When Nana saw me, she stood up and hurried over to touch my forehead. Her smile assured me that my fever was gone. Then, she made me sit at the table and she rolled a few pancakes for me. One had my favorite apricot filling, the other one ground walnuts and honey, and the third one was filled with brown sugar and cinnamon. I ate ravenously. And I knew I would not stop after the third pancake. My Nana was happy to see that my appetite had returned in full force.

When I finished the sixth pancake and there was no room for more, I lay in bed and watched the soap opera with Nana.

Outside, my father and neighbors got to the stage where all of them were singing and laughing, and I knew that soon the neighbors' wives would come to look for their husbands. Rakija really worked miracles with my fever. And, obviously, it performed wonders with the grown-ups as well. It brought them back to their childhood. Once they overdosed on rakija, they forgot about their stupid, serious political arguments and complaints. You didn't hear them talking about low salaries, high prices, ridiculous taxes, corrupt government, bad bosses, and a lot of work. All you heard was laughing, jokes, and singing. Sometimes, when they continued their hanging out with rakija until late at night, they would even play games: hide and seek, hopscotch, jump rope, or Monkey in the Middle. Then I would sneak out of my bed and, through the window overlooking our backyard, I would watch them and laugh. Those were hilarious scenes. I don't remember any TV show that was funnier and more interesting. And those were moments when I liked grown-ups the most. 📖

*Urban Life: Parking*, Photograph, by Manit Chaotragoongit

# Cold

## April Vomvas

I gaze out the barred window
At the sky—blue
I smell the fresh cut grass
Out on the yard—green
I feel the cold metal bunk
Through my thin mat—hard
I hear the shouted orders
Of the guards—mean
I see my freedom
In my mind—distant
I taste the food
On my brown tray—old
I hear my child's voice
On the phone—sad
I touch my friends
Through thick glass—cold

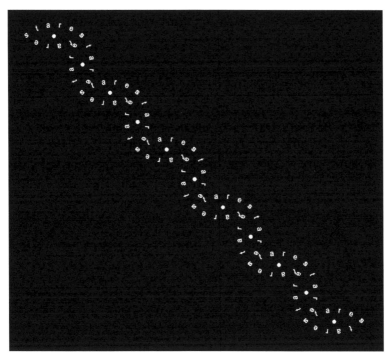

*Stares/Stairs*, Digital Writing, by Jack Williams

# Sealed Records

## Sarah Brown Weitzman

The man at the county adoption records office says:

"Your mother had every right to keep herself hidden

in sealed records. You have no right to know

anything about her, certainly not her name

not even the color of her hair though

it could have been red like yours or possibly

the father had red hair." I go away

with that new clue, picturing a red-haired man.

Butcher? baker? candlestick maker? jailor? rapist?

# Zabavnik

## Vladimir Vulović

### Parents

Belgrade, Yugoslavia, January 5, 1952—some twenty months before my birth. My father buys the first post-war issue of *Politika's Entertainer*—or *Politikin Zabavnik*, in Serbian. *Zabavnik* is called *Politikin* because it's published by the same company that publishes the most popular Yugoslav daily: *Politika*. But there is no politics in *Zabavnik*. Just comics and articles of interest "For everyone from 7 to 77," as they advertised it at the time. It might even cheer up my mother who's in the hospital for multiple operations to treat her wounds from the German bombardments in 1941.

My parents are both about to graduate from the School of Electrical Engineering, University of Belgrade. Married for two years already, they live on the second floor of an apartment building, in a single tiny room, with no running water, the outhouse in the courtyard, a bare light bulb hanging from the ceiling, and a hot-pot to heat up food.

Laughter and merriment were scarce in post-war Yugoslavia. But did my father, when purchasing that first *Zabavnik*, also have in mind entertainment for his future children, my brother and me?

He continues purchasing *Zabavnik* until my mother's release from the hospital in early May. They continue buying it together from then on. My mother continues buying it after my father leaves to serve his military duty. They continue buying it a year later after he returns. They are still buying it on a business trip in snow-bound Montenegro, where I am conceived. And through her pregnancy. And after my birth. And a month later, when my father is called up for military exercises, and my mother—without his help—moves all their possessions and month-old me into a larger "flat": two tiny adjacent rooms, and again, no running water, an outhouse nearby, one bare bulb in each room. They keep buying *Zabavniks* and storing them.

They keep buying them and storing them even after the birth of my brother four years later when we move to a modern flat, with running water, a real bathroom, a sink, chandeliers, tile stoves, a hallway, a tiny terrace, a pantry, a "maid's" room, a bedroom, a kitchen, a living room—luxury and splendor. And yet the happiest day for my brother and me comes several years later when our parents present us with bound volumes of *Zabavnik*.

One tome for each year. Each tome eighteen inches tall, twelve and a half wide, and two to three inches thick, depending on the year (tomes of later years are thicker). Tomes big and heavy for little children. My brother looks at the comics in them though he doesn't know how to read. He learns to read just so he can read *Zabavnik*. We read these tomes, sitting, kneeling, and crouching on the carpet, in front of them, to the side of them, and most often leaning above them, on our elbows and knees. They are our world.

There are comics, mostly Disney comics, but not just comics in *Zabavnik*. There is also a plethora of enchanting and informative articles. Educational! Fun, fun, fun!

You are never poor, depressed or lonely reading *Zabavnik*. *Zabavnik* is your gate, your window, your access to the world. *Zabavnik* is the world.

## Comics —Foreign

A partial list of my *Zabavnik* buddies: Miki Maus, Donald Duck, Goofy, Pluto, Robin Hood, Hiawatha, Flash Gordon, Zarkov, Popeye, Olive Oyl, Bim and Bum, and on, and on, and on. Most of them are of foreign origin, mostly Disney creations, but who cares? They are all my friends and they have their own friends in turn.

Major characters with their supporting actors: Mickey with Minnie, Pluto, and Goofy; Donald with Daisy, Huey, Dewey, and Louie; Flash with Dale and Zarkov; Hiawatha with animals and Indians; Ming Foo with little Johnnie and sailor Tom; Lambert, the sheepish lion, with his foster mother and the wolf; Popeye with Olive Oyl, Swee'Pea, Oscar, and Wimpy; Katzenjammer

Kids (Hans and Fritz) with Captain, Inspector, Rollo, Lena, Mama, Miss Twiddle, and King Bongo.

Nobody lives in a vacuum; we all need others to survive. The more friends you have the bigger your world is. The truer your friendships are the better your world is. These are the lessons of *Zabavnik*.

Each character was also unique.

Mickey brought us to unusual places: a haunted hotel, an island of antediluvian animals, a kingdom of his double. With Mickey we learned how to behave reasonably in unreasonable circumstances.

Donald was a normalizer. In his everyday tantrums I recognized my mother, myself, my brother, even my father. Donald made our fractious family seem normal.

Goofy taught me that being nutty also means being endearing and happy. (I'm still goofy!)

Flash brought us interstellar adventures where fantasy ruled. He nurtured my physics quest to understand the cosmos, and all things even more mysterious than the skies.

Ming Foo (in our Serbian translation inexplicably dubbed Shang Lin) unearthed wisdom even in the most difficult situations. I still remember: "A brave man dies once, and a coward a thousand times."

Popeye's girlfriend, in our Serbian translation not Olive Oyl but "Oliva," was very dear. I enjoyed her simple charm. I'm glad I did not know the true meaning of her name for I don't like when people—even cartoonists—denigrate their creations. But above all I loved Wimpy —always on the move to finagle another hamburger. I cherish his Serbian name—Pera Ždera, or "Peter the Devourer"—a vast improvement to the English original.

Humor was an antidote to my yelling mother, my scowling father, my own envy toward my all-too-cute little brother. Humor allowed me to laugh at myself and my shortcomings. *Zabavnik* fostered my imagination, erased boundaries, made everything possible.

# Donald Duck

Donald Duck was my alter ego: same temper, same maturity level, same unpleasant voice—his raspy, mine nasal. He's the most human of all Disney's creations: easily thrown off, subject to bad luck, venting his anger against his nephews, his fiancé, passersby, neighbors, squirrels, life as we know it —like Charlie Chaplin's Little Tramp, like Buster Keaton himself, he's another modern-life hero.

You don't have to be perfect to be lovable! Too much restraint, too much moderation, kills life. Celebrate the Donald in all of us!

I love his name in Serbian—Paja Patak, or "Pat the Duck"— as ingenious as the English original. Kudos to our Serbian translators!

Stories with Donald Duck rarely evolve from one issue to another, the way they do with Flash Gordon or even Mickey Mouse. Humor has a hard time with long arcs. But Donald's short strips, where the entire story happens on a single page or a half, are unsurpassable.

At a boxing match Donald keeps taunting the losing boxer, only to find himself, on a tram ride home, sitting next to this same giant. At home Donald worries over his nephews learning acrobatics on a wire, only to trip over one. On a walk outdoors, Donald carries an umbrella, but ends up soaking wet. In winter time, Donald dresses for the weather, but ends up almost naked. Donald is a sore loser and therefore funny and dear.

As a child, spending long summers on the farm with Nana, Grandpa and Great-Grandma, I read *Zabavnik*. One morning, Grandpa returned from field work to have a drink, saw me reading *Zabavnik* and said in a rough voice: "Oh, how I would slap his butt!"

"Who, Grandpa?" I asked, scanning the comics in front of me.

"That one, with the big white butt," he said, pointing at Donald.

"But Grandpa, what did Paja do to you?"

"You think it's all true?"

"But no, Grandpa. I read it only because it's funny."

"So, you don't believe in that?"

"Not one bit. "

"Well then, you can continue to read."

My grandpa was a peasant with three years of elementary school, but to my reckoning, one of the brightest people I knew. He worried about me being hoodwinked by modern charms, the way a number of peasant folk were. I'm glad I reassured him about Paja Patak.

## Color

The first issue of *Zabavnik* used just black and red and anything that could be obtained by mixing and diluting these colors. In subsequent issues the red was replaced in turn with teal, green, yellow, etc. —but in each issue, in addition to black there was just one chromatic color. Ours was the world of a socialist palette.

We didn't mind. That single chromatic color, in its different hues, accompanied by grays, conjured up all the colors. When the spirit is ready, it easily soars. To this day, as I leaf through *Zabavnik* tomes, I don't notice a single chromatic color changing from one issue to another: instead, it seems to me that every issue contains all colors!

Opulence and extravagance are abhorrent to me. Too many colors I find garish. They unnerve me. Restraint is needed. Don't treat me like a bull in a ring, let me Imagine!

My American wife thinks this esthetic stance of mine is due to my growing up in socialist-era Belgrade. Okay. Even I might find today's Belgrade a bit too gray, drab, and gritty. But so what? All that gray helps me appreciate colors more, like the rare flower in a park, or yellowing trees.

## Katzenjammer Kids

Few people in America have ever heard of the Katzenjammer Kids, let alone read them or loved them. But in Yugoslavia everybody knew of Bim and Bum—the names we knew them by.

Had we known of their German origin, would we have ever read them? All hints of German were removed in our translation. We didn't know its characters spoke English with a strong German accent. We didn't know the prankster kids had German names. We didn't know the strip's original creators were German. We didn't know that the strip idea came from German folk tales. In Yugoslavia after World War II nothing related to Germans would have been funny. This scrubbing of anything German from the comic was a necessary, and good choice.

Because they were funny.

In this comic, kids engender all kinds of pranks, the grownups punish the kids, the kids take revenge. Sometimes even grownups, especially Captain and Inspector, make pranks. Fifty years later, reading Bim and Bum, I still hiss like a gander, laughing to tears.

Bim and Bum are the leading characters but not always victorious. Sometimes they get the short end of the stick, sometimes their nemesis Rollo, sometimes Lena, or Inspector, Captain, Miss Twiddle, or even Mama or King Bongo. On an island where they live, hierarchy rules and Mama is the strongest, but everybody trips up somebody sometimes. The fact that in each issue somebody else may win gives it freshness and cheer.

Yet, why are they so dear to me still? Is it because of their large family which reminds me of my own extended family? Is it because their slapstick humor liberates me—like when my mother bit on a pickled cucumber and squirted liquid on to Uncle Jovan's new white shirt, and we all burst out laughing? In laughter, my mother was sweet, my father was kind, and my brother and I were on the same side.

## Mickey Mouse

Among Disney's creations, Mickey comes closest to perfection. I used to love him. In our fantasy realm, he led, I followed. But now things are different. Now I'm old. Now I find him too smug, too sweet, too staid. Or am I simply envious?

But truly, he's too nice, too measured, too good. Without his friends or external problems, he's a yawn. Lucky for us, he's rarely alone: there is Goofy with his silliness, Pluto with his moles. Lucky for us, he ventures to interesting places: the island of dinosaurs, a haunted hotel, the kingdom of his double. Lucky for him, he's enterprising and brave, so for many years he starred on *Zabavnik's* front page.

I loved his energy. In those early comics he went on to explore, travel, examine, solve problems, help others, make friends, even grieve. An exemplary person. Perhaps too chaste.

Some of this chasteness was lost on me in elementary school, in seventh grade. One day, a group of us visited Zoran Marić, one of the worst students in our class section. He was at home recovering from an illness. Glad to see us. At one moment, jolly with our visit, he unexpectedly shared his circlejerk usage of comics. His hand wrapped around an imaginary penis, he stroked twice in beat while chanting "Mickey, Goofy," and with one winning stroke, accompanied with a wide grin, erupted "Pinocchio!"

## Comics —Domestic

In *Zabavnik*, we had Yugoslav comics as well. Not just short strips ending in a line or two, but also comics occupying an entire page and with action developing from one issue to another. In one such comic, dubbed here "Cookie Steeple Chase" (since I forgot its title), sweets race over barriers, ditches, ponds, and all along one mean cookie (Pretzel Đura?) plays dirty tricks on a good cookie, Marzipan Brana. Brana wins.

There was also a comic called "The Wedding of Tsar Dušan," based on an eponymous epic folk poem. In this comic, Miloš Vojinović, a nephew of tsar Dušan, joins his wedding procession disguised as a Bulgarian shepherd. Other participants want to drive him away, but the Tsar lets him stay. And then, in moments of dire difficulty for the Tsar, Miloš saves him —jumps over three horses, shoots the apple from afar, beats the best Latin duelist, recognizes the bride, and on the way back defeats the three-headed Duke Balačko.

And there was the "Adventures of little Raško, a chess player and a rascal"—all in rhyme. Little Raško cheats in chess against his smaller sister—denies he stole a pawn, makes her cry. Later, after falling asleep, he's surrounded by chess pieces come alive. War is pending in the chessland, and Raško is blamed for the missing pawn, and the vile, treacherous, scheming black bishop has it in for Raško. At a moment of extreme distress due to this bishop, Raško says: "By my chess-player's honor, my thieving days are over."

Raško wakes up, angry with the bishop. But will Raško himself improve? We hoped he would. For we all knew our own faults, and in rooting for Raško, we rooted for ourselves.

And then of course there was comic True-Steel, or Baš Čelik in Serbian—where a young, brave, and modest prince, defeats in the end a mythical, nearly-immortal being. Years later, I used to tell this uniquely Serbian tale to my American-born son.

Seeing our own legends, inventions, and stories in *Zabavnik* made our hearts swell. Our culture was not inferior to what the West had. We were on par with the world.

Texts

Ever since my childhood I longed to find one particular science fiction novel, a novel I read long ago, a novel about a man who changed the course of the Gulf Stream—a novel I couldn't find for the longest time. Imagine my surprise when I found it recently in the 1952-1953 tomes of *Zabavnik*!

*Zabavnik* was not just a compendium of comics. Even more space was devoted to columns and articles. Often trivia for sure, but also amazing, important, informative texts on far away countries, common and exotic animals, important people from all over, legends, customs, planets, stars, continents—anything that could intrigue anyone from "7 to 77." That was *Zabavnik's* motto. Later—addressing the concern of one aging fan—the editors changed it to "7 to 107."

Columns: Grandpa's skills; Do you know?; Wonders of faraway lands; From our past; Have you already heard that?; Little encyclopedia; This minute—every minute; Anthology of true wonders; Whose biography is this?; Wondrous square; Crosswords puzzle.

Bits from the first few issues: (a) Every minute rats in the U.S. cost its economy 300 dollars; (b) In Bosnia, in 1897, when people started eating tree roots due to famine, the Austrian authorities started taxing the roots; (c) In Bolivia, during some parts of the year, it's colder indoors than outdoors, so only indoors do people wear coats.

Longer texts serialized in the first two years: *Burning Daylight* by Jack London, *The Gold-Bug* by Edgar Allan Poe, *The Man Who Stole the Gulf Stream* by Georges-G Toudouze, *How I found Livingston* by H. M. Stanley, and *Wanted: 7 Fearless Engineers!* by Warner Van Lorne.

Yugoslav history too was represented with its legions of freedom fighters, rulers, scientists, writers, historians, artists, politicians. World War II events were portrayed so as not place blame on any particular Yugoslav ethnic group. In the same spirit, whenever the exact ethnicity of a particular hero could be subject to dispute, editors eschewed terms like Serb or Croat and wrote simply "our man" or "our woman."

Everything we read in *Zabavnik* sparked our curiosity, expanded our horizon beyond our daily routine, made our entire planet, the cosmos even, not just wondrous, but accessible. And even the most terrible events—like famines and wars—were presented with no malice to anybody. As a consumer of American media for many decades now, I only wish they had *Zabavnik*-like editors.

## Flash Gordon

In 1934, Alex Raymond invented the characters Flash Gordon, Dale Arden, and Dr. Hans Zarkov. But from our *Zabavnik* issues in the late 50s and early 60s I never learned that Flash was a quarterback for the New York Jets—I did not know about American football—nor that he had strange blond hair, nor that Zarkov, his buddy, was somewhat crazy and of German descent. Had I known these things they would have probably detracted from my pleasure. Instead, Flash, Dale, and Zarkov were just fearless explorers of the unknown universe and earth. Deep-sea monsters, sea-of-fire monsters, human-like aliens of extraordinary abilities, life-important riddles, merciless emperors, swooning princesses, space ships, harpoons, tridents, and the gold globe gobbling up anyone harboring even a speck of gold—all of this was innocent and exciting with Flash.

His comic-stories, all long, developed from one issue to the next. *Zabavnik* after Flash was no longer the same. I missed him, my friend. The aspiring scientist in me felt kinship with a man who knew that oxygen was the eighth element in the Mendeleev Periodic Table. I missed him in graduate school at Princeton too. So when my fellow students announced some movie with Flash Gordon, I waited in suspense. It turned out to be Flesh Gordon, in a soft-porn movie. America sometimes disgusts me.

Flash influenced me even when I didn't know it. Some eight years after his *Zabavnik* adventures in Atlantis, I got this school assignment: Describe one day in your life in year 2000.

We had ninety minutes to do so. I was fifteen-years old then and it was hard to imagine being forty-six. So old. Everything that mattered would be over by then. Whose life at forty-six mattered? All my heroes were much younger, except maybe for Zarkov, but he was balding, and not as cool as Flash.

I imagined myself being a deep-sea excavator in the Mediterranean Sea. Working my life of drudgery, when one day, exactly on my forty-sixth birthday, I dug up the ruins of Atlantis. It made my life worthwhile.

A copycat feat this may have been, but to this day my Atlantis discovery remains my biggest achievement.

## Changes

Nothing remains unchanged. In 1968, *Zabavnik* changed its format—reduced its page size from newspaper size to magazine size—and introduced true colors. I did not like this smaller format. I did not like those gaudy colors. I found the comics less funny, the articles less interesting.

Up until 1972, *Zabavnik* was published in Serbian Cyrillic only. That year, it started coming out also in Serbian Latin alphabet and in Slovenian.

Its circulation in the mid-1970s reached 330,000. If Yugoslavia then were as big as the U.S. is now, that would proportionately have meant SIX million copies. A mega brand!

But, in our family, we were losing interest in *Zabavnik*. In earlier years, after I wrote my initials in cursive on some pages, my brother retaliated by writing in large capital letters "Owner Miodrag Vulović" on many more pages, even on the bound covers. Like dogs soiling utility poles, we were besmirching *Zabavnik*.

That stopped.

We were still buying *Zabavnik*, we were still reading it, we were still piling its copies in order, but we were not binding them, and we stopped re-reading them. By that time, I was a math and physics freak. And after graduating from college, I left for America to seek different dreams, different worlds, different stars.

Back in Yugoslavia, my great-grandma, nana, and grandpa died. And some time later, my parents moved all our bound and unbound issues from their apartment in Belgrade to our grandparents' house in the village. They sat there for decades, gathering dust.

One summer, I chose three of these tomes and brought them with me back to America. I did this with my parents' and my brother's permission. Many more tomes and even more years of unbound issues remained in the village. And yet I felt like a thief. The only thing that diminished my guilt for having taken something dear to my brother were the layers of dust on the remaining *Zabavniks*, thicker and thicker on each subsequent visit.

And then my parents died. I still kept coming to visit my brother, his family, our extended family, our parents' graves in Belgrade, our grandparents' graves in Ropočevo, our village house there, and *Zabavniks*.

On my last visit, in the fall of 2017, I didn't see any magazines. I asked Miša about them. He said that the man who takes care of our property there had told him that mice were chewing up the *Zabavniks*. Miša directed him to toss out whatever was affected.

I'm glad the remaining three tomes are with me in Bellevue. They're my raft to my past, to my nuclear family, when I was loved, when we were happy, healthy, innocent, and strong. When we laughed. When my grandparents were alive. When Yugoslavia seemed prosperous and everything seemed on an upward spiral. Before it all came crashing down.

## Meaning

Every time I visit Serbia, I buy a current *Zabavnik* issue. Usually just one. For such issues now bring on headaches and sadness. The colors are garish. The comics are ugly. The stories are shallow and depressing. I can't relate to its new aesthetic.

Is it perhaps my nostalgia to blame for this? For though I love best the issues from the years 1952 to 1965, my cousin Dobri, who started reading *Zabavnik* in the late 60s, swears by his own tomes, and worships them like a bible.

Others, like my Godbrother Dejan, agree with me that the level of *Zabavnik* has declined, precipitously so. What was so unique about the magazine at its best?

When it appeared in 1952, there were no other comic books in Yugoslavia, and later, when they did appear, proliferated even, none of them covered more than their own particular group of comic characters, and none of them offered articles, stories, imaginative texts.

*Zabavnik* was not just sugar for the mind, it offered proteins and vegetables as well. Not just exotic ideas and facts, but also practical tips: how to remove a stain from a sofa, how to lighten our hair with chamomile, how to make mashed potatoes yummy with nutmeg. Now we have The Internet and YouTube instead.

## Indians

We in Europe, Yugoslavia especially, always loved, adored, romanticized American Indians. In large part it is due to Karl May. This German author, largely unknown in the U.S., a man who suffered from a slew of psychological ailments, wrote romantic novels about the Old American West, without ever having stepped forth on the American Continent. He is so much better than his American counterpart, Zane Gray.

We loved Indians, and *Zabavnik* carried a Disney comic strip starring the ever-so-cute Little Hiawatha. But it also published long articles, in a number of issues, on the real Hiawatha, the American mythic hero, his enemies, his friends.

And even though some Yugoslavs watching American Westerns yelled "Hajde Džone!" when encountering John Wayne, my brother and I never did so, and in our street games with other kids, we refused to play cowboys; we only played Indians.

My brother has a fantastic imagination. He should have been the writer, not I. As a lad of eleven he started, and continued through at least age seventeen, to walk around the apartment, talking aloud to his imaginary friends. Mother, Father and I looked the other way. We never teased him about it. Only, when a visitor would drop by and discreetly ask about Miša's talking, my dad would say: "Miša is chasing Indians." And then we would all burst out laughing, for we all knew Miša and knew that Dad meant that Miša, with his Indian buddies, was chasing dreams, living his dreams.

That was then. For many years now, my brother has been a serious man, a family man, a good provider, an esteemed engineer, but in his free time he still devours science fiction—still chasing dreams.

And me? Same. For what was my mania for physics, my desire to surpass Einstein, and now my writing attempts in my native tongue that I keep forgetting and in my adopted tongue the I keep enduring like a straightjacket?

Both my brother and I still run with the Indians, both of us still chase dreams, both live in the land of *Zabavnik*, and neither of us would want it any other way. 📖

# Closing Time

## Richard Widerkehr

When certain streets
shine under streetlights,
we're like clock hands at midnight,
your hand in mine.

In dark bars, chairs piled
on tables, upside down.
We don't mention the past.

Hands gather light to them.
What we expected
hasn't happened.
It's all right.

*Fantastic Flying Lamp*, 2018, Digital Art, by Drake Truber

# One Night, One Morning

## Richard Widerkehr

One night someone stood under a tin awning
on a loading dock, waiting for rain to stop.

On another coast, a bald eagle on the naked branch
of a stunted Douglas fir would one day tear at breakfast.

As I write this at Fort Worden in a beige living room
whose tan-and-red carpet has gold swirls,

I think of you and my '77 Chevy Vega,
rust spots near the taillights, one dented fender,

*an Indian car,* my Lummi student called it.
At first, I thought the eagle was a raven,

lugging something white over the beach.
I don't know if you've come home from work,

if you're sitting on our green couch knitting,
fending off Gracie as her claws snarl

your crimson yarn. Maybe, you say, *Gracie, no.*
*You're not helping,* your voice

rising like the sail of the windsurfer
I saw this morning, how he leaned and swung

like a keel under his yellow crescent. The love
and irritation in your voice as you tell Gracie *No.*

I never saw you loved me, till you paced
back and forth, yelled, *I am not a dud.*

Back then I didn't think a woman loved me
unless she clawed my back and screamed,

and even then I wasn't sure. Didn't know
the difference between *dust and summer,*

*rain and the smell of rain,* I would come to write.
Hadn't told you about the loading dock

where I prayed, *Please take my life,*
as if I were a piece of paper.

I'm not waiting for rain or my Vega
to get creamed in a demolition derby,

get rebuilt as a stock car with a Corvette engine
and run 250 thousand miles.

Something keeps burning, a fuse on a runway,
two coastlines that never meet,

an eagle tearing at the privacy of breakfast.
In sunlight, I write this for you.

# Changing Roads

## Jeanette Weaskus

He scanned the bar for prey and was thankful for the many party girls to choose from that were always plentiful on Friday nights. The older ones were easy to get although they did not taste as good and were often guarded by younger nieces who watched over their vulnerable aunties with the fierce vigilance found in Native kinship that he did not care to engage. When he could find an older party girl that was alone it was her misfortune to become the nourishment for his body. The older women knew the traditional ways of the drunken dance and had practiced the looks and the easy score for many decades. They knew no other kind of love than the empty bar embrace. First there was the spark that came when the two souls found the appearance of each other acceptable. There wasn't much more after that because the true love of their lives was the party.

The women in the bars trusted him despite his being a stranger in every community because he had the features of a full blood Native man although he was only half on his mother's side. His father was the immortal Chief of the Elk Nation which made him half spirit. Since he belonged to the spirit world there were rules that applied to him like he could only come out at night. He had been punished by his father when he broke his only taboo and ate elk meat. The Elk Chief had cursed him with a burning hunger for the putrid flesh of drunks. He used his powers to make himself look very beautiful to women but the rule was that only drunk women could see the amazing beauty that he was able to generate for himself. Sober women saw him for what he was, elk from the waist down, human from the waist up with a terrifying mouth of shark-like teeth that had the rotting meat of his last victim wedged between every tooth. He also smelled of death but all this was invisible to anyone with a buzz.

In cursing his son to hunger for human meat, the Elk Chief forced him to walk an evil road all alone. The first people he consumed were from his mother's family and they exiled him from their love and companionship. There were no friends for him among the human beings or the vast elk nation although he did have friends among the other spirit beings. He prayed several times a day to the Creator who was the only father he had left until the Elk Chief forgave him. The Creator loved him no matter what and watched over him as he traveled between Indian reservations. He was spirit rule-bound to stay within his mother's homeland so he traveled the Indian bars and cultural events in a seasonal food cycle. Part of his curse was that he could eat only Native women which was both difficult and easy at the same time. Spring was just now starting so it was time to travel upwards from where he wintered on the Klamath Indian Reservation to the Nez Perce Indian Reservation.

He loved the Oregon high desert at this time of the year. The farmers were not out plowing yet and he could run through the miles of farmland across the deer trails all the way to Wallowa Lake where he would find his cousins, the Bigfoots, and visit there for a while. The Bigfoots are the eldest children of the Creator still alive and they know more than any other beings on the earth. Their name for him was Koo-yeh which meant half elk. That was the name he went by in the human world although the women did not know it was given to him by the sacred Eldest Children. Most Native women recognized his name as indigenous language and sometimes they asked what tribe he was from. If a woman did speak his language, which was very rare in these times, he would tell her the truth, that his name was from another language and it meant "Elk." It was one of those uncommon women who spoke his mother tongue that he met one night at the Lewiston Airport Bar.

It was a packed Saturday night of exceptional circumstance, both a tribal payday and a basketball tournament weekend which meant there would be strangers from other reservations flooding the Indian bars after the ball game. He felt like it was his lucky night to find someone good. Tournament weekends were when he could get a delicious twenty-something to leave the bar with him and he could feast under the stars until dawn. Koo-yeh slipped into the crowd and took a look around to see what the men looked like who were getting all the female attention. He went into the bathroom to shape-shift himself into an Eddy Spears-looking Rez guy which was always the right choice for tournament weekends and made his way into the center of the dance floor to begin his hunt. It was then that he heard his language being spoken and searched for who was saying the holy words aloud in a bar.

She had already seen Koo-yeh trapped in the middle of the dance floor.

"Look, it's that fucken hoof monster thing, back on our Rez again," she said to her companion.

"Where?" the young lady with her asked.

"That ugly one with the stupid western trench coat," she said.

"That fine-ass Native that looks like Dreamkeeper Eddy Spears?"

"Is that what you see, Cuz?" she replied, "interesting."

And then she further insulted him by telling him to leave forever in his own language. The young woman watched his face turn sour at these words and then she smiled as if in victory that he understood what was said. He began to make his way towards her. She sat at the bar smoking a cigar. That was appropriate for such an offensive woman; he was thinking about eating her to rid the earth of such insolence.

"You wanna dance, Monster?" she asked and stood up keeping his gaze. She took some kind of battle-ready stance and whipped out a bowie knife from the inside of her jean jacket. Koo-yeh had never seen a woman rise up to challenge him and was snapped out of his righteous anger. A group of large, mean-looking Native men came over and got around them.

"This fool botherin' you, Sister?" one of them asked.

She put her knife away and said, "Kut-see (thanks) but naw, I'm just being crazy Native chick status." She embraced Koo-yeh, kissed him on the cheek and said, "Stop lookin' at bitches you fucker."

The men smiled and melted back into the crowd. She had just saved him from a terrible beating. Even though he was part spirit, men could still hurt him. He had been caught and beaten several times over the last two centuries. Koo-yeh could die and he could feel the pain of being beaten, but unlike humans, he would come back to life and walk away after dying.

"Why?" he asked. She ordered a couple of beers and set one before him.

"Have a beer with me," she held his hand for a minute, "tell me if the stories are true, are you really the son of Hall-Paw-Win-My (Dawn Woman)? She is my ancestor and if you are her son that makes us related," she said.

Koo-yeh caved at hearing his mother's name. He hung his head and let the tears come free after two hundred years. She put her arm around him and he rested his head on her shoulder and just wept and shook until the episode ended. Koo-yeh gulped down his beer and she pushed hers over in front of him. He gulped this one too and she took out a pack of cigarettes and put one into his mouth and lit it. They both smoked and he finally calmed down enough to ask her name.

"Ruby," she said, "and my Indian name is Tom-mom-min."

"Cake?" he asked and couldn't stop laughing for a minute.

Crying and laughing were human acts that he hadn't done since the 1700s when his people still loved him. It was bringing him to another place in the landscape of his heart and mind. She fed him another cigarette and studied his face. "I wonder how different your life would have been with elk for the top half and human for the bottom half?"

They laughed while imagining Koo-yeh with a huge rack of antlers and stout neck supported by a man's lower half. Falling over all the time from being top heavy and relieved to shed his antlers in the early spring. The night went on like that with Koo-yeh answering a myriad of historical questions that Ruby had always wanted to know about language and mythology. And Ruby making them both laugh and smoke cigarettes until they were sick. She told him many wonderful things she learned from other Indians like the Maidu storytellers who told her there were "Wup-toe-lee" which were half human and half fish that lived in the rivers of Northern California. Since Koo-yeh wintered on the

Klamath Indian Reservation, he could venture southeast until he found the Feather River where the Wup-toe-lee live.

"You could marry a Wup-toe-lee," she said, "you're both half human on top, animal on the bottom and spirit beings."

Koo-yeh loved this idea, "I can't go past the Klamath Indian Reservation, though," he said.

"Your father could fix that, let's get you a Wup-toe-lee," Ruby said.

The first thing they had to do was get his curse lifted. Ruby was a scholar of legends and knew the stories about the Elk Chief and his half human son, Koo-yeh. She was also brave enough to try things like bugling for the Elk Chief at the only time he could come to the human world which was under an orange moon. Crazy ass Ruby also sprinkled elk urine to lure him to the creek that he was known to favor. They hid and waited. Ruby kept bugling but he did not come to them on that orange moon. She did not give up. The time came when they did see his father and Ruby came out and placed a fine gift of tobacco and berries before the great Elk Chief. She prayed to him. Ruby asked that the curse afflicting his son be lifted so that Koo-yeh can get himself a Wup-toe-lee wife from the Feather River. She prayed for the great Elk Chief to forgive his son and start to enjoy the grandkids they would have. She prayed for love to return to the family and that they all be blessed by the Creator.

Koo-yeh now walked a new road. He did not go to the bars or eat Native women anymore. With his father's help he was now able to transcend the boundary limitations and travel southeast of the Klamath Indian Reservation to the north and middle forks of the Feather River where the Wup-toe-lee were said to live. Ruby told him to bring pearls and cowrie shells for the Wup-toe-lee. She strung dozens of shell necklaces as gifts for them. Koo-yeh felt the weight of the pearls in his backpack and thought it would be a good time to set them down and have a smoke. He began to sing his favorite song, "Don't Stop Believin'," by Journey. 📖

*Twisted Crow2*, 2008, Photograph, by Rayn Roberts

# In my little room

## Danae Wright

In my little room
I have one chair
for the company
that never comes.
It sits in the corner,
vacant, lacking
even cobwebs.

# The Putting-Off Dance

## Carolyne Wright

Humming a blues riff from far inland,
you lay the moon shells I give you
on your table's little dune of letters
that have piled up for days, unopened
as the bodies of sand dollars.
You are the man
with whom I share a wall.

> All morning in adjacent studios, we move
> between kitchen and work table, each footstep
> tracking its shadow analogue.
> November's ten-knot gale
> rattles the veranda, the sidelong
> windows empty of sky. In diorama

this row of studios opens to its cutaway
dilemmas. In jokes you press a stethoscope
to my wall, X-ray vision switched on full
like figments of wishful thinking.
Moon shells pile up, signs of the zodiac
look both ways. Who says *No*
is out of the question? When I type

> your voice is the sea in my ear.
> When I pause, a chair scrapes
> on your side of the wallboards,
> you cat-walk down the veranda
> to my door. It's too late to outwit
> the moment, redoubling the keystrokes'

arbitrary gabble to reverse your steps,
erase your profile through my Venetian
blinds. Your honey and mulled wine
win this round, your tongue-tied plea
I never quite believe, but my alibis
ride a tilting raft. You give me a turquoise
amulet with broken clasp, its damage

       unexplained as women who ring for you
       on the downstairs phone. I set an African
       violet on the sill, its petals meant to deflect
       you. *Who leads?* I ask the season's waltz card.
       *Who follows?* Our moves tell the future
       in mirrors. You stumble whenever the phone

switches long-distance partners. Your zodiac
unknown: what sign would claim us
from dream's shifting dune-house?
We go back to our desks as if
to lovers, the phone downstairs
ringing its two-tone note: *Decide.*
*Decide.* Words fly out of the letter piles

       clamoring for answers, my blood's
       divided longings. When bedroom lights go out
       in this coastal town, our footsteps
       echo across the floorboards,
       so much diverted sleep between us.
       Stalling for time, I name old lovers,

quote from *The Complete Guide
to Rejection*. Rain squalls off and on
all evening like a difficult conversation.
Doesn't night's unbroken sky

arch like a serious intent, our ends and beginnings
threaded on the same strand, each single
constellation tied to consequence? I fear

       your universe with its own rules. Traceries
       of North Atlantic sand between my quilted
       comforter and pillows, I scribble
       predictions in the dark while the town
       sleeps, inventing one last reason
       it wouldn't work, my body up against
       that wall, braced for giving in.

# Gertrude Bell

## Marjory Woodfield

In the Sheikh of Daja's goat-hair tent there are scattered carpets. Pomegranate, saffron, indigo. There are women behind curtains. Shadows in corners. The men smoke Shisha and call you *al-Khatun*. You sit cross-legged among them. Use fingers to eat the roasted lamb that comes on trays piled high with rice. Drink small cups of dark coffee. Discuss the latest tribal raids. How things are in Egypt. Share ancient texts. You open the Mu'allaqat. Suspended odes, placed on the Ka'aba. Written in gold on Coptic cloth. Bend heads together over the fire. From hand to hand pass the book.

*The Women's March, Edition 4*, Photograph, by Julia Justo

# Just a Kiss

## Janet Yoder

You were my advisor for one year in 1977, before I entered graduate school at the University of Washington. You were the one assigned to guide me through the academic limbo of being a fifth-year student. You suggested courses and faculty who knew their stuff in linguistics and anthropology. We had conversations about language, culture, and politics, about what aspect of language may be hardwired into the brain. We discussed Chomsky's theory of nativism and the Sapir-Whorf hypothesis of linguistic determination. Is thinking formed by language or language formed by thinking? If a language has no past tense verbs but only a past marker that comes at the end of the sentence, does a speaker think more in the present? What is the difference between these two sentences? I went to the market and then I cooked dinner. I go to the market and then I cook dinner yesterday. You revealed your deep knowledge by asking provocative questions about shared assumptions packaged into language or setting problems of justice, race, and status expressed through dialect. You helped me see how everything mixed in the rich estuary of language.

You complimented me on my analysis of the Chomsky texts we discussed. You invited me to join a seminar group of your graduate students. I was flattered and went once. But it was too many academics talking too much abstraction. So I opted to just visit your office monthly to check in.

Somewhere in the months, you began asking personal questions. Gradually I revealed that I had separated from my boyfriend, Robby, and that I had met someone new but was still somehow attached to Robby. I was newly back from a year in Mexico and considering how speaking Spanish had changed me. I was baking quiches part time at the Surrogate Hostess. You revealed that your wife was dying of cancer and your eyes teared up as you spoke of her. You had concerns about how your grown children would handle what lay ahead.

While in eastern Washington visiting my parents, I bought a box of McIntosh apples. Back in Seattle I made applesauce. I dropped a jar by your office door with a note. You called the next day to ask how I knew your wife had passed away. I hadn't known but told you I was sorry for your loss. You insisted I come to your office the next week when you would be back.

It was late afternoon. Out your office window I saw rowers on Lake Washington. You seemed cooped up, wound up. "I have to get out of here," you said. "Do you want to grab a bite with me at Tai Tung?" I said yes and we trekked down all those steps on the east side of Padelford Hall to your car. There was winter light in the sky. We drove down to Chinatown in just a few minutes and parked right near Tai Tung. We took a booth where you pressed a button in the wall when we were ready to order. A waiter came and we made our wishes known. We started with a soup of dark mushrooms. We drank jasmine tea. Then was it chicken chop suey for you and egg foo yung for me? You told me how it was at the end with your wife, that your children were taking the loss hard and each differently. You thanked me again for the applesauce and you picked up the tab.

Then you drove up Capitol Hill to my apartment on Bellevue Avenue. There was no parking so you double parked. I turned to thank you for dinner. You grabbed me and began kissing me hard on the mouth, pushing with your tongue. My surprise slowed me for a second, then I pulled away.

"Why not?" you said. "It's just a kiss."

"I have to go." I grabbed my book bag and jumped out of your car.

I went up the steps to the entry door and then on upstairs to my apartment. My apartment faced the street so I didn't turn on the lights. I walked to the window and watched your car make its way down the street. I closed the curtains and sat down. I felt suddenly shaky and betrayed. Had all of our meetings, discussions, the invitation to the brainy seminar, the advice about courses, had that all been for the purpose of a pushy, mushy kiss? Or more?

I never went back to your office. Shortly after that, I got into my program and got a new advisor who supported me through my studies and on into the teaching world. I'd like to say I never saw you again, but a couple of years later I ran into you at a bakery near Green Lake. It was summer and I had just jogged the lake. I was standing in line when I felt someone's eyes on me. I turned and caught your gaze. You were with a young woman. Was she your daughter? Or a student you were advising? I walked out of the bakery.

More years later I heard you had been accused of sexual harassment. Not rape. Not assault. But unwanted hugs and kisses. You reportedly repositioned the charges, stating you were, "trying to find or create the margin where the power differential between professor and student, an inequality imposed by the institution and its rank-based definition of authority, can be set aside by those who wish to be more free than the usual definitions allow." When I read this, I knew that I should have spoken to someone back in 1977. We both know there are many reasons why I didn't. And we both know that your kiss was not just a kiss. &#128366;

# The Man Who Read My Novel Twice

## Nicole Yurcaba

is the wind sweeping, filling the car
as I race two-lane highways, one hand
steering, the other wiping wisps of hair
from my mouth, Rob Zombie's "Dragula"
smearing from the speakers, blending
openness-howl, exposing dressed wounds,
peeling, redressing, peeling, redressing
with Lidocaine-laced gauze I discovered
in a cabinet where a needle pricked
eighty on the speedometer.

*Transposition*, Drypoint Etch & Aquatint Print,
by John Timothy Robinson

# Random Notes on Seattle's Red Sky Poetry Theatre:
## The Poet's Gymnasium

### Thomas R. Prince

It is an interesting phenomenon that people often don't realize the cultural importance of their work while they are in the process of achieving their personal goals. The individuals who founded Red Sky Poetry Theatre (RSPT) are among them. The brainchild of Don Wilsun, RSPT and its affiliated organizations would shape the literary and performance arts culture of Seattle, the West Coast, and beyond. Red Sky was the longest running open mike poetry series in Seattle history.

But one would not call RSPT a school of poetry. Founding member Matt Lennon said that they specifically were not attempting to create a new school of writing. They were trying to create a venue that was accessible to new authors. They were creating a safe place for those not formally trained to read or write poetry or prose. The "Open Mike"—allowing anyone to sign up to read—was central to that philosophy. It was literally open to all who wished to perform.

Red Sky Poetry Theatre was much more than just the work of its founders. It was already a community of poets, performance artists, and publishers when it was incorporated in 1982. RSPT was more than Spoken Word readers.

Founder Don Wilsun came from a working-poor family. The child of a single mother in the New Orleans of the 1950s and 60s, autodidact Wilsun learned to write the hard way. He learned to drum from his Cajun family. He approached life differently than the academic poets that dominated the Seattle literary scene in the 1980s. In Wilsun's view, Poetry as Art was storytelling intended to entertain the masses as they struggled through their daily lives. Poetry wasn't meant for an elite few who could afford literary art classes. Poetry was not meant to be stiff and rigid. Poetry was meant to be loose and fun.

Red Sky Poetry Theatre was a place to practice one's work. It has been called the "poets' gymnasium." I have heard the origin of this phrase attributed to Don Wilsun, Matt Lennon, Charlie Burks, and RSPT founding member Bill Shively. Wilsun would tell *The Seattle Times*, in 1986, that Burks said it. Burks would say Lennon said it. Lennon would say Shively said it. Shively would say Wilsun said it. One can imagine the four of them, as a joke, intentionally obfuscating who originally coined the term. Not one of them ever took credit for the expression. That is the kind of folks they were.

Red Sky Poetry Theatre had been active for a couple of years before it became an official non-profit organization. Descended from Dogtown Poetry Theatre, which ran briefly in the mid-1970s and was also co-founded by Don Wilsun, RSPT coordinated with organizations like Campus Poets & Writers, a performance group run by Seattle Central Community College instructor JT Stewart and made up of her friends and colleagues.

A short history of Bumbershoot and Red Sky Poetry Theater: another RSPT founding member, Tom Parsons, organized a small press bookfair component for the festival, and RSPT beloved affiliate, Charlie Burks, essentially created Bumbershoot Writers in Performance but left after one year. That chair was filled by someone new each year until One Reel took over producing the festival in 1980. They hired Judith Roche to run the literary arts section of the festival. Up until then, the literary arts performers were all picked by the University of Washington's English Department. These were usually authors who came to Seattle to promote their books. They would read but they weren't necessarily performers. Bill Shively said that the academic readers all sounded exactly the same. Everyone would read in the precise cadence that was the style of the day. Shively emphatically stated that they were just plain boring.

When One Reel took over Bumbershoot they decided it would be a good idea to get some community input. (These were the days when Bumbershoot's mission was still to bring Arts to the general public who otherwise could not afford such things.) They decided to have a town hall-style forum.

This gathering attracted writers from all over the region with one idea in mind: open up the Literary Arts Performance section to local writers and performers. In attendance were Burks, Paul Dorpat, JT Stewart, *Poetry Exchange* publisher Don Glover, who owned Horizon Books, Jeanne Yeasting, and many others who would influence Seattle's growing performance arts scene.

This forum was tumultuous. The old school academics were adamant that only published writers be allowed to perform. The more experimental, underground writers and performers wanted to be able to present innovative work. A compromise was finally reached and in the future the UW would pick only some of the performers. As Judith Roche was already affiliated with Red Sky Poetry Theatre, it was agreed that RSPT would be tasked with supplying local performers.

The Bumbershoot Festival changed how Red Sky Poetry Theatre had to operate: it needed to become an officially-recognized non-profit organization. Six people put their names to the incorporation papers: Don Wilsun, the inspirational father of RSPT, Tom Parsons, Judith Roche, Matt Lennon, who would later become a member of the Seattle Arts Commission, Bill Shively, and Joe Keppler.

Now that Red Sky Poetry Theatre was legit, the board needed to come up with a way to determine who would read at Bumbershoot. They decided to have competitions during the spring with selected judges determining who would read that Labor Day Weekend. People would sign up to read at an open microphone; a number were chosen to come back and perform again, and the judges chose a lucky few to perform in front of an audience of hundreds, then thousands.

By its very nature, Red Sky Poetry Theatre was able to adapt to multiple venues; RSPT was versatile. It could present quiet, intellectual readings at quaint little coffeehouses like Anna's Café, the Cause Celebré, or the Still Life Café in Fremont. Equally, RSPT could be at home promoting raucous, multimedia performances at early grunge venues such as the Five-0 Tavern, the Ditto Tavern, or Squid Row.

The Bumbershoot competitions facilitated by RSPT were truly equal opportunity events. These predated Poetry Slams by fifteen years.

Joe Keppler was not fond of the open mike format so he left to create his own venue and magazine, *Poets. Painters. Composers.*

Shortly before Keppler left, Elliott Bronstein was voted onto the RSPT board. Soon afterwards Trudy Mercer, Michael Hureaux (a future Choreopoet), and Marion Kimes were elected to join the board.

Don Wilsun went back to New Orleans to care for his ailing mom in 1986. Kimes and Bronstein would take over administration of RSPT, roles they would perform until 2005.

Elliott Bronstein (who worked as a Public Information Officer at the Seattle Office for Civil Rights for years) claims he wasn't actually a poet; he was a prose writer. He was attracted to RSPT because of his love for literature in general. He met Don Wilsun at the Pike Place Market and decided to see what this "Poetry Theatre" was really about. Once he witnessed a performance, he was hooked for life. Bronstein had a talent for administration that helped keep RSPT solvent.

Poet Marion Kimes was a tiny woman with a huge presence. She was voted acting president of Red Sky Poetry Theatre in 1986, and retained that position for nearly twenty years. The title was a mere formality; in practice, RSPT generally acted by consensus of the whole board. Kimes was extremely supportive of new authors. It didn't matter how raw and unpolished someone's material was. She would lift their spirits and give them the inspiration to improve themselves. In the same way, she constantly strived to be a better writer and performer herself.

Judith Roche tells a wonderful story about an exuberant Kimes co-hosting the Writers in Performance events with acclaimed poet Sam Hamill. "Marion was there with her cheerleader thing, beating a drum, and he (Hamill) hated it."

Red Sky Poetry Theatre-affiliated authors would be published in myriad magazines, journals, chapbooks and plain, old, black and white Xerox rags. (For those of you who are too young to know, Xerox was the first copy machine for public use. They held a patent for many years.) There was a community of artists who would contribute to publications as well as writers, creating a marvelous synthesis of poetry and form.

RSPT left a huge written legacy. There were the Bumbershoot Anthology books. There was Red Sky Press which published magazines *SkyViews, Open Sound, Open Sky,* (self-published work by contributing writers and artists and coordinated by Bill Shively for many years), and, in 1996, *Nobody's Orphan Child,* an anthology of work by sixty-four writers. Much of this legacy is still available in the marketplace. Some of it can be found in the University of Washington Libraries Special Collections.

In the late 1980s, margareta waterman became a RSPT board member, bringing nine muses books with her—a collection of books and recordings by Charlie Burks, Wally Shoup, Louise Dovell, Michael Hureaux, Roberto Valenza, Don Wilsun, etc.

Matt Lennon and Don Wilsun had radio shows on the Seattle non-commerical radio station KRAB-FM 107.7 in the late 1970s, early 1980s. *Red Sky at Night* was one; *Talk Art* was the other. They would take turns hosting and would sometimes have a guest host like Charlie Burks or Joe Keppler. Recordings of these radio performances have been lost to the sands of time, though earlier readings by Charlie Burks are in KRAB's online archives .

Red Sky Poetry Theatre was an early adopter of the Public-access television format. Television cable companies were required by law to provide free broadcast access to the general public through narrowcast public-access cable TV channels. A lottery system selected who would get TV time slots. Martina and Alan Goodin, RSPT board members since 1984, won excellent evening spots. Their first A & M Production was called *Paramount Poets.* They were still on a learning curve but they recorded several well-known Seattle poets. It ran for one year. Their next show was *Cactus Poets,* which was more polished. They also published a *Cactus Poets* chapbook of the favorite poems of each performer in that two-year series. Their final series was called *Red Sky Live.* Whereas the prior two shows were prerecorded, *Red Sky Live* was, as titled, broadcast in real time. They included an innovative idea called "Phone a Poem," where members of the viewing audience could call in and read something. This was unique and moderately successful.

All of the ¾ inch U-matic master tapes of *Paramount Poets*, *Cactus Poets*, and *Red Sky Live* were lost when the grade school where Alan Goodin taught was remodeled. The stored tapes were tossed in the trash heap while he was away. Very few VHS copies remained. Most performances have vanished from history.

Roberto Valenza, the bad boy poet of Red Sky, once told me personally, "Alternative to Loud Boats is summer camp for Red Sky Poetry." Jeanne Yeasting describes Valenza, the magnificent Phoebe Bosché, and herself, sitting around in a room at the Ontario Hotel. They decided that the Blue Angels [U.S. Navy squadron of fighter aircraft] were just too much noise. Valenza and Bosché, members of the Red Sky board, went to work and created one of the most awaited annual events in Seattle arts.

Organized in 1985, Alternative to Loud Boats (ATLB) happened annually for about ten years. It was more than poetry, much like RSPT itself. It was music, art installations, and performance art theatre. The first ATLB on August 4, 1985, at the Seattle Center, featured Red Sky regulars Willie Smith, Patrick McCabe, Jesse Minkert, Roberto Valenza, Marion Kimes, Bill Shively, Jesse Bernstein, Phoebe Bosché, and musicians Rob Angus, Michael Monhart, Jeff Greinke, and the Tibetan American Jazz Ensemble.

In 1997, after much debate, Red Sky Poetry Theatre left Squid Row Tavern and moved to the Globe Cafe, a vegetarian/vegan cafe. Paul Nelson, founder of the Seattle Poetics LAB (SPLAB), joined the board at this point.

Red Sky Poetry Theatre had twenty-eight official board members over the course of twenty-five plus years. Bronstein and Kimes held RSPT together for twenty years. They finally ran out of steam. Evoked like an exploding sun, RSPT went out with a whimper, not a bang. 📖

MARCH

1
SHELLY NAMEROFF

8
DUNCAN McNAUGHTON

15
SHARON DOUBIAGO

22
CARLETTA WILSON
THERESA CLARK

RED SKY POETRY:

STILL LIFE IN FREMONT
COFFEEHOUSE/ 709
N . 35TH
547 - 9850
29
JOSEPH KEPPLER
MICHAEL MONHART
ARSENIO ORTEZA

*Red Sky Poetry Theater flyer, SkyViews Vol. II, No. III,* March, 1987,
Red Sky Press, Editor Phoebe Bosché,
Contributing Editors James Maloney, Peter Sawicki

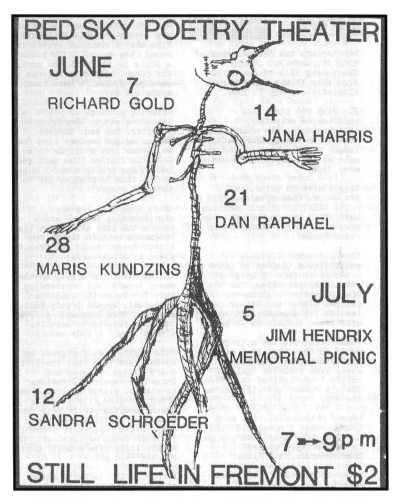

*Red Sky Poetry Theater flyer, SkyViews Vol. II, No. 5,* June-July, 1987, Red Sky Press, Editor Phoebe Bosché, Associate Editor Peter Sawicki, Contributing Editor James Maloney, Poetry Editor Arsenio Orteza

*Red Sky Poetry Theater flyer, SkyViews Vol. II, No. 6,* July, 1987,
Red Sky Press, Editors Phoebe Bosché, James Maloney
Poetry Editor Arsenio Orteza, Associate Editor, Peter Sawicki

"Typical nonsense as I try to write," Drawing, by Saint James Harris Wood

# VIII

## RANTS, RAVES, AND REVIEWS

# turning homeward

restoring hope and nature in the urban wild

adrienne ross scanlan

# Turning Homeward, Restoring Hope and Nature in the Urban Wild

by *Adrienne Ross Scanlan*
Mountaineers Books, Seattle, https://www.mountaineers.org/
ISBN: 978-1-68051-062-1
2016, hardback, 160 pp., $17.95

## Reviewed by Thomas Hubbard

In our beautiful Salish Sea, salmon and other marine wildlife are experiencing an existential crisis, resulting from the presence of ... us. Here's a book, *Turning Homeward*, that discusses the harm we're doing and shows how caring people are working to save, to restore, habitat for Pacific Salmon and other wildlife.

TWISTING WEAKLY in the thick mud, half out of the shallow water, a male sockeye struggled to make his way back to Cottage Lake Creek. The fish had swum underneath the partially raised roots of a cedar and wound up, not in the part of the creek thick with females, but in a tiny mud puddle. He had lost the genetic race. None of the sockeye had eaten since they left the ocean weeks before to make their way upstream to where they were born. Their sole drive was to reproduce, and here was this male—literally and figuratively — stuck in the mud. One of the men on the Sierra Club field trip waded into the black mud, grabbed the struggling sockeye, and tossed it back into the creek. A brief, heated discussion of the ethics of interfering with natural selection ensued, but it ended when someone said, "We can't afford to lose a single one." [p. 22]

Each day, each week, Seattle goes about business as usual. Cargo vessels enter and leave our ports, semis load and unload, freight trains come and go, toilets flush, freeways load up with traffic. Waste, sewage overflow, and pollutants from innumerable sources all wash "away" into our watershed. Exhaust particles from surface and air traffic precipitate to the hard surfaces of roads, roofs, and parking lots, and, with the rain water, wash "away" into our watershed. Truth is, "away" doesn't exist—all the poisons and pollutants end up in our streams, which dump into Puget Sound. And that is killing off our wildlife.

When they return from the ocean into our poisoned bays, rivers, and creeks where the watershed deposits everything that runs off, everything that washes "away," salmon struggle to survive long enough to spawn. Some among us devote hours, days, even decades of labor to save and hopefully to restore the wildlife habitat that our "business as usual" is steadily poisoning. The author of this book is one such person.

Adrienne Ross Scanlan, from the eastern edge of North America, came here seeking a home. Quickly—through her labors—she learned more than most natives and long-timers know about this area's wildlife, especially our urban wildlife. In the excerpt above, she describes a stranded Sockeye salmon, exemplifying the problems she set out to solve.

Scanlan relocated to Seattle from New York in the late 80s, searching for a place to call home. She immediately began a decades-long effort to understand this place. In the forward to her fascinating book, *Turning Homeward*, she explains: "I found home largely through discovering and helping to restore Pacific salmon, a group of creatures that journey from their place of birth, change and grow, and then return home, changed again." Scanlan's book tells a story of her long service to the continuing effort at repairing the damaged relationship between wild Pacific salmon and the beautiful Pacific Northwest that they nourish. This book, and her years of service, substantiate her right to call Seattle *home*.

In claiming Seattle, Scanlan says she followed the Jewish tenet of *Tikkun Olam*: repairing the world. Upon her arrival here, she became aware of serious harm being done to the Pacific Northwest and its resident wildlife by humans, especially those of us identifying as part of the five-century influx of Europeans and the resulting American capitalism. She labored for years to repair what she could of this harm—braving cold, soaking, muddy, laborious days along area creeks and waterways—and this book records her efforts, her successes. Chapters of Scanlan's book bear the names of creeks and drainage areas in and around Seattle, such as "Cottage Lake Creek," "East King County," and "Phinney Ridge." These creeks and wild areas remaining here are the sites of ongoing give-and-take between destruction and repair.

Scanlan pictures the terrible waste of adult salmon returning from the ocean to spawn, but instead dying (often, almost immediately upon entering one of our polluted creeks) before they can find a mate and create the next generation.

> I thought back to that day long ago at Kelsey Creek when I'd held fertilized coho eggs in my hands before placing them in incubation tubes. Pre-spawn mortality was revealed just a few years after that. In the late 1990s, Seattle Public Utilities and Washington Trout (now the Wild Fish Conservancy) conducted field studies to see if habitat restoration was making it possible for adult salmon to reach and spawn in urban streams. Up and down creeks were seemingly healthy coho females bulging with eggs, or males with milt (which holds sperm cells and body fluids), but nearly all were dead or dying before spawning, and many were still in their ocean-phase colors, indicating that they had been in freshwater for a relatively short time. [p. 96]

A parallel effort Scanlan writes about is the removal of "invasive" plants—those not native to the Pacific Northwest. In her process of learning about the area's wildlife and plants, she became familiar with many local species, both invasive and native. But after cutting, snipping, and ripping out Himalayan blackberries for some time, she came to respect them, equating them with the starlings—a few non-native birds imported in the 1700s, that have come to inhabit nearly every U.S. city. Eventually she came to identify herself as a "non-native species." She notes that having moved here from another region causes her to be more aware and alert to the plants and animals around her. She finally has come to respect the invasives for their hardiness.

Speaking again as a weed, I'd have to say that tenacity counts. Maybe the Himalayan blackberry has earned its place, if only because it's so hard to get rid of. More than a few restoration volunteers I've spoken to voice my concern: Why penalize the plant for being hardy and able to tolerate new environments? [p. 84]

In her long labors to repair damages in this place she has claimed as her home, Scanlan has gained a more forgiving attitude. "I had a personal issue to wrestle with as I snipped thorny spines of Himalayan blackberry, smelling the fragrance of verdant life with each cut. I'm ambivalent about weeds because it took a weed to help me make a home." [p. 86] Such character development is a classic marker for stories considered important to this and most other cultures. It's a human value.

Hard-gained tolerance doesn't, however, lessen her dedication to repairing the damage we've done, as she works to restore salmon habitat. Nor does she limit her concern to salmon. Scanlan's effort extents to habitat in general. She advocates for natural areas with diverse flora, to attract and support what she poetically calls "an ever-changing kaleidoscope of bird species."

The last chapter of Scanlan's book, titled "Green Lake Park," tells of the successful (albeit premature) birth of her daughter, Arielle, and of taking her to Green Lake. "Her second spring, I wheeled Arielle in her stroller around Green Lake to show her turtles. Turtles, cattails, red-winged blackbirds, daffodils—it was all the same to Arielle, all part of a big world she had yet to discover." [p. 145]

At the end of *Turning Homeward* Scanlan includes a few pages not only listing, but introducing and discussing her sources. This book belongs in the backpack of anyone exploring and learning about Seattle and the Pacific Northwest, especially those of us looking to call it home. 📖

*On Anzio Beach*

Elizabeth Alexander

# On Anzio Beach

by *Elizabeth Alexander*
Ravenna Press, Edmonds, WA 98020
Order info: *www.ravennapress.com*
ISBN: 978-0-9985463-6-0
2017, hardback, 130 pp., $12.95

## Reviewed by Larry Laurence

What do talking dogs (one is a temporary reincarnation of a chain-smoking, whisky-drinking obstetrician who continues these habits as a Scottish terrier), a talking black bear, a talking grandfather clock, a talking angelfish (another reincarnation, this time the mother of the narrator's best friend), a sentient carpet, thermostat, car, hat, and a marble seagull who also flies and eats crumbs, have in common? Wait, there's more: a recurring, several hundred year-old daemon (guardian angel) now in the form of a sarcastic, mostly well-meaning but ineffectual, talking dashboard doll who has (mostly) lived in Dallas since the city's founding (1841). And more: God, St. Peter, The Pearly Gates, angels, souls, spirits, specters. And more: historical figures including Civil Rights icons Sojourner Truth and Fannie Lou Hamer; Jane Heap, influential supporter of Modernist literature and co-editor of *The Little Review* (1914–1929); artists, including French artist Yves Klein and Algerian artist Rachid Koraïchi. And more: historical events and settings including WWI and II; 1920s Paris; Algerian struggle for independence from France (1954–62); 1950s–70s Dallas, replete with KKK, Jim Crow, segregation, and a long-delayed (some thirty years after Brown v. Board of Education) integration, as well as visits back to contemporary Dallas; a girls' school, a graduate school in theology plus a Methodist ministry in the late 1970s–early 80s New England; and the beginnings of the U.S.–Afghanistan War (2001).

As I'm sure you've guessed by now, all of the above (and more!) are in Elizabeth Alexander's highly imaginative and genre-busting collection of short stories, *On Anzio Beach.* "Genre-busting" because many of these stories can be described as surreal and experimental: part fable, part memoir, part coming-of-age, and part historical, societal, and aesthetics essay, as well as political-religious satire.

On my first reading of these thirteen short stories, I was sure I would write about the title story, "On Anzio Beach," the longest of the collection and a lovely story with a numinous ending. It is a dream-within-a-dream concerning several of the collection's recurring characters: two white families with daughters who are all best friends in conservative Christian, white, segregated 50s-60s Dallas, and a girl (the narrator, Elizabeth) who rebelled as a young woman and left Dallas for college in New England. Elizabeth is now a middle-aged woman back in Dallas, caring for her elderly, dying mother. Elizabeth's father died some thirty years earlier. I would describe the story as a coming-of-age tale, part two. It is something we Baby Boomers and some aging Gen-Xers know well: We become parent/caretaker of our parents and inevitably find we have "unfinished business" with our parents even if we thought we had settled things. Elizabeth believes in life and death but death does not mean the end of existence: "I knew that Daddy existed. I sensed him. I had dreamed him. . . . As to where Daddy was: that was the question. Only a great detective could find the answer."

That detective turns out to be a dog, the above-mentioned "temporary reincarnation of a chain-smoking, whisky-drinking obstetrician who continues these habits as a Scottish Terrier" who was in life (but remember he still exists somewhere and somehow) the best friend of Elizabeth's father (also an obstetrician) and mother. We embark on a dream journey which includes a visit to Elizabeth's present-day mother, then to 1920s Paris, and lastly to WWII Italy and Anzio Beach. Historically, Anzio Beach is nicknamed "Hell's Half Acre," a fierce WWII Allied Forces–Nazi battle site where Elizabeth's father served as a surgeon in a U.S. Army mobile surgery (MASH unit)—basically a collection of large medical surgery tents well within range of Nazi artillery and bombs.

But on my second reading of this collection (when I review a book, I always do at least a second reading), I realized I must write about "Transpositions," a brave, religious, political, social, civil rights satire which I originally thought was a minimally disguised, darkly comic riff on Donald Trump. The story, or perhaps parable is a better term, begins in October 2001, with George W. Bush's "Operation Enduring Freedom," the U.S.–Afghanistan War, America's second-longest (and continuing) war. Do you remember the mass U.S. bombing raids, antipersonnel cluster bomblets, thousands of civilian deaths? Obviously, Elizabeth Alexander remembers. However, she doesn't place her story in Afghanistan or in the U.S. The setting is Christian Heaven at The Pearly Gates. Let's look at some excerpts from the first few pages of "Transpositions," and perhaps you'll see why I thought Alexander was actually writing about Trump:

If she had died only two days earlier, Synthia Comer would have breezed her way into Heaven.

Unfortunately, Synthia had her fatal aneurysm on October 5, 2001, when Saint Peter imposed a quota of zero Americans in heaven.
God demanded an explanation.
"Americans are nothing but trouble," Saint Peter declared. A doubt flickered in his hard blue eyes but passed away. "Moreover, even You cannot guarantee their security. Not after the bombing—"
"—What bombing?"

God saw what he had made and, behold, it was no longer good. God cried for the physical world and every living thing. His tears fell as blossoms: apricot, orange, apple, plum, dogwood, and pear. They softened the world. They cushioned Synthia's fall.

Saint Peter likewise believed that the dead—those who had behaved on Earth—would return to God. Saint Peter had, however, inadvertently created an imbroglio in the mechanism: When he barricaded the pearly gates against Americans, a gap in the back fence appeared. Anyone at all could gain admittance.

Saint Peter called for volunteers to mend the gap, but none came forth. Mrs. Fannie Lou Hamer had aroused the opposition. She addressed Saint Peter with the same searing authority with which she testified before the Credentials Committee, on behalf of the Mississippi Freedom Democratic Party, in 1964.

Standing tall, without crutches or cane, her left eye clear as the right, Mrs. Hamer planted herself before Saint Peter. "What are you afraid of?" she demanded. "Some kind of jihad?"

Saint Peter blushed.

A quartet of angels formed a semicircle around Mrs. Hamer. "Precious Lord, take my hand lead me home," the angels sang.

Saint Peter lifted his eyes unto the hills. "Regretfully, we cannot revisit our decision at this time."

Mrs. Hamer shook him by the wings. "Shame on you! Who made you Pope?"

Saint Peter looked to his right, but God had flown the coop.

Still thinking that "Transpositions" was, in fact, a satiric riff on Trump and his so-called immigration policies, I looked to see if the story had been published prior to its inclusion in *On Anzio Beach*. It so happens that "Transpositions" first appeared in the online journal, BlazeVOX, in 2013. So, Elizabeth Alexander is not only a skilled, highly imaginative writer. She's also prescient!

I'll conclude this review with my own attempt at prescience: On finishing reading this wondrously, odd collection of short stories, the reader, if the reader is like me, will be wonderfully awed. 📖

# Snake Medicine

(First Step)

Laura Lee Bennett

# Snake Medicine (First Step)

*by Laura Lee Bennett*
Nine Muses Books,
3541 Kent Creek Road, Winston, OR 97496
ISBN: 1-878888-76-5
2017, paper, 16 pp., $7.50

## Reviewed by Jim Maloney

*Snake Medicine*, Laura Lee Bennett's newly released chapbook, is a prose poem tracing a decent into drugs and desire. But this is no journal scribbling. Whatever autobiographical details originated the piece have been polished down to totemic images. The narrator has no name, and her nemesis is only referred to as The Outlaw—who she circles around irrevocably attracted and waiting to get burned.

There is an outlaw living in your house.

He came for the weekend and brought his laundry. You didn't know that outlaws did things like laundry, and actually they don't. Instead they leave deposits of their bodily functions around your house: milky yellow wads of tissue, misty drops of urine, dried semen, salty tears. They also leave the richly colored patina of their habits on your fine wood furniture: sticky marijuana resin, empty whiskey bottles filled with cigarettes long dropped inside of them. But mostly it is the smell the outlaws leave behind. The *smell*.

Things proceed from attraction to obsession to addiction.

Little did you know that the outlaw has brought another lover with him: a powdery sprite that he carries in a round tin case. He summons this lover often, in the form of tiny glassy flakes, and spreads her intricate particles carefully across a piece of agate. He offers you the silt of this lover, he offers you the straw.

He wants you to make this lover yours also, and you do. You want to be where the outlaw has been, you want to wear all his shapes.

And of course the end is predetermined but recounted with a wry sense of humor.

One evening you return and the outlaw is gone. There is hair in the shower drain and fresh spoor in the ashtray. The Yellow Pages are open to T for Taxicabs. He has showered, shaved, and gone. However, he has left his laundry, which by now is a pile as high as the ceiling. Your house reeks of the outlaw and his feet.

This makes you angry. You feel an anger and desperation unparalleled. You feel ferocious and vengeful. You grab all the laundry and stuff it into a large garbage bag. You shove the bag of laundry into the back of your car. You grab a bottle of Bushmill's and you hit the road, in search of him.

The bottom is approaching.

The next thing you know there is a loud juicy smack, and your head bounces off the steering wheel. Somewhere nearby glass is grinding and metal is crunching. There are lights everywhere, red and white lights. Someone is knocking at your window. You roll the window down. Someone is asking you to please get out of the car ma'am.

And then comes the recovery. First rehab:

They tell you that you must join Alcoholics Anonymous. They tell you that you must write your First Step. That you must confess your sins. You must admit that your life has become unmanageable due to drugs and alcohol. You must call upon your Higher Power. You are a sick person trying to get well. You have a disease, like diabetes. You can't get well by yourself, and you can't get well while you're using. You must ask the forgiveness of God. You must ask His support in helping you kick your habit. Let go and let God, they say. Let go.

Where is the loving self-acceptance in that?

Then there is mysticism retrieving past lives:

You and the outlaw were members of a devil-worshiping cult. There were nine of you. You lived with this cult from the age of ten to the age of 96. You were involved in torturing animals and small children. There was bestiality. Sex. Fire.

But ultimately the narrator is left to pull it all together.

*Snake Medicine* is a humorous, well-crafted journey, well worth the read. The book is elegantly produced by nine muses books, and has original cover art by Crystal Edwards.

[Note: this story was first read at Red Sky Poetry Theatre, Ditto Tavern, Seattle, Washington, in April, 1993.] 📖

*Lost Glove*, Seattle, 2018, Photograph, by Kevin J. O'Conner

# IX

# RAVEN NOTES

# NOTES, PERMISSIONS, AND
# PUBLICATION CREDITS

**Anna Bálint:** " 'Ilonka's List' came about in relation to trying to learn more about my own history and some huge holes—the disappearances of whole swaths of my Hungarian family—and conflicting stories of our Roma ancestry. While I've learned a lot about the Roma and myself through the research that accompanied this personal search—and that included numerous trips to Hungary and reconnecting with family—I've also encountered many more holes, missing puzzle pieces. I wrote this story as part of trying to negotiate holes. Specifically, in trying to make sense of the Roma experience of seeking compensation for their suffering during the Holocaust, about which I could find almost no information. All I had to go on was that a) some Roma eventually were compensated in the 1970s; b) many Roma never applied for compensation due to a variety of reasons, including illiteracy, suspicion/fear, not receiving relevant information, etc. Hence, this story took me, and Ilkona, on a wild, dream-like chase that had little to do with hard facts and yet in the end felt completely true."

**Paul Bamberger:** "And Then On To Palookaville," will be published in his next book of poems, *A Country of Long Winters*, by Deerbrook Editions in fall, 2018.

**Michael Daley:** "The Virgin Knife" was published by the online magazine *Fungi* in 2018. Reprinted by the permission of the author.

**Sharon Goldberg:** "Many thanks to my cousin, author Hollace Ava Weiner, whose research provided the basis for the early part of my essay, 'Searching for My Name.' "

**Rafael Jesús González:** "One Way of Looking at Thirteen Blackbirds/Un modo de ver trece pájaros negros," a tanka, is Rafael's response to Wallace Stevens' poem, and to the Katsushika Hokusai painting, *Willows and Birds*.

**Steve Griggs:** Thanks to the support of the Seattle Office of Arts & Culture's CityArtists program for the creation of "Blues for John T. Williams."

**Katsushika Hokusai:** (Japanese, 1760-1849) The painting, *Willows and Birds*, is in the public domain.

**Sue Gale Pace:** "The External Me," a creative non-fiction piece, was previously published, in a slightly different version, in an online-only journal, *Epiphany*, which no longer exists.

**Belle Randall** on **Mary Randall:** "The story, 'The True Vocation, was written by my mother Mary Randall in 1949. I'm getting Mary's writings published in a couple of different places. Her letters to American philosopher Stanley Cavell are part of the special-collections archive at the Bancroft Library, UC Berkeley, and she is clearly identified as Mary Randall. I've been tempted to 'Honor my mother' by allowing her to use my name, as she did when submitting 'The True Vocation.' I kind of honor her and get payback at the same time."

**Jack Remick:** "The Wisdom of Finishing" and "The Arrogance of the Princely Mind" are essays included in Remick's manuscript in preparation, *What Do I know? Wisdom in the Twenty-first Century* (2018).

*Friend in a Teacup*, Photograph, by Jury S. Judge

# BIOGRAPHICAL NOTES
## Artists / Illustrators

Seattle-based artist **Alfredo Arreguín** has exhibited his work internationally, recently at the Museo de Cadiz in Spain (2015). He has exhibited solo shows at Linda Hodges Gallery since 2001. In 1980, he received a fellowship from the National Endowment for the Arts. In 1988 Arreguin won the commission to design the poster for the Centennial Celebration of the State of Washington (the image was his painting Washingtonia); that same year he was invited to design the White House Easter Egg. Perhaps the climatic moment of his success came in 1994, when the Smithsonian Institution acquired his triptych, *Sueño* (*Dream: Eve Before Adam*), for inclusion in the collection of the National Museum of American Art. Arreguin's work is now in the permanent collections of two Smithsonian Museums: The National Museum of American Art and the National Portrait Gallery.

**Kree Arvanitas** is a mixed-media artist based in Seattle, with cultural roots in Greece and Western Europe (Netherlands). An autodidact, she has been illustrating or drawing since childhood. Currently she is focusing on acrylic, altered photos, mixed-media, and collage as her "weapons of choice" under the name RebelDog Studio. She co-curated the exhibit *Artful Henna* in 2010 (with artist Jeanie Lewis), which featured henna-inspired art on and off the human body from internationally acclaimed body artists; she curated *Tesseract: 4 Artists, 4 Dimensions* in 2015, featuring three other artists (Matthew Potter, Lesley Rialto and Jeanie Lewis). Kree is Art Director for a new online magazine, *Enzyme Arts Magazine* (*https://www.facebook.com/enzymemag/*), and is a member of CoCA Seattle (Center On Contemporary Art) and A/NT Gallery in Seattle, Washington.

**Toni La Ree Bennett** is both a photographer and writer. She attended the University of Washington, where she received a PhD in English, and a Certificate in Photography. Visual work has appeared in *Women Arts Quarterly* (cover), *Cimarron Review* (cover), *Nassau Review* (upcoming), *Rappahannock Review, Glassworks, Gravel, Grief Diaries, Memoir, Poetry Review, Atomic Petals*, and others. Her work is online at *tonibennett.com*. "*Peach Beach* was taken from the Santa Monica pier. With the haze and ocean foam and distance from the scene, I felt I was looking at a scene from the past, at people that, at least on that day, let the waves wash all their troubles away. *Bus Tunnel* was also taken from a distant view. Tunnels frighten me, and I was confronting that nightmare I have of being trapped in a tunnel or watching a monster come out of it. Or the nightmare of just missing the #41 back to Northgate."

**Angela Boyle** is a natural science illustrator and cartoonist who runs the natural history anthology, *Awesome 'Possum*. She spends entirely too much time working freelance at home, alone, and is perhaps becoming a little more morbid every day. You can find her online at *angelaboyle.flyingdodostudio.com*, and at Twitter, Instagram, and Tumblr as *angelabcomics*. "Living in Seattle, I would often walk with my boyfriend and two dogs, and we would see an abundance of crows. We wondered what they were so loudly discussing, and hence *Oooh, Shiny!* was born. These are pages 8–11 of the original comic from 2011. The comic was made using linocut, with hand lettering on each of the eight original sets of prints."

**Anita K. Boyle** is a poet, artist, and publisher of Washington State poets in handmade, limited editions through Egress Studio Press. As an artist, she makes paper and prints, paintings in watercolor and oil, assemblages, and handmade one-of-a-kind books with materials from nature and handmade paper. She has four eight-page natural science comics in three of the four *Awesome 'Possum Natural Science Comic Anthologies*. "Who doesn't love a corvid? Crows have the attitude toward life that we desire, but seem unable to fully grasp. Just like my best friends, crows are intelligent, playful, sneaky, kind, and generous. They tell great jokes. They play music in the early morning light. As I drew this swaggering one in graphite on paper, I thought about all that."

Santa Monica, California-based artist **Gregg Chadwick** has been painting for three decades. His current studio is an old airplane hangar where the flurry of takeoffs and landings on the runway outside seems to creep into Chadwick's paintings as he explores the movement of past, present, and future within his light-filled paintings. His current series of paintings is entitled *Mystery Train,* and evokes the railways of America, steel rivers that Chadwick says run in his blood. His grandfather worked as a fireman stoking coal in steam engines before advancing to train engineer on the Jersey Central Railroad Line. "*The Passerby*: In a cafe on 1st Avenue in Seattle, John Coltrane played on the sound system, pulling me back in time. Outside, streetcars used to rumble down the avenue. My mind drifted, shifting time and location. *Under the El*: Above us, the trains thundered. In the maze of traffic under the El, she seemed to search for something. Her taxi? Her Uber? Her friend? A car radio played. I knew that song. What was that song?"

**Manit Chaotragoongit** was born in Bangkok, Thailand, and earned a BA in Political Science and Public Administration. Currently he works for the Port Authority of Thailand, and studies photography. "I prefer conceptual photography and street life. My artwork is all about life. [In my photos] I stopped the movement of story around myself before it changed or [was] lost in time. I took a photo and collected a moment of something or somewhere that impressed me and had meaning. I could not live without a memory, experience, or feeling from [an] event . . . The memory is important for the present and the future."

**E. Grace Dager** received a BFA from Cornish College of the Arts, and is currently operating an Artist Loft Bed 'n' Breakfast and "live in" gallery, Gold E. Lofts, in Everett, Washington. "I work in many mediums, but find photography especially poignant in capturing the mood of the street. The images are from a series of photographs documenting the changing graffiti in and around Seattle."

**Patrick Dixon** is a writer/photographer retired from careers in teaching and commercial fishing. His photographs have been published in *Cirque Literary Journal, Oregon Coast, The Smithsonian,* and several fishing trade magazines, including *National Fisherman.* Patrick received an Artist Trust Grant for Artists to edit *Anchored in Deep Water: The FisherPoets Anthology,* published in 2014. His poetry chapbook *Arc of Visibility* won the 2015 Alabama State Poetry Morris Memorial Award." The photo, *Raven in Snow,* was taken in 2008, in Kodiak, Alaska. I have been connected with ravens ever since a couple of them greeted me when I moved to Alaska. I love their intelligence, personality, and stark beauty. The image was posterized and manipulated in Photoshop."

**Kathleen Gunton** is a poet/photographer. She believes one art feeds another. Committed to literary journals, her work has graced the cover and inside pages of *Thema, Flint Hills Review, Arts & Letters, Potomac Review,* and *Broad River Review*—to name a few. She posts to her blog "Discursion" (*http://kathleengunton.blogspot. com*). "Birds are a gift. As a photographer I am always challenged in trying to capture them. On my daily walks I carry my small Canon PowerShot with a zoom on it so exact that I can catch a bird's eye—which is what I did with this corvid, captured on June 24, 2017, while I was on my daily walk near Santiago Creek in Orange, California. Eye to eye is always my goal. *Raven Chronicles* had publisheda couple of my images in the past, so, of course, my first thought was what is this bird saying with his quick glance? 'Remember Me.' Yes. And then he was off to his world of sky."

**Katsushika Hokusai**—professional names Shunrō, Sōri, Kakō, Taito, Gakyōjin, Iitsu, and Manji (born October 1760, Edo [now Tokyo], Japan, died May 10, 1849, Edo)—was a Japanese master artist and printmaker of the ukiyo-e ("pictures of the floating world") school. His early works represent the full spectrum of ukiyo-e art, including single-sheet prints of landscapes and actors, hand paintings, and surimono ("printed things"), such as greetings and announcements. His famous print series, *Thirty-six Views of Mount Fuji,* published between 1826 and 1833, marked the sum-mit in the history of the Japanese landscape print.

**Jury S. Judge** is an internationally-published cartoonist, writer, and artist. His political cartoons are featured in his column, "Comic Quarters," of *The Noise*, a literary arts and news magazine. His cartoons are also published in the *Lowell Observer*. His artwork has been published in several literary magazines, *Dodging The Rain*, *The Manhattanville Review*, and *New Plains Review*. He graduated Magna Cum Laude with a BFA from the University of Houston-Clear Lake in 2014.

**Julia Justo** is an Argentinian-born American artist. She combines digital technology, embroidery, and collage to create mixed media works, often working from vintage pictures that give her work a sense of history. She holds an MFA from the National University of Argentina. Her awards include a 2017 Certificate of Recognition from Laura Phipps, Curator, The Whitney Museum of American Art. "My work reflects on the social and political powers that affect me, an immigrant and a Latin woman, and my community. According to historical archives, in the the 1960s and 1970s a main focus of the NYPD was to spy on civil rights groups. The recent increase in protesters reminds me of those struggles. I ignore the boundaries between then and now, art and document, figuration and abstraction. I believe that present social struggles remain from what came before, and the role of the artist is to give society the tools to resist discrimination. . . ."

**J.I. Kleinberg** is artist, poet, freelance writer, and co-editor of *56 Days of August* (Five Oaks Press, 2017) and *Noisy Water: Poetry from Whatcom County, Washington* (Other Mind Press, 2015). She lives in Bellingham, Washington, and blogs most days at *thepoetrydepartment.wordpress.com*. "These visual poems are from an ongoing series of collages (1600+) built from phrases created unintentionally through the accident of magazine page design. Each chunk of text (roughly the equivalent of a poetic line) is entirely removed from its original sense and syntax. The text is not altered and includes no attributable phrases. The lines of each collage are sourced from different magazines."

**vivian linder levi:** "The so-called homo sapiens, those shards continue to emit the echoes of the ones who were erased from existence; the resonance comes through study, contact with the people, dreams, ancient Hebrew letters, and, last, but not least, the music."

**Kevin J. O'Conner** mostly works with words these days, but he has been photographing things since early childhood. His photographs have been published in *Spindrift*, and featured prominently in his 2016 poetry collection, *This Is Fifty-three*. "This was one of those 'found art' opportunities. I was leaving Third Place Books [in Seattle] on a rainy Friday afternoon, and spotted the glove on the pavement next to a car parked a couple spaces away from mine. I almost kept walking, but changed my mind, took out my phone, and got the shot. Whatever the story was behind the glove (and the broken chopsticks next to it), it ended in that parking lot."

**Willie Pugh** is a long time Seattle photographer and an Alabama native. He attended an all-black high school in Selma, Alabama during the height of the civil rights movement. At age fifteen he took part in the Selma to Montgomery marches. It was during this period that he first became interested in photography as a way of recording and remembering the world in which he lived. His photos have appeared in such diverse places as *Ebony Magazine*, *Beacon Hill Times*, and *Raven Chronicles*.

**Rayn Roberts'** work is found in printed anthologies and journals. He is author of *Jazz Cocktails and Soapbox Songs*, *The Fires of Spring*, and *Of One and Many Worlds*. In his home state, Washington, he's often heard at local readings and on KSER Radio FM 90.7 for PoetsWest. He hosts a reading series at Green Lake Public Library in Seattle. His latest book, *These Boys, These Men*, will be published in fall 2018.

**Sabrina Roberts**, photographer, collaborated with poet Joan Fiset on a series of poems and photos in this issue. Sabrina lives in Bothell, Washington. Her photographs have appeared in *Assisi*,

*Trickhouse, Shots Magazine, Washington English Journal*, and *Press*. Group exhibitions include: Photographic Center Northwest, 10th Annual Photographic Competition Exhibition, Opus, University of Maine at Augusta, and the Maine Media Workshops, Rockport, Maine.Visit her at *www.sabrinaroberts.com*.

**John Timothy Robinson** is a traditional, mainstream citizen and a ten-year educator for Mason County Schools in Mason County, West Virginia. In Printmaking, his primary medium is Monotype and Monoprint process with an interest in collagraph, lithography, etching and nature prints. "*The Primordial Geology* edition is a series of nine prints created through drypoint etching. I attempted to illustrate changes in texture and line. The idea of working and then reworking the same plate seemed to complement the idea that the initial print sketch resembled a rock face or similar geological feature. I kept working the idea through the nine prints until in the final print, *Transformed*, I added an aquatint to make a few contrasting gradations while keeping the outer lines of the print image."

Years before acquiring his first camera, **Joel Sackett** discovered photography in a suitcase full of albums of black pages and deckle-edged photographs. He attended the University of Copenhagen, the Praestegaard Experimental Film School in Denmark, and the San Francisco Art Institute. He lived in Japan from 1980 to 1990, working as an editorial and documentary photographer. He photographed for *Backstage at Bunraku* and *Rikishi, The Men of Sumo*, both published by John Weatherhill, Inc. Sackett moved to Bainbridge Island in 1990 with his wife, Michiko and their two children. He produced a series of annual exhibits about the island and the books, *In Praise of Island Stewards* and *An Island in Time*. "The liveaboard photographs attest to my belief that when all is said and seen, there is no greater priveldge than contributing to the historical record."

**Judith Skillman** is interested in feelings engendered by the natural world. Her medium is oil on canvas and oil on board; her works range from representational to abstract. Her art has appeared in *Minerva Rising, Cirque, The Penn Review, The Remembered Arts,* and elsewhere. She studied at Pratt Fine Arts Center, and the Seattle Artist's League under the mentorship of Ruthie V. Shows include The Pratt. Visit her at *jkpaintings.com.*

**George L. Stein** is a writer and photographer living in Michigan City, in Northwest Indiana. George works in both film and digital formats in the urban decay, architecture, fetish, and street photography genres. His emphasis is on composition with the juxtaposition of beauty and decay lying at the center of his aesthetic. Northwest Indiana's rust-belt legacy provides ample locations for industrial backdrops. George has been published in *Midwestern Gothic, Gravel, Foliate Oak, After Hours, Hoosier Lit, Gulf Stream Magazine, 3Elements, Stoneboat, Occulum, the Gnu Journal, Iliinot Review* and *Darkside Magazine.*

**Don Swartzentruber** is a contemporary artist; he holds an MFA from Vermont College of Norwich University. His work has been featured in magazines such as *Footsteps to Oxford, The 2River View, Wisconsin Review, 5 Trope, Indiana Review, Forge, Driftwood, Rhubarb-Winnipeg, Half Drunk Muse, The Agonist: Thoughtful, Global, Timely, The Lampshade, Winamop,* among others. Don has taught college and secondary classes since 1993, and is the recipient of numerous awards such as Indiana Arts Commission Grants, Lilly Creativity Fellowship Awards, International Graphic Arts Trust Scholarship, etc. Follow him on Instagram and Facebook as *carnivalsage* or visit *www.swartzentruber.com.*

**Drake Truber's** sketches are recognized for their emotional energy and narrative qualities. His work has been exhibited at The Rochester Contemporary Art Center, Fort Wayne Museum of Art, and the National Department of Education. His interest in interactive learning nurtured the creation of a Latin language learning video game, Vindac, which was entered in the Independent Games Festival. Drake is currently studying entertainment and fine art illustration at Art Center College of Design in Pasadena, California. Follow Truber's work on Instagram, Twitter (@ drake.truber), and *www.draketruber.com*.

**Theodore C. Van Alst, Jr.** lives and works in Missoula, Montana. His short story collection about sort of growing up in Chicago, *Sacred Smokes*, is forthcoming from the University of New Mexico Press. His writing and photography have been published in *The Rumpus, Entropy, Electric Literature, The Raven Chronicles, High Desert Journal, Indian Country Today, Literary Orphans*, and *Yellow Medicine Review*, among others. "I am fortunate to live in Montana and also to have the ability to travel. The West and Northwest present a tapestry so visually rich it can be difficult some days to decide where to rest your eye. But whether walking, driving, or flying, I'm always ready for that light that's just about to become magic, that self-composing vista, that relative from the woods or the sky who I only have to ask for a picture. I hope I've shown at least a little of the inspiration I'm blessed to see daily."

**Daniel Staub Weinberg** is a pen and ink and colored pencil Wordartist. He has had a number of group shows and two solo shows in the Chicago area. "After travels to Germany long ago, and Israel not so long ago, I realize that the world is inhabited by creatures that sense distances in different ways, and that spaces between people are flexible and prone to change. Languages used to interest me, now I see art as a unique language. . . ." Visit him at *www.artpal.com*, then search for *weinbergsart*.

**Jack Williams** is a multidisciplinary artist who specializes in text-based art and video art, and sometimes a convergence between the two. He studied Performance Writing at Dartington College of Arts, and earned a MA in Film and Screen Studies at Goldsmiths College, University of London. "This piece of concrete poetry was created using a prominent example of a homonym. The word *stares* is represented semantically, whereas *stairs* is evoked structurally. With text-based art I believe that spatiality is often as crucial as the text itself."

**Saint James Harris Wood** was on the road with his psychedelic punk blues band, The Saint James Catastrophe, when he picked up the heroin smoking habit. This inevitably led to a California high desert penal colony where he reinvented himself as a writer of the darkly absurd. His poetry, fiction, and essays have been published in *Confrontation, Meridian, Tears In The Fence, On Spec, Lynx Eye, The Sun,* and other less reputable literary gazettes.

**Judy Xie's** work has been nationally recognized by Scholastic Art and Writing Awards, and she has been published in *Polyphony H.S,* An International Literary Magazine for High School Writers and Editors. She attends Mountain Lakes High School in Mountain Lakes, New Jersey, and will be graduating in the year 2020.

**Mary Zore** is an artist from southern New Hampshire. Her background includes a BS in Fine Art from the University of Wisconsin in Madison, and an MFA in Studio Teaching from Boston University. She teaches drawing and art appreciation at a local college, and continues to work on her art along with raising three children. She mainly works with drawing in various media, and likes to experiment with mixed media. She considers her art to have an expressive nature, which can include recognizable images along with abstract marks and presentation.

# BIOGRAPHICAL NOTES
## Writers

**Linda Amundson:** A recent transplant from San Diego, she has been working on her craft for fifty+ years. Published in *Thunderclap, Hummingbird Review,* and the *San Diego Poetry Annual* for many years.

**Sara Bailey** is a native Arkansan. She earned her BA in Writing and Rhetoric with a minor in English from the University of Central Arkansas, and her MFA in Creative Writing from Murray State University. Her work has been included in the *New Madrid Journal of Contemporary Literature, Torrid Literature Journal,* and *Adelaide Literary Magazine,* and will appear in upcoming editions of *The Garfield Lake Review* and *Big Muddy.* Most recently, Bailey was selected as a short list winner nominee for the Adelaide Voices Literary Contest, 2018.

**Anna Bálint** edited *Words From the Café* (2016), an anthology of writing from people in recovery. She is also the author of *Horse Thief,* a collection of short fiction spanning cultures and continents, and two earlier books of poetry. Currently, she teaches adults in recovery from the traumas of homelessness, addiction, and mental illness with Seattle's Path With Art, and at the Safe Place Writing Circle at Recovery Café in Seattle.

**Paul Bamberger** has published several books of poetry, including *Down by the River,* Islington Briar Press. Deerbrook Editions is publishing *A Country of Long Winters* in 2018.

A native Virginian, **Jane Blanchard** lives and writes in Augusta, Georgia. Her two poetry collections—*Unloosed* and *Tides & Currents*—are available from Kelsay Books.

**Barbara Bloom** moved to the Pacific Northwest in 2016, after living in Santa Cruz, California for over forty years where she taught writing and literature. Her childhood was spent on a remote coastal homestead in British Columbia, where she learned many skills, like cutting and splitting wood, pruning fruit trees, and cod-jigging. She has two book publications: *On the Water Meridian* and *Pulling Down the Heavens*.

**Judith Borenin** has been writing poetry ever since she was subjected to the hands of Sisters in a convent in Lesmurdie, Western Australia, when she was in the fourth grade. She survived the Great Alaska Quake in '64, and has since lived in numerous U.S. states. She has moved over twenty-five times, but now writes, reads, and lives in Port Townsend, Washington.

**Jessica Brown** is a freelance journalist and writer living in the UK, where she writes about people, places, and the stories sparked by their coexistence.

**Thomas Brush** has had work published in *Poetry Northwest, The Indiana Review, The Iowa Review, Prairie Schooner, Quarterly West, The North American Review, The Cimarron Review, The Texas Observer* and other magazines and anthologies. His most recent books are from Lynx House Press: *Last Night*, 2012, *Open Heat*, 2015, and *God's Laughter*, fall 2018.

A fourth generation West Coast native, **C.W. Buckley** lives and works in Seattle with his family. He reads regularly at Easy Speak Seattle in northeast Seattle. His work has appeared in *Tiferet: A Journal of Spiritual Literature, Rock & Sling*—*a journal of witness, Lummox Journal, POESY Magazine*, and the *Bay Area Poets Coalition Anthology 23*. He is the author of *Bluing*, a chapbook forthcoming in 2018 from Finishing Line Press. You can follow him as *@chris_buckley* on Twitter.

A founder of Floating Bridge Press, **T. Clear's** poetry has appeared in many magazines and anthologies, most recently in *Terrain.org, Scoundrel Time, UCity Review, The Rise Up Review*, and *56 Days of August: Poetry Postcards*. Her work has been nominated for a

Pushcart Award and Independent Best American Poetry Award. She is a lifelong resident of Seattle, and has the good fortune to spend her days inventing new color combinations to paint on sandblasted glass, allowing her to make her living as an artist.

**Terri Cohlene's** poetry has appeared in such publications as *Godiva Speaks, Pontoon 8 & 9, Floating Bridge Review, Arnazella, Switched on Gutenberg,* and the anthology, *America at War.* She edited two adult poetry anthologies, *Godiva Speaks I & II.* She has taught at Richard Hugo House, Shoreline and Whatcom Community Colleges, and Hypatia-in-the Woods. Currently, she serves on the board of Olympia Poetry Network, and is a freelance editor in Olympia, Washington.

**Minnie A. Collins** lives in Seattle, and is the author of *The Purple Wash* (2013) and *Palm Power: Hearts in Harmony* (May, 2018). Her work is published in *Raven Chronicles, Fly to the Assemblies!: Seattle and the Rise of the Resistance, Emerald Reflections, Threads, Voices That Matter, Quiet Shorts, Blackpast.org,* and in other publications. Among her regular spoken word/open mike venues are Writers Read, a monthly program at Seattle's Columbia City Library, The Elliott Bay Book Company, and Third Place Books-Seward Park. She also reads her work at Northwest African American Museum and Onyx Fine Arts Collective exhibits.

**Linda Conroy,** a retired social worker, believes that poetry serves to honor the complexity and simplicity of human nature. "In the process of writing we discover the unexpected in ourselves and others, the ordinary and the unique." Her poems have recently appeared or are forthcoming in *Shot Glass, Washington 129+* (a limited-edition digital chapbook), *Third Wednesday* and *The Penwood Review,* as well as in local anthologies.

**Cathy Cook** has been published in *The Chaffey Review, 3Elements Literary Review,* and in three editions of *Conceptions Southwest.* Her focus is on writing about bodies, especially her own, and exploring the wonder in the everyday, especially domestic existence. For the last two years, she has performed slam poetry in Las Cruces, New Mexico and enviorons, which has made her poetry more visceral and more politically engaged.

**Mary Eliza Crane** is a native of New England who migrated to the Pacific Northwest three decades ago and settled into the Cascade foothills east of Puget Sound. Mary has two volumes of poetry, *What I Can Hold In My Hands* (Gazoobi Tales Publishing, 2009), and *At First Light* (Gazoobi Tales Publishing, 2011). Her work has appeared in *Raven Chronicles, The Cartier Street Review, Tuesday Poems, Quill and Parchment, The Far Field, Avocet,* and several anthologies, including *The LitFUSE Anthology,* and, most recently, *WA 129: Poets of Washington,* poems selected by past Washington State Poet Laureate, Tod Marshall.

**Michael Daley** was born and raised in Dorchester, Massachusetts, and is a retired teacher. His poems, essays and stories have been published widely. His collections of poetry are: *The Straits, To Curve, Moonlight in the Redemptive Forest,* and *Of a Feather.* He's published a book of essays, two books of translation, and several chapbooks. He lives near Deception Pass, Washington.

**Lauren Davis** is a poet living on the Olympic Peninsula. She has an MFA from the Bennington Writing Seminars, and her work can be found in publications such as *Prairie Schooner, Spillway,* and *Lunch Ticket.* She is an editor at *The Tishman Review,* and teaches at The Writers' Workshoppe in Port Townsend, Washington.

**Risa Denenberg** lives in Sequim, Washington, where she works as a nurse practitioner. She reviews poetry for *The American Journal of Nursing,* and is a co-founder and editor at Headmistress Press. Her most recent poetry collection, *slight faith,* was published by MoonPath Press in April, 2018.

**DC Diamondopolous's** stories have appeared in over eighty-five anthologies and online literary publications, including *Lunch Ticket,* Silver Pen's *Fabula Argentea,* and *Fiction on the Web.* His stories "Billy Luck" and "Slapstick Blues" were Semi-Finalists in the Screencraft Cinematic Short Story 2017 Contest., and "Billy Luck" was nominated for *Best of the Net 2017 Anthology*. The international art and literary magazine, *The Missing Slate*, honored DC as author of the month for the short story "Boots" in August, 2016.

**Mike Dillon** lives in Indianola, Washington, a small town on Puget Sound, northwest of Seattle. His book, *Departures*, a narrative in poetry and prose about the forced removal of Bainbridge Island's Japanese Americans after Pearl Harbor, will be published by Unsolicited Press in April, 2019.

**Patrick Dixon** is a writer and photographer retired from careers in teaching and commercial fishing. Published in *Cirque Literary Journal, Panoplyzine*, and the anthologies *FISH 2015* and *WA 129: Poets of Washington*, he is the poetry editor of *National Fisherman Magazine's* quarterly, *North Pacific Focus*. Patrick received an Artist Trust Grant for Artists to edit *Anchored in Deep Water: The Fisherpoets Anthology*, published in 2014. His chapbook, *Arc of Visibility*, won the 2015 Alabama State Poetry Morris Memorial Award.

**Bruce Louis Dodson** is an expat living in Borlänge, Sweden, where he practices photography, and writes fiction and poetry. Recent work has appeared in *Breadline Press West Coast Poetry Anthology, Foreign & Far Away—Writers Abroad Anthology, Sleeping Cat Books—Trip of a Lifetime Anthology, The Crucible, Sounds of Solace—Meditative Verse Anthology, Cordite Poetry Review, Buffalo Almanac, mgversion2>datura, Whitefish Review, Smoky Blue Lit & Arts, Permafrost*, and *Art Ascent*, among other publications.

A professional archaeologist, **Chris Espenshade** branched into creative writing in 2017. His work appears in *The Write Launch, The Paragon Journal, The RavensPerch, The Dead Mule School of Southern Literature* (thrice), *The Raven Chronicles Journal* (twice), *Life in the Finger Lakes* online (twice), and *Georgia Outdoor News*.

**Alex Everette** is a Boston-based writer working on an English degree. What free time he has is split between witchcraft, hiking, and his pets. His writing can be found in *Up The Staircase Quarterly* and *Into The Void Magazine*.

**Catherine Fahey** is a poet and librarian from Salem, Massachusetts. She is the Managing Editor and Poetry Co-Editor of *Soundings East*. When she's not reading and writing, she's knitting or dancing. You can read more of her work at *www.magpiepoems.com*.

**Rebeka Fergusson-Lutz** is a full-time professional high school English teacher, and part-time semi-professional creative person. She has taught in Romania, Washington, D.C., Qatar, Oman, Honduras, and China. When she's not writing lesson plans and grading papers, she works as a freelance writer, editor, and researcher. When she's not chained to her laptop with those side-hustles, she experiments with drawing, painting, sewing, printmaking, collage, and various combinations thereof.

**Joan Fiset** lives in Seattle. She's a psychotherapist and a teacher. Currently she offers Second Wind Writing Groups. Her book of memoir prose poems, *Now the Day is Over* (Blue Begonia Press, 1997) won the King County Publication Award. Her book of prose poems, *Namesake*, was published by Blue Begonia in 2016. Her poems and short fiction appear in *Trickhouse*, *Tarpaulin Sky*, *The Seattle Review*, *Kirkus Review*, *Calyx* and others. Visit her website: *joanfiset.com*.

**Anne Frantilla** was born and raised in Seattle. After fifteen years in Michigan, she was happy to return to the left coast. In her job as Seattle City Archivist she cares for voices from the past, working to connect them with people in the present. She has been published in *Hippocampus* and *Raven Chronicles*.

**Rich Furman** is the author or editor of over fifteen books, including a collection of flash-nonfiction/prose poems, *Compañero* (Main Street Rag, 2007). Other books include *Detaining the*

*Immigrant Other: Global and Transnational Issues* (Oxford University Press, 2016), *Social Work Practice with Men at Risk* (Columbia University Press, 2010), and *Practical Tips for Publishing Scholarly Articles* (Oxford University Press, 2012). His poetry and creative nonfiction have been published in *Another Chicago Magazine, Chiron Review, Sweet, Hawai'i Review, Evergreen Review, Black Bear Review, Red Rock Review, Penn Review,* and many others. He is a professor of social work at University of Washington Tacoma, and is currently a student of creative nonfiction at Queens University's MFA-Latin America program.

**Sharon Goldberg** lives in the Seattle area and was once an advertising copywriter. Her work has appeared in *The Gettysburg Review, New Letters, The Louisville Review, Cold Mountain Review, Under the Sun, Chicago Quarterly Review, The Dalhousie Review, Gold Man Review,* three fiction anthologies, and elsewhere. Sharon was the second place winner of the 2012 On the Premises Humor Contest, and Fiction Attic Press's 2013 Flash in the Attic Contest. She is an avid but cautious skier and enthusiastic world traveler.

**Rafael Jesús González**, Professor Emeritus of literature and creative writing, was born and raised biculturally/bilingually in El Paso, Texas/Cd. Juárez, Chihuahua, and taught at University of Oregon, Western State Collage of Colorado, Central Washington State University, University of Texas El Paso (Visiting Professor of Philosophy), and Laney College, Oakland, California, where he founded the Department of Mexican and Latin-American Studies. His collection of poems, *La musa lunática/ The Lunatic Muse,* was published in 2009, with a second printing in 2010. He was honored by the City of Berkeley with a Lifetime Achievement Award at the 13th Annual Berkeley Poetry Festival in 2015. He was named the first Poet Laureate of Berkeley in 2017. Visit his blog at *http://rjgonzalez.blogspot.com/.*

**James Grabill's** work appears in *Caliban, Harvard Review, Terrain, Mobius, Shenandoah, Seattle Review, Stand,* and many other publications. His books are *Poem Rising Out of the Earth* (1994),

*An Indigo Scent after the Rain* (2003), Lynx House Press. Environmental prose poems are *Sea-Level Nerve: Books One* (2014), *Two* (2015), Wordcraft of Oregon. For many years, he taught all kinds of writing as well as "systems thinking" and global issues relative to sustainability.

**John Grey** is an Australian poet, and U.S. resident. His work was recently published in *Fall/Lines*, *Euphony* and *Columbia Review*, with work upcoming in *Cape Rock*, *Poetry East* and *Midwest Quarterly*.

**Steve Griggs** has written for the *The Seattle Times*, *Seattle Weekly*, and *Earshot Jazz*. His work has also been published in *Rhythm in the Rain: Jazz in the Pacific Northwest*, *Stories of Music Volume 2*, and *Creative Colloquy Volume 3*. "Blues for John T. Williams" is a script for a performance of music at the John T. Williams Honor Totem on August 30, 2017, the seventh anniversary of his death. It was commissioned through a CityArtist grant from the Seattle Office of Arts & Culture. Ian Devier filmed the performance for broadcast on the Seattle Channel.

**Mare Heron Hake** is a poet, artist, editor, and teacher, living in the greater Tacoma area. She has conversations with crows, dialogs with her dog, and adores most wildlife, but admits to a life-long distrust of spiders. Her most recent work can be seen at the *Hips & Curves* blog, and as Poetry Editor for *Tahoma Literary Review*.

**Sharon Hashimoto** teaches at Highline College in Des Moines, Washington. Her book of poetry, *The Crane Wife* (Story Line Press, 2003), was co-winner of the Nicholas Roerich Prize. She is a recipient of a National Endowment for the Arts fellowship in poetry. Her recent fiction and poetry have appeared or is forthcoming in *Shenandoah*, *Moss*, *River Styx*, *North American Review* and *Footbridge Above the Falls* (Rose Alley Press). She is currently at work on a novel.

**Alicia Hokanson,** retired from forty years of teaching English, now devotes her time to writing, reading, tutoring, and political activism in Seattle and on Waldron Island, Washington. Her first collection of poems, *Mapping the Distance*, was selected by Carolyn Kizer for a King County Arts Commission publication prize. Two chapbooks from Brooding Heron Press are *Insistent in the Skin* and *Phosphorous*.

**Thomas Hubbard**, a retired writing instructor and spoken word performer, authored *Nail and other hardworking poems*, Year of the Dragon Press, 1994; *Junkyard Dogz* (also available on audio CD); and *Injunz*, a chapbook. He designed and published *Children Remember Their Fathers* (an anthology) and books by seven other authors. His book reviews have appeared in *Square Lake*, *Raven Chronicles*, *New Pages* and *The Cartier Street Review*. Recent publication credits include poems in *Yellow Medicine Review, I Was Indian*, Foothills Publishing, and *Florida Review*, and short stories in *Red Ink* and *Yellow Medicine Review*.

**Kathryn Hunt** makes her home on the coast of the Salish Sea. Her poems have appeared in *The Sun, Orion, The Missouri Review*, and *Narrative*. Her collection of poems, *Long Way Through Ruin*, was published by Blue Begonia Press, and she's recently completed a second collection of poems, *You Won't Find It on a Map*, a finalist for the 2017 Idaho Prize from Lost Horse Press. She made films for many years; her film *No Place Like Home* premiered at the Venice Film Festival, in Italy. She's worked as a waitress, shipscaler, short-order cook, bookseller, printer, food bank coordinator, filmmaker, and freelance writer. Visit her at *kathrynhunt.net*.

**Paul Hunter** has published fine letterpress poetry under the imprint of Wood Works Press since 1994. His poems have appeared in numerous journals, as well as in seven full-length books and three chapbooks. His first collection of farming poems, *Breaking Ground*, Silverfish Review Press, 2004, was reviewed in *The New York Times*, and received the 2004 Washington State Book Award. A second volume of farming poems, *Ripening*, was published in

2007, a third companion volume, *Come the Harvest*, appeared in 2008, and the fourth, from the same publisher, *Stubble Field*, appeared in 2012. He has been a featured poet on *The News Hour*, and has a prose book on small-scale, sustainable farming, *One Seed to Another: The New Small Farming*, published by the *Small Farmer's Journal*. His book of prose poetry, *Clownery, In lieu of a life spent in harness*, was published in 2017, by Davila Art & Books, Sisters, Oregon.

**Heikki Huotari** is a retired professor of mathematics. In a past century, he attended a one-room country school and spent summers on a forest-fire lookout tower. His poems appear in numerous journals, recently in *The Journal* and *The Penn Review*, and he's the winner of the 2016 Gambling the Aisle chapbook contest. Forthcoming books will be published by Lynx House, Willow Springs, and *After The Pause* online magazine).

**Ann Batchelor Hursey's** poems have appeared on Seattle buses, in *The Seattle Review* and *Crab Creek Review*, among others. Besides collaborating with a variety of artists, she has written poems to compost and hand-made-things. Her chapbook, *A Certain Hold*, was published by Finishing Line Press, 2014. Her poem, "Pike Place Market: Prelude," is haibun-style and is the first poem in her chapbook-in-progress, "She Who Watches" (working title).

**Christopher J. Jarmick** is a Seattle-area writer and a former Los Angeles TV producer who has curated and hosted monthly poetry readings and special events since 2001. In November of 2016, he became the owner of BookTree, Kirkland, Washington's only new and gently-used independent bookstore (http://www.booktreekirkland.com/). His writings and poetry have been published in several literary presses, newspapers, magazines, and online (including *Raven Chronicles*). His newest collection of poetry, *Not Aloud*, was published in 2015 by MoonPath Press.

**Lynn Knapp** is a poet, memoirist, musician, and teacher. She is the author of *Giving Ground* (2017), a book of poetry celebrating her Spanish-speaking neighborhood. The grit, grime, and unexpected beauty of the central city inspire her life and her writing. Her poem "Crossing" has been nominated for a Pushcart Prize: Best of Small Press Awards, for poetry published in 2017.

**Jeff LaBrache**: "I am not a writer; Charlie Burks was my best friend. Throughout our journey through life Charlie inspired me, calmed me down, and gave me good advise and his friendship. His passing has left a deep hole in my heart. I have been a musician since I was ten years old. I stopped playing in 1987, but the chops are still in my head. I have been bringing legal Chinese Antiques out of China for the last twenty-five years."

**Andrew Lafleche** is a poet, author, and journalist. Andrew enlisted in the Canadian Forces in 2007, and received an honorable discharge in 2014. He is the recipient of the 2016 John Newlove Poetry Award. His work has appeared in *SunMedia, Bywords, Snapdragon, The Manhattanville Review, The Poet's Haven, Lummox Press, CommuterLit,* and various other national and international publications. He has five books, including *A Pardonable Offence* (2017), *Ashes* (2017), and *One Hundred Little Victories* (2018). Connect with Andrew online at: *www.AJLafleche.com.*

**Dr. Elizabeth Landrum** has retired from a private practice of clinical psychology, and is enjoying living a quiet life with her wife and dog on an island in the Pacific Northwest where she enjoys the beauty and quiet surroundings for reflection and writing. Her poems have appeared in *Cirque, Shark Reef, Southern Women's Review, Grey Sparrow, Soundings Review,* and *3 Elements Review.*

**Larry Laurence's** books are a full-length volume of poems, *Life Of The Bones To Come,* Black Heron Press, chosen as a National Poetry Month selection by NACS, the National Association Of College Stores; a chapbook, *Scenes Beginning With The Footbridge At The Lake,* Brooding Heron Press; and an e-chapbook, *Successions Of Words Are So,* E-Ratio Editions, New York. His poems have appeared in the anthologies *How Much Earth: The*

*Fresno Poets*, Roundhouse Press, and *Jack Straw Writers Anthology*, Jack Straw Productions, Seattle, and in journals including *CutBank, Floating Bridge Review, Poetry Northwest, POOL, Raven Chronicles*, and *Southern Poetry Review*. Laurence earned an MA in English, at California State University, Fresno, studying poetry under Philip Levine.

**Yvonne Higgins Leach** is the author of *Another Autumn* (WordTech Editions, 2014). Her poems have appeared in many journals and anthologies, including *The South Carolina Review, South Dakota Review, Spoon River Review* and *POEM*. A native of Washington state, she earned a MFA from Eastern Washington University. She spent decades balancing a career in communications and public relations, raising a family, and pursuing her love of writing poetry. Now a full-time poet, she splits her time living on Vashon Island and in Spokane, Washington. For more information, visit *www.yvonnehigginsleach.com.*

Tutoring English and writing at North Seattle College, **Loreen Lilyn Lee** is a Seattle writer whose writing often reflects her three cultures: Chinese (ethnicity), American (nationality), and Hawaiian (nativity). Willow Books Literature Awards has selected her memoir *The Lava Never Sleeps: A Honolulu Memoir* for its 2018 Grand Prize Winner, Prose, with publication by Aquarius Press. Publications include *The Jack Straw Writers Anthology* and *Burningword Literary Journal*. She has read her work in numerous venues in Seattle and Portland, including being selected for the Seattle performance of "Listen To Your Mother," which was produced in forty-one cities in 2016.

**Simone Liggins** earned her MFA in Writing at the Jack Kerouac School of Disembodied Poetics at Naropa University. The foundation for her love of writing and literature was paved at an early age, and blossomed during her teenage years through the kind of tortured freedom that only the ostracism of high school can grant a person. Her various influences include, but are not limited to, Sylvia Plath, Kurt Vonnegut, Dorothy Parker, Audre

Lorde, Lenore Kandel, Laurell K. Hamilton, Octavia Butler, The Beatles, Lady Gaga, Fiona Apple, and Jimi Hendrix.

**brenna lilly** is a writer from New Hampshire. She is a graduate of the *Kenyon Review's* Young Writers Workshop for high school students; she features weekly essays on *liminalexistence.com*. Her chapbook, *everything will all come together*, was released in 2016.

**Kaye Linden**, born and raised in Australia, is a Registered Nurse with an MFA in fiction from the Northwest Institute of Literary Arts on Whidbey Island. She is the previous flash fiction, poetry editor, and current prose poetry, fiction editor for the *Bacopa Literary Review*. Kaye's publications are extensive, and include honors, awards, and nominations for a Pushcart Prize. Kaye's latest books in her teaching series include 35 *Tips For Writing A Brilliant Flash Story* and 35 *Tips for Writing Powerful Prose Poems*. Kaye enjoys supporting and mentoring new writers. Visit Kaye at *www.kayelinden.com*.

**Martha McAvoy Linehan** is a Seattle-based poet, art maker, chemical dependency professional, and Integrated Movement Therapist (IMT). She co-founded, with her sister Jennie Linehan, Word UP SHOT, a photography and poetry project designed for adolescent girls in recovery. She later adapted the scope of the project to address the specific needs of young women who have been commercially sexually exploited. Martha currently works as a counselor, yoga instructor, and art facilitator with the Organization for Prostitution Survivors (OPS)(*www.seattleops.org*). Poetry Around Press published her book of poems, *Au Revoir Georgette*.

**Anna Odessa Linzer** is the author of the award-winning novel, *Ghost Dancing*, and of *A River Story*, which was adapted into a two-person performance piece. Anna's home waters are the Salish Sea. Her childhood summers were spent along the beaches and her life since has been lived along these same beaches. The beaches have washed up bits of stories, and like the people she has known, they have entered into her work. *Home Waters*, a trilogy of three novels—*Blind Virgil, Dancing On Water,* and *A River Story*—was published as a limited edition by Marquand Editions, Seattle.

**Alice Lowe** reads and writes about life and literature, food, and family. Her personal essays have appeared in more than sixty literary journals, including, this past year, *Baltimore Review, Stonecoast Review, Citron Review, Eclectica, Room,* and *Pilcrow & Dagger.* Her work is cited among the Notable Essays in the *2016 Best American Essays,* and was nominated for the *Best of the Net Anthology.* Alice is the author of numerous essays and reviews on Virginia Woolf's life and work, including two monographs published by Cecil Woolf Publishers in London. She lives in San Diego, California, and blogs at *www.aliceloweblogs.wordpress.com.*

**Megan McInnis,** a Washington native, descends on one side from early Issaquah settlers on Lake Sammamish, on the other side from Detroit Mafiosi. She was first published in Raven Chronicles in 2013, performed in the Stand Up for Harm Reduction Comedy Showcase and The Gay Uncle Time in 2015, and was published in the anthology Words from the Café in 2016—a book produced by members of Seattle's miraculous Recovery Café and edited by the magnificent Anna Bálint.

**Tim McNulty** is a poet, essayist, and nature writer. He is the author of three poetry collections, including *Ascendance,* Pleasure Boat Studio, New York (2013), and eleven books on natural history, including *Olympic National Park: A Natural History,* University of Washington Press (2009). Tim has received a Washington State Book Award, and the National Outdoor Book Award, among other honors. He lives on Washington's Olympic Peninsula. Visit him at *timmcnultypoet.com.*

**Jim Maloney,** a writer of sorts, "back in the day," has mostly switched from words to wine (Madrona Wine Merchants in Seattle). Occasionally he still comes up with a literary opinion or two. He was co-editor of Red Sky Poetry's mag *Skyviews,* and edited/published an eclectic zine, *Fishwrap,* back in the day.

**Terry Martin** used to teach, but now she doesn't. She has published hundreds of poems, articles, and essays, and has edited journals, books, and anthologies. Her most recent book of poems, *The Light You Find*, was published by Blue Begonia Press (2014). She lives in Yakima, Washington—The Fruit Bowl of the Nation.

**Michelle Matthees**'s previous poems have appeared in numerous journals, including *Memorious, The Baltimore Review, Superstition Review, J Journal*, and *The Prose Poem Project*. In October of 2016, New Rivers Press published her first book-length collection of poems, *Flucht*. She earned an MFA from the University of Minnesota Creative Writing Program. For more information about her work visit *michellematthees.com*.

**Jessica (Tyner) Mehta** is a poet and novelist, and member of the Cherokee Nation. Jessica is the author of ten books, including the forthcoming *Savagery* and *Drag Me Through the Mess*. Previous books include *Constellations of My Body, Secret-Telling Bones, Orygun, The Last Exotic Petting Zoo*, and *The Wrong Kind of Indian*. She's been awarded numerous poet-in-residencies posts, including positions at Shakespeare Birthplace Trust in Stratford-Upon-Avon, England, Paris Lit Up in France, and the Acequia Madre House in Santa Fe, New Mexico. Jessica is the recipient of a Barbara Deming Memorial Fund in Poetry. Visit Jessica's site at *www.jessicatynermehta.com*.

**John Mifsu**d was born in Sliema, Malta, and currently lives in Seattle. He is a playwright and filmmaker, and has been published in three anthologies, including *Boyhood: Growing Up Male*, a multicultural anthology from University of Wisconsin Press. He has written and directed several original scripts for the theatre including *Lavender Horizons, They Called Her Moses, At Second Sight* and *Angels' Wings Flyin'*. Mifsud won the 2001 Jack Straw Writer's Award in Creative Non-Fiction, and curated the same program in 2005. He produced, directed, and scripted a national award-winning PBS documentary about gay and lesbian youth, *Speaking for Ourselves*. In 2006, he published *All Clear*, a recollection of family stories about surviving Nazi aggression in Malta and immigration to Canada. It is available at *allclearmalta.com*.

**Jack Miller** is a student who primarily writes poetry, inspired by his experiences with schizophrenia as well as the Modernist writing and music movement. Born in North Carolina but raised in San Francisco, he is a senior at Abraham Lincoln High School. There, he is a member of the queer community. His poem "Love Drive" was published in Sacred Heart Cathedral's *Oracle*, 2015, and his short story, "Mushroom Hunt Gone Wrong," appeared in the magazine *TeenInk* and won an Editor's Choice Award.

**Kevin Miller** lives in Tacoma, Washington. Pleasure Boat Studio published his third collection *Home & Away: The Old Town Poems* in 2009. Blue Begonia Press published his first two collections *Everywhere Was Far* and *Light That Whispers Morning*.

**Rita Mookerjee's** poetry is featured or forthcoming in *Lavender Review, Cosmonauts Avenue, Spider Mirror Journal*, and others. Her critical work has been featured in *The Routledge Companion to Literature and Food, The Bloomsbury Handbook of Literary and Cultural Theory*, and *The Bloomsbury Handbook of 21-Century Feminist Theory*. She currently teaches ethnic minority fiction and women's literature at Florida State University, where she is a PhD candidate specializing in contemporary Caribbean literature with a focus on queer theory. Her current research deals with the fiction of Edwidge Danticat.

**Rocio Muñoz** is a student currently studying poetry. "I have never been a person to write poetry; however, I love reading it. Because of my poetry class, I fell in love with poetry and the wonderful process of writing it. The process of poetry has helped me grow as a person and writer."

**C.A. Murray** is getting his MFA at the University of Alaska in Anchorage. His poetry is featured in *Foliate Oak's Online Literary Magazine*, and his fiction in *West Texas Literary Review*.

**Jed Myers** lives in Seattle. He is author of *Watching the Perseids* (Sacramento Poetry Center Book Award), *The Marriage of Space and Time* (MoonPath Press, forthcoming), and two chapbooks. Recent honors include the Prime Number Magazine Award for Poetry, The Southeast Review's Gearhart Poetry Prize, and The Tishman Review's Edna St. Vincent Millay Poetry Prize. Recent poems can be found in *Rattle, Poetry Northwest, Southern Poetry Review, The Greensboro Review, Terrain.org, Valparaiso Poetry Review, Solstice, Canary,* and elsewhere. He is Poetry Editor for the journal *Bracken*.

**Kevin J. O'Conner** writes daily, and publishes the best (or least horrible) of each day's poems on his blog, "Ordinary Average Thoughts." Once he has accumulated enough poems he deems worthy, he publishes them in book form. Kevin's latest collection is *The Lilac Years*; his poems have also appeared in *Spindrift, Lament for the Dead,* the Kirkland Art Center Exhibition, *Clay? VI,* and the African-American Writers' Alliance's anthology, *Voices That Matter.* He lives near Seattle with his cat, Trixie, who likes to sit on top of the refrigerator.

**John Olson** is the author of numerous books of poetry and prose poetry, including *Echo Regime, Free Stream Velocity, Backscatter: New and Selected Poems, Larynx Galaxy* and *Dada Budapest.* He was the recipient in 2004 of *The Stranger's* annual Genius Award for Literature, and in 2012 was one of eight finalists for the Washington State Arts Innovator Award. He has also published four novels, including *Souls of Wind* (shortlisted for The Believer Book of the Year Award), *The Nothing That Is, The Seeing Machine,* and *In Advance of the Broken Justy.* He lives in Seattle with his wife and cat.

**Sue Pace** has work in over 120 publications in Australia, the UK, Canada, and the U.S. Sue writes poetry, short fiction, flash fiction, and creative personal essays. Her collection of related short stories, *Driving Sharon Crazy,* is available through Amazon and will also be available though Audible in 2018. In 2017 she was in Manchester, England giving a workshop on the use of words to portray emotions.

**Chris Pierson** is a teacher in Port Townsend, Washington, where he loves to sail, garden, kayak, teach, and write. He studied creative writing and literature at Kansas State University.

**Thomas R. Prince** is a poet, playwright, and published journalist. Born in Chicago, he was a woodwind player until he broke his hand in a fall in 1981. Excepting a couple of brief sojourns, he has resided in Seattle since 1973. A political activist, Prince has organized unorthodox marches such as the January 2001 Funeral for Democracy. He is currently producing a documentary with the working title "Red Sky Poetry Theatre: An Alternative Seattle."

**Mary Randall** (1920-2004) grew up in West Seattle and attended West Seattle High, where she showed unusual promise as a creative writing student, winning a national short story contest sponsored by *Scholastic Magazine*, with an entry that prompted John Steinbeck to call her "a damn fine writer."

**Jack Remick** is the author of seventeen books—novels, short stories, non-fiction, poetry, and screenplays. He co-authored *The Weekend Novelist Writes a Mystery* (Dell) with Robert J. Ray. His novel *Gabriela and the Widow: A Story of Memory, Immortality and Redemption* (Coffeetown Press) was a finalist for the Montaigne Medal, as well as a finalist in the Foreword Book of the Year Award. Recent work appears in *The Helicon West Anthology*, and is forthcoming in *Red Wheelbarrow Anthology*.

**Sherry Rind** is the author of four out-of-print collections of poetry, and editor of two books about Airedale Terriers. She has received awards from the National Endowment for the Arts, Anhinga Press, Artist Trust, Seattle Arts Commission, and King County Arts Commission. Her poems have appeared recently in *Cloudbank, Marathon Literary Review, Crosswinds, Weatherbeaten,* and *Shark Reef Review*.

**Frank Rossini** grew up in New York City and moved to Eugene, Oregon, in 1972. He taught at the University of Oregon and Lane Community College for thirty-eight years. He has published work in various journals, including the *Seattle Review, Chiron Review, Clackamas Review, Raven Chronicles, Más Tequila Review* and *Paterson Literary Review*. Silverfish Review Press published his poetry chapbook, *sparking the rain*. In 2012, sight|for|sight books, an offshoot of Silverfish Review Books, published *midnight the blues*, poems.

**Martin Rutley** has been writing short fiction for more than a decade. He is influenced by a variety of writers, including Frank Kafka, Harold Pinter, Charles Bukowski ,and William Burroughs. He lives in Manchester, England.

**Vaibhav Saini** grew up in India, visiting family in the dusty villages of Haryana, and in the concrete jungles of New Delhi. Parts of his unpublished novel, "Innocence Lives in an Eyrie," excerpted in this issue, are based on his experiences. He was longlisted for The Man Asian Literary Prize in 2008. Vaibhav moved to the U.S. for graduate school, worked as an Instructor in Medicine at Harvard Medical School, and currently serves as the Licensing Director (Life Sciences) at the University of Connecticut. He is seeking an agent and/or publisher for his novel, "Innocence Lives in an Eyrie." He can be reached at *vaibhav.saini@gmail.com*.

**Catherine Sutthoff Slaton** received her BA in English, Creative Writing from the University of Washington in 1980. Her poems have been published in *Soundings Review* (Pushcart nominee), *Switched-On Gutenberg, Till, Hummingbird Press, Raven Chronicles, Tupelo*, and Metro Transits' 2017 Poetry on Buses Series. Catherine lives in Chimacum, Washington—"the most beautiful place in the world."

**Kathleen Smith** is a northwest poet with roots in Montana's Flathead Valley. Her work has appeared in *Cirque, Helen: A Literary Journal, Rise Up Review, Baseball Bard*, and *The Far Field*;

and included in several regional anthologies: *Okanogan Poems Volumes 2 and 3, Floating Bridge Review #7, Poets Unite: LitFuse @10 Anthology, Yakima Coffee House Poets Twenty Second*, and *WA129+ Digital Chapbook*. She lives and works in the community of Roslyn, Washington.

**Matthew J. Spireng's** book, *What Focus Is*, was published in 2011 by WordTech Communications. *Out of Body*, Bluestem Press (2006) won the 2004 Bluestem Poetry Award. Chapbooks include *Clear Cut, Young Farmer; Encounters, Inspiration Point*, winner of the 2000 Bright Hill Press Poetry Chapbook Competition, and *Just This*. Since 1990, his poems have appeared in publications across the U.S., including *North American Review, Tar River Poetry, Rattle, Louisiana Literature, English Journal* and *Timberline Review*. He is an eight-time Pushcart Prize nominee.

**Joannie Stangeland** is the author of *The Scene You See, In Both Hands*, and *Into the Rumored Spring*, all from Ravenna Press, as well as three chapbooks. Her poems have appeared in *Prairie Schooner, Mid-American Review, The Southern Review*, and other journals. Joannie is currently in the MFA program at Rainier Writing Workshop at Pacific Lutheran University in Tacoma.

**JT Stewart** (poet, playwright, public artist, editor, teacher) has performed at Bumbershoot Literary Festival, Northwest Folklife Festival, and on NPR. She has received grants from Artist Trust, 4 Culture, and the NEH. Viewers can see her broadsides in the permanent collaborative exhibition *Raven Brings Light To This House Of Stories* in the Allen Library at the University of Washington.She currently serves as a juror (one of eighty from five countries) for the yearly SOVAS Awards (Society of Voice Arts & Sciences).

**Carol R. Sunde**, born and raised in Iowa, now lives in Washington in a fishing-tourist village. Since retiring from a Grays Harbor College counseling position (degree in Social Work), she's been exploring a life-long interest in poetry. She earned a Certificate in Poetry from the University of Washington. Her poems have appeared in *The Lyric, Switched-on Gutenberg, Clover, The Avocet,* and *Any Wednesday.*

**Stephen Thomas** played his role in Seattle's poetry scene of the 80s, 90s and early 00's. He performed often at Red Sky Poetry Theater, at Bumbershoot, and many other regional venues, as well as farther afield. In 1984, he founded and built The Cabaret Hegel, where now an off-ramp leads I-5 traffic into the Industrial Flats. There Stephen presented and performed with many other Northwest writers and musicians, including Jesse Bernstein. He has published his work in many ephemeral magazines, as well as in *Exquisite Corpse, Poetry Northwest, The Malahat Review, Windfall, Malpais Review,* and others. His book *Journeyman* was published by Charles Potts'Tsunami Inc. He currently lives, writes and performs in Germany. He has two new collections, *Jones, as is* and *Bonfire,* which are looking for publishers.

**Mark Trechock** writes from southwestern North Dakota, where he has lived since 1993. His poems have previously appeared in *Raven Chronicles,* and recently in *Mobius* and *Drunk Monkeys.*

**Ana Vidosavljevic** is from Serbia and is currently living in Indonesia. She has work published or forthcoming in *Down in the Dirt* (Scar Publications), *Literary Yard, RYL (Refresh Your Life), The Caterpillar, The Curlew, Eskimo Pie, Coldnoon, Perspectives,* ans *Indiana Voice Journal.* She worked on a GIEE 2011 project, Gender and Interdisciplinary Education for Engineers 2011, as a member of the Institute Mihailo Pupin team. She attended the International Conference, "Bullying and Abuse of Power," in November, 2010, in Prague, Czech Republic, where she presented her paper "Cultural intolerance."

**April Vomvas** was born and raised in sunny Las Vegas, Nevada, and works at a university in an administrative role, in a department that allows her to be surrounded by literary genius on a daily basis. She has had two published poems.

Raised in socialist Yugoslavia, **Vladimir Vulović** excelled in math and physics. To earn his physics PhD, he moved to the U.S., but after two postdocs switched to software programming. Years passed. Yearning for satisfaction and meaning, he started writing about the beloved people and country of his youth, some present day experiences, even fictionalized worlds. His work has appeared in *Literary Journal* (of The Association of Serbian Writers), *Raven Chronicles, Signs of Life, The Cincinnati Review,* and *The Gettysburg Review.*

**Jeanette Weaskus** (Nez Perce) has an MFA in Creative Writing from the University of Idaho, and her work has been published in *Yellow Medicine Review, Borne On Air: Essays of Idaho Writers,* and *Sovereign Bones: New Native American Writing.* She lives in Pullman, Washington, and works for the Nez Perce Tribe as a radio personality for KIYE tribal radio station (88.7 and 105.5). Her on-air personality is "Doctor Jaye." The main focus of her job is oral preservation with the emphasis being on folklore.

**Sarah Brown Weitzman**, a past National Endowment for the Arts Fellow in Poetry, and Pushcart Prize nominee, has had work in hundreds of journals and anthologies, including *The New Ohio Review, Raven Chronicles, The North American Review, The Bellingham Review, Rattle, Mid-American Review, Poet Lore, Miramar,* and elsewhere. Pudding House Press published her chapbook, *The Forbidden.*

Juilliard-trained soprano **Marianne Weltmann** teaches singing in a private studio in Seattle. Her stories from the Belongings Project were the impetus for a Seattle Opera commission, *An American Dream,* which premiered August, 2015. Translator of film scripts, opera, and operetta, her contemporary English text of Mozart's *The Impresario* was the first opera performed at the Seattle Fringe Festival. Her work is published in *Synapse* and *Raven Chronicles.* While awaiting publication of a her memoir, *Grace Notes: Songs Of Love And Loss, Death And Transfiguration,* she continues to hone her craft with Greenwood Poets in Seattle.

**Richard Widerkehr** earned his MA from Columbia University and won two Hopwood first prizes for poetry at the University of Michigan. His second book of poems is *In The Presence of Absence* (MoonPath Press); one poem in it, "Pear Trees on Irving Street," was read by Garrison Keillor on *Writer's Almanac*, and one was posted on *Verse Daily*. Recent work has appeared in *Rattle, Arts & Letters, The Binnacle, Bellevue Literary Review, The MacGuffin, Muse/A*, and *Measure*. Other work is forthcoming in *Atlanta Review, Natural Bridge*, and *Chiron Review*. He is a poetry co-editor for *Shark Reef Review*.

A visual and literary artist, **Carletta Carrington Wilson's** poems have been published in *Calyx Journal, Make It True: Poems from Cascadia, Cimarron Review, Obsidian III, The Seattle Review*, and *Raven Chronicles; Beyond the Frontier: African American Poetry for the 21st Century; The Journal*, Book Club of Washington; *Pilgrimage; Uncommon Waters: Women Write About Fishing*, and *Seattle Poets and Photographers: A Millennium Reflection*; and, online, in *Rattapallax: Innovative Northwest Poets* and *Torch*.

**Marjory Woodfield** is a writer and teacher of literature. She has returned to New Zealand after living in Saudi Arabia. She has been published by the *BBC, Stuff* (NZ), and *Nowhere*. Her short fiction has been published in *Flash Frontier*, and she is a Bath Ad Hoc Fiction winner. Her writing inspiration often derives from travel within and around Saudi Arabia.

**Carolyne Wright's** recent book is *This Dream the World: New & Selected Poems* (Lost Horse Press, 2017), whose title poem received a Pushcart Prize and was included in *The Best American Poetry 2009*. Her ground-breaking anthology, *Raising Lilly Ledbetter: Women Poets Occupy the Workspace* (Lost Horse, 2015), received ten Pushcart Prize nominations and was a finalist in the Foreword Review's Book of the Year Awards. Her latest volume in translation is *Map Traces, Blood Traces / Trazas de mapa, trazas de sangre* (Mayapple Press, 2017), a bilingual sequence of poems by Seattle-based Chilean poet, Eugenia Toledo. She teaches for

Richard Hugo House in Seattle, and for national and international literary conferences and festivals.

**Danae Wright** has also had work published in *Prole*. She lives in Seattle.

**Janet Yoder** lives with her husband on their Seattle houseboat, the floating nation of Tui Tui. Her writing has appeared in *Bayou, Porcupine, Passager, The MacGuffin, North Dakota Quarterly, The Evansville Review, The Massachusetts Review, Pilgrimage, River Teeth*, and *Chautauqua*. She is currently at work on a collection of personal essays inspired by her friendship with Skagit tribal elder, the late Vi Hilbert.

**Nicole Yurcaba** is Ukrainian-American, an English instructor, goth (yes, with a lowercase "g"), novelist, essayist, poet. She lives in Mathias, West Virginia.

# BIOGRAPHICAL NOTES
## Editors

**Kathleen Alcalá** (Fiction): is the author of six books of fiction and nonfiction, including *The Deepest Roots: Finding Food and Community on a Pacific Northwest Island*, from the University of Washington Press, 2016. Her work has received the Western States Book Award, the Governor's Writers Award, and a Pacific Northwest Booksellers Association Book Award. Kathleen has a BA in Linguistics from Stanford University, and an MA in Creative Writing from the University of Washington, as well as a Master of Fine Arts from the University of New Orleans. Along with Phoebe Bosché and Phil Red Eagle, she co-founded *The Raven Chronicles* on her dining room table. Read more about her adventures at www.kathleenalcala.com.

**Anna Bálint** (Words From the Café): edited *Words From the Café*, an anthology of writing from people in recovery. She is also the author of *Horse Thief*, a collection of short fiction spanning cultures and continents, and two earlier books of poetry. She teaches adults in recovery from the traumas of homelessness, addiction, and mental illness. She is a teaching artist with Seattle's Path With Art, and the founder of Safe Place Writing Circle at Recovery Café in Seattle.

**Phoebe Bosché** (Managing Editor): is a cultural activist, and has been managing editor of The Raven Chronicles Literary Organization / Raven Chronicles Press since 1991. She is a full-time editor and book designer. Her favorite poet is Archy, the cockroach, whose muse is Mehitabel, the alley cat.

**Gary Copeland Lilley** (Poetry): is the author of seven books of poetry, the most recent being *The Bushman's Medicine Show* from Lost Horse Press (2017). He is originally from North Carolina and now lives in the Pacific Northwest. He has received the Washington, D.C. Commission on the Arts Fellowship for Poetry, and was a finalist for 2018 -2020 Washington State Poet Laureate. He is published in numerous anthologies and journals, including *Best American Poetry 2014, Willow Springs, Waxwing, the Taos International Journal of Poetry & Art,* and the *African American Review* (AAR). He is usually seen attached to a guitar. He is a Cave Canem Fellow.

**Priscilla Long** (Nonfiction) is a Seattle-based writer of poetry, creative nonfiction, science, fiction, and history, and a long-time independent teacher of writing. Her work appears widely and her five books are: *Fire and Stone: Where Do We Come From? What Are We? Where Are We Going?* (University of Georgia Press), *Minding the Muse: A Handbook for Painters, Poets, and Other Creators* (Coffeetown Press), and *Crossing Over: Poems* (University of New Mexico Press). Her how-to-write guide is *The Writer's Portable Mentor: A Guide to Art, Craft, and the Writing Life.* She is also author of *Where the Sun Never Shines: A History of America's Bloody Coal Industry.* Her awards include a National Magazine Award. Her science column, *Science Frictions,* ran for ninety-two weeks in *The American Scholar.* She earned an MFA from the University of Washington, and serves as Founding and Consulting Editor of *http://www.historylink.org,* the online encyclopedia of Washington State history. She grew up on a dairy farm on the eastern shore of Maryland.

# ACKNOWLEDGMENTS

Raven is indebted to our 2018 co-sponsors for partial funding of our programs: the Seattle Office of Arts & Culture (Civic Partners); 4Culture/King County Lodging Tax (Arts Sustained Support Program); the Washington State Arts Commission/ArtsWA, with National Endowment (NEA) funding (Project Support); and all Raven subscribers and donors. Special thanks to the generosity of GIVEBIG 2018 (Seattle Foundation) donors Carl Chew, Minnie A. Collins, Robert Flor, Larry Eickstaedt, Larry Laurence, Anna Linzer (in honor of Dot Fisher-Smith), Lawrence Matsuda, John Mifsud, Pamela Mills, and Anonymous; many thanks for their donations in support of Raven ongoing programs.

Founded in 1991
Vol. 26, Summer, 2018
www.ravenchronicles.org

## PUBLISHER
Raven Chronicles Press,
501(c)(3) Organization

## MANAGING DIRECTOR
PHOEBE BOSCHÉ, SEATTLE

## FOUNDERS
KATHLEEN ALCALÁ
PHOEBE BOSCHÉ
PHILIP H. RED EAGLE

## EDITORS, VOL. 26
KATHLEEN ALCALÁ
ANNA BÁLINT
PHOEBE BOSCHÉ
GARY COPELAND LILLEY
PRISCILLA LONG

## COPY EDITORS:
PHOEBE BOSCHÉ, ANNE FRANTILLA,
PAUL HUNTER

© 2018, Raven Chronicles Press,
a non-profit, 501(c)(3) organization

Made in the USA
San Bernardino, CA
14 July 2018